Faster Smarter

Microsoft
Office System

2003 EDITION

Katherine Murray
*Microsoft Office expert, popular
author and columnist*

CW00351151

PUBLISHED BY
Microsoft Press
A Division of Microsoft Corporation
One Microsoft Way
Redmond, Washington 98052-6399

Copyright © 2004 by Katherine Murray

All rights reserved. No part of the contents of this book may be reproduced or transmitted in any form or by any means without the written permission of the publisher.

Library of Congress Cataloging-in-Publication Data
Murray, Katherine. 1961-
    Faster Smarter Microsoft Office System -- 2003 Edition / Katherine Murray.
        p. cm.
    Includes index.
    ISBN 0-7356-1921-2
    1. Microsoft Office.   2. Business--Computer programs.   I. Title.

    HF5548.4.M525M872   2003
    005.369--dc21   2003052698

Printed and bound in the United States of America.

1 2 3 4 5 6 7 8 9   QWE   8 7 6 5 4 3

Distributed in Canada by H.B. Fenn and Company Ltd.

A CIP catalogue record for this book is available from the British Library.

Microsoft Press books are available through booksellers and distributors worldwide. For further information about international editions, contact your local Microsoft Corporation office or contact Microsoft Press International directly at fax (425) 936-7329. Visit our Web site at www.microsoft.com/mspress. Send comments to *mspinput@microsoft.com*.

ClearType, FrontPage, InfoPath, Microsoft, Microsoft Press, MSN, NetMeeting, the Office logo, OneNote, Outlook, PowerPoint, SharePoint, Visio, Windows, and Windows Server are either registered trademarks or trademarks of Microsoft Corporation in the United States and/or other countries. Other product and company names mentioned herein may be the trademarks of their respective owners.

The example companies, organizations, products, domain names, e-mail addresses, logos, people, places, and events depicted herein are fictitious. No association with any real company, organization, product, domain name, e-mail address, logo, person, place, or event is intended or should be inferred.

Acquisitions Editor: Alex Blanton
Project Editor: Kristen Weatherby

Body Part No. X09-69372

To every computer user who wants to work smarter and faster and get on to the really fun things in life!

Table of Contents

Part 2: Microsoft Word Power: Create Professional Documents

Part 5: Microsoft Outlook: Communicate, Collaborate, and Organize

Acknowledgments

As always, it was a joy to work with everybody at Microsoft Press as we put together Faster Smarter Microsoft Office System – 2003 Edition for you. The goal was to update, improve, and streamline the earlier edition, giving you the techniques and know-how you need to accomplish your tasks in the shortest possible time. I think we hit the mark (you'll have to let us know <g>). But we couldn't have pulled it off without the talent and perseverance of a number of excellent publishing professionals. I want to send a huge THANK YOU to Kristen Weatherby (you're missed!), Alex Blanton, Laura Sackerman, Carmen Corral-Reid, Thomas Keegan, and Donald Cowan for their terrific work on this project. Also, a special fond thank you to my agent, Claudette Moore, who introduced me to Microsoft Press way back when and continues to provide terrific ideas, insight, and guidance on each of the books we do together.

Introduction

Welcome to *Faster Smarter Microsoft Office System – 2003 Edition*, the book that's going to show you how to best take advantage of Office features to get your work done by the fastest route. As you know, in the Office System there's a lot to learn—and this book will help you focus on completing your daily tasks efficiently and accurately, hopefully enabling you to pick up a number of new techniques along the way for streamlining your work in other areas as well.

The Microsoft Office System includes all the applications you need to work with information in a variety of forms. Writing a letter to all your national salespeople? Microsoft Word is the program you need. Are you on the phone half the day? Capture your conversations in Notes view in Microsoft Outlook. Are you responsible for creating data lists in worksheets you distribute to department managers? Excel gives you powerful tools that enable you to enter, manage, sort, and save data in smart ways for easy reuse later. These applications, as well as Microsoft Access and Microsoft FrontPage, are covered fully in this book, presented in a way that helps you get to key items quickly.

Focus on *Fast*

Faster Smarter Microsoft Office System – 2003 Edition spotlights the tasks you most need to accomplish in a given day and gives you the fastest path from beginning to end. We skip the background chat and extraneous information and provide, in a friendly, easy-to-read style, the bare necessities you need and the extra tips you want. How is this book faster than others? Here are a few of the ways we've focused on *fast* for you:

- **Giving you what you need**   Our close ties with Microsoft Corporation give us access to the latest research on what information workers need to accomplish their daily tasks. We know which tasks are most common and which are most troublesome, and we can provide the information readers most need and want to address those topics. In reality, we don't have to look any further than our own offices—we each use Office in various capacities every day.

- **Climbing quickly up the learning curve**   We're assuming that you've been working with computers for a while but you may be new to some or all of the Microsoft Office System applications. This assumption allows us to leave out the extreme basics ("To turn on your computer, push the Power button...") and get to the higher-end, task-oriented procedures more quickly.

- **Showing you time-saving procedures**   Most people use only a small percentage (common lore is 20 percent) of their programs' capabilities. This book seeks to help you discover the time-saving features you may be missing in your current use of your favorite Office applications and pick up some new tools along the way.

Focus on *Smart*

How many times have you heard the phrase, "Work smarter, not harder"? Most of us—inundated with data in countless forms and from every direction—couldn't work any harder if we had to. Working smarter is our only option to getting more done in the same amount of time. The following items show you how we focus on helping you work smarter:

- **More Value, Less Time**   Working smarter means getting more value from the work you do by reusing your data in a way that shortens your pile of busywork and cuts down on the margin for error. Examples and ideas in this book show you how to prepare your data to be reused in documents, worksheets, presentations, Web pages, and more.

- **More Cooperation, Less Duplication**   Effective teams can divide up tasks and work smarter—and faster—to meet a common goal. Examples in this book show you how to use the Office System's enhanced collaboration features to work collaboratively using several of the core Office applications.

- **More Knowledge, Less Learning**   Working smarter means knowing the ins and outs of the Office System programs so that you can use them effectively together. This book helps you leverage your learning by providing prompts for ways in which you can use the various Office applications together.

This Book Is for You

Chances are that you're pretty comfortable with computers but your just haven't had the time or inclination to get too close to the Office System. Perhaps your office just licensed the program for the first time, or you decided recently that after a number of years, it's time for your small business to upgrade to a program that can truly do it all.

Whatever your reason for learning the Office System now, welcome! Here are just a few of the things you can expect to find in this book:

- Information about each of the Office applications that is relevant to the tasks you do everyday

- Procedures that are easy to follow and to-the-point, providing the fastest path to accomplishing a certain goal

- Clear language explaining new concepts, applications, and procedures

- Examples of ways in which you can use the Office System features to streamline your own work

- Illustrations that show how various features can be used

- Tables and diagrams to help present key concepts quickly in an easy-to-remember format

What's in This Book?

We've divided *Faster Smarter Microsoft Office System – 2003 Edition* into seven parts to give you a good look at each of the individual applications and explore the common features of the program. Here's how it breaks out:

Part 1, "The Microsoft Office System Common Features—Fast and Functional," introduces you to the Microsoft Office System and shows you how to perform all the tasks that are common to the various applications. You'll also learn to work with multiple programs and organize and manage files in this part of the book.

Part 2, "Microsoft Word Power: Create Professional Documents," shines a spotlight on Word 2003 and shows you how to make the most of the world's most popular word-processing application. Here you'll learn everything you need to know about mastering a library of tasks in Word—from creating documents to editing, formatting, enhancing, printing, and distributing them. Along the way you'll learn about special Word features, shared documents, macros, pictures, XML, and more.

Part 3, "Effective Microsoft Office Excel 2003: Analyze and Organize Data," moves quickly through the tasks involved in creating a spreadsheet and shows you how to organize and work with data in data lists, PivotTables, charts, reports, and more. You'll also master common worksheet tasks, such as naming and working with ranges, editing, formatting, printing, and charting. This part of the book also introduces the new visual mapping tool used to tag your Excel data for XML documents.

Part 4, "Microsoft Office PowerPoint 2003: Present Ideas Powerfully," takes you quickly through the process of capturing your ideas and putting them in slide form. In this part of the book, you learn to create presentations quickly by using the professional designs built into the program. You also learn to work with styles, colors, animations, and more to get and keep the attention of your audience. Finally, you learn to time and navigate your presentation—and use ink features to annotate slides on the fly.

Part 5, "Microsoft Outlook: Communicate, Collaborate, and Organize," shows you how to take advantage of the many organizing and connecting features in Microsoft Outlook. This part begins by showing you how to let Outlook handle your online communications—creating, sending, receiving, and filtering e-mail. You also learn how to work with instant messaging to connect with others in real-time. But the capabilities of Outlook go far beyond simple messaging; you can also use the Calendar, Journal, Address Book, Notes, and Task features to further organize your daily tasks.

Part 6, "Managing Data with Microsoft Office Access 2003," focuses on applying the powerful but accessible features of this data management program to gather, organize, and work with the data integral to your business operations. In this part of the book, you'll learn to create a database; work with tables, forms, and queries; produce reports; coordinate with SharePoint Team Services, and much more.

Part 7, "Microsoft Office FrontPage 2003: Design Effective Web Pages," gives you the straight story on creating Web pages that look and feel professional. This part starts right off showing you how to create a simple site and builds on the basics by walking you through adding graphics, working with color, creating and managing links, adding tables and frames, creating rollovers, and using the new enhanced code editor. You'll also learn how to preview your pages in multiple browsers and publish your pages to the Web.

This book winds down with four appendixes. Appendix A provides the step-by-step of installing the Office System. Appendix B lists the Office System shortcut keys found in various applications. Appendix C offers a number of references to other sources you can consult to continue your learning about the Office System and its specific core programs. And Appendix D gives you a bird's-eye view of all the changes throughout the Office System, along with some of the behind-the-scenes rationale for resolving common business challenges.

Special Book Elements

Icons and special elements can help you find extra information quickly as you're reading through the book. That's our intent with the special elements we've added to *Faster Smarter Microsoft Office System – 2003 Edition*.

- **Aha!** items point out tips, tricks, and special techniques that can help you work more productively with the Office System.

- **Notes** provide additional information related to the task at hand. A note might provide quick background information on a feature or offer a Web site you can refer to for more information.

- **Cautions** help you avoid trouble by pointing out potential problems and suggesting alternate routes.

- **Lingo** tips clearly define concepts and technical terms that are shown in italics in the text.

- **See Also** tips provide references to other areas of the book that relate to the current discussion.

System Requirements

For the Office System to run optimally on your system, Microsoft recommends that you have the following hardware and software capabilities:

- Pentium 133 or Pentium III computer

- Microsoft Windows 2000 with Service Pack 3 or Windows XP

- At least 64 MB RAM (128 MB recommended) for the operating system, plus 8 MB for each application running

- 245 MB hard disk space

- CD-ROM drive
- Super VGA monitor (or better) with 800-by-600 pixel resolution and 256 colors
- Mouse or other pointing device (trackball, touchpad, stylus, etc.)

In addition to these system basics, you may need other devices depending on what you want to do with the Office System. Check out this list for additional items:

- A Windows-compatible printer
- A scanner or digital camera for importing graphics
- Microphone for speech recognition
- Extra RAM for media-intensive operations
- 14,400-baud modem (or faster)
- Internet connection with an Internet Service Provider

Getting Support

Every effort has been made to ensure the accuracy of this book. Microsoft Press provides corrections for books at the following address:

http://mspress.microsoft.com/support/

If you have comments, questions, or ideas regarding this book, please send them to Microsoft Press via e-mail to the following address:

mspinput@microsoft.com

or via postal mail to:

Microsoft Press
Attn: Faster Smarter Series Editor
One Microsoft Way
Redmond, WA 98052-6399

You can also contact the author directly at kmurray@iquest.net or via her BlogOfficeXP web site, *http://www.revisionsplus.com/blogofficexp.html*, which covers both Office XP and the Office System applications. For product support issues, please contact Microsoft Press at one of the addresses listed above.

Part 1
The Microsoft Office System Common Features—Fast and Functional

Ready to get started using the Microsoft Office System? Good. This first part of the book walks you quickly through the basics so you can get busy doing the things you want to do with Office System applications. Chapter 1, "A First Look at the Microsoft Office System," shows you how to get into the program and take a quick look around. You also learn about the new features introduced or enhanced in the Office System, and find out how to use the Help system—just in case you need it later.

Chapter 2, "Working with Programs and Files," shows you how to work with several different programs at once, so that you can share data and features. You also discover the nitty-gritty of multiple window management—how to display multiple open windows, switch among them, and close them when you're through. Also in this chapter, you learn how to perform some of the tasks that the applications have in common—tasks such as opening, saving, printing, and closing files.

A First Look at the Microsoft Office System

10-Second Summary

- ■ Learn what's included with the Office System
- ■ Find out about the new features
- ■ Get ideas for ways you will use the Office System
- ■ Start the Office System applications
- ■ Get the help you need as you work

Welcome to a new generation of Microsoft Office! If you're completely new to Office, you will find it easier than you might think to get comfortable accomplishing your daily tasks. If you're familiar with Office but new to the Office System, you'll discover that the newest features of Office make your work easier by bringing additional tools and resources directly into the familiar Office interface. This chapter gives you the "big picture" of the Office System and walks you quickly through all the basics you need to begin using the Office System applications.

Note First things first. If installing the program is up to you and you haven't done it yet, take a moment now and, using Appendix A as your guide, install the Office System. If you are using the Office System on a network and you are not the network administrator, talk to the powers that be so you can get the program installed and begin using it as soon as possible.

What's Included with the Office System?

Microsoft Office has been around in one form or another for more than a decade, and the Office System is the latest and greatest release in a long line of successful programs. The Office System is actually a *system* of applications, meaning that it is a collection of complementary programs that work together to help you accomplish what you need to do. These are the core programs at the heart of the Office System:

- ■ Microsoft Word 2003, a word-processing program you'll use to write letters, create reports, publish newsletters, and more.

- Microsoft Excel 2003, a spreadsheet program capable of performing simple-to-complex financial operations, sorting and analyzing data, charting, and reporting.

- Microsoft PowerPoint 2003, a presentation graphics program you'll use to create slide shows for presentations, kiosk displays, and even broadcasting on the Web.

- Microsoft Outlook 2003, an information and communication manager you'll use to send and receive e-mail, organize your calendar, and keep track of notes, tasks, and your personal and business contacts.

In addition to the core programs, the following applications may be included with your version of the Office System:

- Microsoft Access 2003, a relational data management program that enables you to organize, track, sort, filter, and report on your data.

- Microsoft Publisher 2003, an easy-to-use desktop publishing program that provides designs, art, and more for producing marketing materials.

- Microsoft Office Business Contact Manager 2003, a contact manager that adds functionality to Outlook 2003, enabling you to carefully track, organize, and work with leads and client information.

- Microsoft Office OneNote 2003, an exciting new notetaking application that enables you to capture thoughts and ideas in just about any form and use them with your other Office applications.

- Microsoft Office InfoPath 2003, a new application that enables you to create XML-based forms to capture your critical data in an industry standard format for easy and smart storage and exchange.

Aha!   Different Needs, Different Versions

In reponse to customer feedback, Microsoft is offering a number of different versions of the Microsoft Office System to meet different types of professional needs. This enables you to choose the Office system that best fits the needs of your particular business. The different product editions (also called SKUs, or *stock keeping units*) are as follows:
* Microsoft Office Professional Enterprise Edition 2003
* Microsoft Office Professional Edition 2003
* Microsoft Office Small Business Edition 2003
* Microsoft Office Basic Edition 2003
* Microsoft Office Student and Teacher Edition 2003
For a listing of the individual applications and features included with each of these product editions, visit Microsoft online at *www.microsoft.com/presspass/ newsroom/office/factsheet/OfficeSKUFS.asp*.

> **Note**   Microsoft FrontPage 2003, a professional-level Web page creation pro-
> gram, is now available only as a stand-alone product. For more information, go to
> *www.microsoft.com/office/preview/frontpage/default.asp.*

A Quick Look at the Office System New Features

The keystones underlying changes in the Office System are *collaboration* and *communication.* Now working in groups is easier than ever. New features—built right into the task
panes of selected applications—enable you to reach team members, share tasks, and work
on documents with a click of the mouse. Also, in the Office Professional editions, support
for the universal Extensible Markup Language (XML) standard enables you to share data
with coworkers and between applications more easily. In addition to the collaboration and
XML features, the Office System includes these enhancements:

- Instant messaging capability now extends through smart tags to all Office applications. This means you can contact any team member who is currently online
  when you're working on a document that lists his or her name—no matter
  where you're working.

  Lingo *Instant messaging* is a real-time communication tool that enables you to see which
  of your contacts are currently online and send them a quick note in a window that pops up
  over other applications.

- XML support in Word, Excel, and Access now allows you to open, use, and save
  files as XML data (Office Professional editons only).

  Lingo *XML* is an acronym for "Extensible Markup Language," a universal, customizable
  metalanguage that allows users to develop and apply a simple tagging system to identify
  the content and structure of data.

- SharePoint Team Services features are now built into Word, Excel, and
  PowerPoint, enabling you to work collaboratively in a shared space online.

- Improvements in smart tags and the addition of XML-driven InfoPath forms
  and smart documents give you (and your business) additional power to gather
  and use data through the familiar Office interface.

- Office Help now extends automatically online to Microsoft.com, giving you
  access to virtually unlimited Help resources in the form of conventional Help
  articles, tutorials, and more.

- The Office System now makes working remotely easier than ever by adding full
  support for the Tablet PC, with ink support that enables you to transform handwritten notes into typed text ready to be edited, e-mailed, printed, or shared.

- Additional security features in the Office System and improvements in setup make upgrading, deploying, and maintaining Office easier.

- Improvements in each of the applications (the new Reading view in Word; a visual mapping tool in Excel; backup support in Access; a great new editor in FrontPage; and a whole new look for Outlook) streamline your computing experience and give you more power to apply to your Office creations.

Information Rights Management in the Office System

One of the challenges to sharing information and working collaboratively is the question of how to make sure that proprietary data is protected. How do you control the distribution and modification of your key documents? In the Office System, a new feature known as Information Rights Management enables you to protect your documents by controlling access and editing features. In other words, you control who views, prints, edits, or forwards your document—and set the limits on what, if anything, you want them to be able to change.

What Can You Do with the Office System?

As you can see just from the preceding list, the Office System presents you with a huge array of tools you can use to perform all sorts of tasks related to capturing, working with, and sharing information. Whether you work with words, numbers, images, Web content, or data, there's a program in the Office System that was created to do just what you want to do. Whether you write memos, produce reports, design Web pages, manage data, schedule presentations, or create e-mail campaigns, you can accomplish it all with the Office System. Here are just a few ways you can use the Office System:

- You can create the company newsletter in Word, route it to your supervisor for approval, turn it into Web content using FrontPage, and send out an e-mail version using Outlook.

- You can store the inventory records for your small bookstore in an Access database; track sales and accounts receivable and payable in Excel; and do a mass mailing to your entire customer base using the mail-merge feature of Word, all the while saving the data in XML format so it can be used in an unlimited number of ways.

- You can create a professional-level corporate Web site using FrontPage, using SharePoint Team Services to assign individual articles to different departments; compose the annual report in Word; and import charts you created in Excel to show the company's happy financial picture.

■ You can use Outlook to help organize your calendar, schedule meetings with your staff, track employee information, assign tasks (for yourself and others), add notes to reviewed documents, and manage your ever-growing contact list. You can also use the new Meeting Workspace to share documents, files, and links related to an upcoming meeting with your team.

> **Aha!**   How Will You Use the Office System?
>
> The best use of the Office System is, of course, whatever *you* plan to do with it. How will the Office System applications help you in your day-to-day work? As we go along, think through the tasks you do either manually or with another program and ask yourself how you would like to improve or streamline those tasks can help you get the most out of Office.

Starting the Office System

If you've been around the block with Windows XP, you know how to start a program. When it comes to the Office System, your major choice is deciding whether you want to open a program directly (by choosing Microsoft Office Word 2003 after choosing Start, All Programs, Microsoft Office, as shown in Figure 1-1), or by opening a new or existing Office document. Here's what to choose when:

Figure 1-1   The most common way to start an Office System application begins with the Start menu.

In previous versions of Office, you could use the Office Shortcut bar to launch various documents in the different applications. But don't go looking for it in the Office System—it's not there. Instead, you can use the New Office Document option at the top of the

All Programs menu to display the New Office Document dialog box shown in Figure 1-2 and choose the type of Office document you want to create.

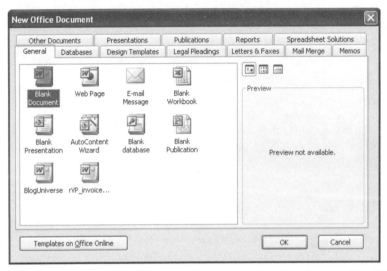

Figure 1-2   Choose the New Office Document command at the top of the All Programs menu when you want to begin a new document in the Office System.

Launch Your Favorite Applications—Fast

Here are a few tips for putting your favorite Office System icons where you can reach them quickly—in the Start menu, on the desktop, and in the Quick Launch bar:

- To add a favorite icon to the Start menu, click Start, choose All Programs, point to Microsoft Office, and then point to the application you want to use. Click and drag the program icon to the application area of the Start menu; then release the mouse button. The program icon appears in the left panel of the Start menu where you can click it easily.

- Add an Office application to your desktop by dragging the program icon from the All Programs menu to your desktop. A shortcut is automatically created that shows the program name and symbol.

- Add your favorite Office applications to the Quick Launch area of the taskbar (the area immediately to the right of the Start button) by dragging the program icon to that area and releasing. The small icon is placed in the taskbar, where you can launch the program easily.

The Quick Launch bar must be active before you can add an application to it. Right-click the Start button and choose Properties. Click the Taskbar tab and make sure Show Quick Launch is selected. Click OK to close the dialog box.

> **Aha!**   Easy Opening After First Use
>
> Because Windows XP has "smart" menus that customize themselves to show choices you've recently made, the next time you open the Start menu you may see the Office application you just opened in the top portion of the Start menu. To start that application, simply click it.

Exiting Programs

Although you can leave all your Office applications open at the same time, it may use up your computer's resources, depending on the amount of memory your system has. To close programs you no longer need, either click the Close box in the upper right corner of the application window, or choose Exit from the File menu of the application.

If you have entered information or modified the file, the program will ask you whether you want to save the file. If you do, enter a file name (or, if you are working with an existing file, leave the file name as it appears) and click Save.

Getting Help in the Office System

Everybody needs a little help now and then, and the Help system in the Office System can bring a Web full of resources to your desktop. When you're working in any Office application, you can get help several different ways:

- Search for help in the Getting Started task pane
- Enter a question or phrase in the Ask-A-Question box
- Press F1 to display the Help task pane and choose your options

Searching for Help

One of the big changes in the Office System is the easy integration of Microsoft.com with the Help system throughout Office. Now the Getting Started task pane in Word, Excel, PowerPoint, and FrontPage provides a Help search box you can use to look for information on a topic that's stumping you. When you enter a word or phrase and click the Start Searching button (or press Enter), the Help utility searches the Help files on your computer and the Help database at Microsoft.com and displays the results in the Search Results task pane (see Figure 1-3).

Figure 1-3 Office searches online to display results related to the topic you enter.

Aha!   Easily Modify Search Settings

If you are not connected to the Internet when you enter a search phrase, Help will search the files residing on your computer by default. If you want to keep Office from searching the files on Office Online, click the Online Content Settings link in the bottom of the Help task pane and click the Search Office Online Content Automatically When Connected check box. Click OK and the search feature is disabled.

Click an item to display its contents. When you are finished reviewing the information, click the Close box in the Help window to return to the application you were using.

Note   Sometimes it can be difficult to find the specific help you need if the words you're using are too general. Try narrowing your terms to identify the specific issue as concisely as possible; for example, format header, number images, export workbook, and so on.

Aha!   Ask a Question, Get an Answer

The Ask-A-Question box is located in the upper right corner of each application window. Enter a word or phrase, press Enter, and the Help system displays the results in the Search Results window.

Microsoft Office Online

In addition to the expansion of the help resources to include the online Help database, now you can move quickly from any Office application directly to the new, improved Office Web site, Microsoft Office Online. Just press F1 to display the Help task pane (see Figure 1-4), and you can choose to jump immediately to assistance, get online training, join a community, or check to see whether any new updates are available.

Figure 1-4 Press F1 to display Help choices that take you to Office Online.

The offerings on the Help task pane take you to the following areas:

- **Assistance**   The Assistance Home page provides all kinds of articles to help you find the answers to common questions, explore key features in each of the programs, look for specific help in newsgroups, or report a problem.

- **Training**   Office Online Training offers online classes, Web-based interactive training, and self-paced practices. In the Training section of Office Online, you'll find specific task-oriented projects to help you accomplish a particular goal (for example, create a baby growth chart, a party guest list, or a "Car For Sale" sign). You can also find more general, application-oriented introductions (create an outline in Word or use Excel as a calculator, for instance). And there are online courses to explore in the various applications (Word, Outlook, Excel, FrontPage, Visio, Access, Publisher, InfoPath, and PowerPoint).

> **Aha!**   Want to learn more about InfoPath?
>
> If InfoPath, the new XML-based forms application, has piqued your interest, you can take an online course to find out more about it on the Training Home page of Office Online.

In addition to these Help features, you can click Connect To Office on Microsoft.com to find the following helpful areas on the Microsoft Office Online home page:

- **Templates**   The templates link takes you to a Templates Home page with dozens of professionally designed templates for common business and personal uses (see Figure 1-5).

Figure 1-5 The Templates Home page offers dozens of document templates for download.

- **Clip Art and Media**   The Clip Art and Media link on Office Online allows you to download thousands of pieces of clip art and animations for use in your documents and business (or fun) presentations.

- **Downloads**   Click the Downloads link to find the latest on Office System upgrades and check out templates and files available for downloading.

- **Office Marketplace**   The Office Marketplace offers third-party Web services that complement the services included in the Office System.

Wondering about the Office Assistant?

Even though the Help system has been almost entirely revamped, the Office Assistant lives on in the many faces of Clippit, Dot, F1, Merlin, and the others. The Office Assistant is an animated help personality that recognizes common tasks and provides prompts, questions, and support to help you learn basic procedures and solve problems. The Assistant is hidden by default, but you can display it by choosing Show the Office Assistant from the Help menu. Clippit, a friendly little paperclip, appears the first time you display the Assistant, but you can choose other personalities by right-clicking the Assistant, choosing Options, and clicking the Gallery tab.

Detecting and Repairing Problems

Sometimes your version of Office may just start acting squirrelly. Not long ago, after months and months of use, I found that I could not quit Outlook without an error occurring. Each time I tried to close the program, a dialog box would appear, telling me that the program was not responding and asking me whether I wanted to send an error report. What happened? Most likely, a file that Outlook regularly uses to quit the program was damaged in some way. The solution? Detect And Repair.

The Detect And Repair option is available in the Help menus of all the Office System programs. When you select the command, the Detect And Repair dialog box appears (as shown in Figure 1-6), giving you two basic choices:

- You can have Office restore your shortcuts while doing the repairs (this returns the original shortcuts to your Windows desktop).

- You can have the utility discard any changes you've made to the program and return the program to its default settings.

Figure 1-6   Detect And Repair can be your answer when an Office program is behaving strangely.

Click Start. The first thing Detect And Repair will ask you to do is quit all open Office programs. A list appears in the Close Office Programs dialog box; quit the programs and return to the dialog box, and then click Retry. The Microsoft Office Profile Wizard scans your hard disk, restores any damaged files, and displays a message saying everything's fine. Click OK to close the message box and return to your cleaner, healthier program.

You Know You Need Detect And Repair When . . .

Refer to the following list to determine when you need to use the Detect And Repair tool:

- Your program keeps locking up at a certain point in a familiar process.

- The program seems to take an inordinately long time to do a routine task (such as opening or saving a file).

- The screen update in an application is very slow; for example, a dialog box "blocks out" part of the application window that is not immediately refreshed.

- The program is acting inconsistently; for example, Word might begin substituting odd styles for styles you *know* you've created correctly; information might appear in the wrong formats or disappear altogether (don't panic—most likely the data isn't really *gone*; the screen just hasn't updated its display).

Talking to Microsoft

One of the major enhancements in the Office System is what's known as the "customer feedback loop." Microsoft wants to hear what we have to say so that they can learn what we love and what we avoid in the various Office applications. For this reason, you'll find feedback buttons in Help windows, on the Web page, and built into the Help menu of the Office programs. When you click Contact Us in the Help menu, you are taken immediately to the Contact Us page of Office Online so that you can make suggestions, search the knowledge base, and more.

Fast Wrap-Up

- The Office System is available in five different versions: Professional Enterprise, Professional, Small Business, Basic, and Student and Teacher editions.

- The new features in the Office System focus on collaboration and communication—now teamwork and reuse of data is easier than ever.

- Create a new Office document by choosing New Office Document from the All Programs menu, or launch an application directly by choosing the program name in the Microsoft Office submenu.

- You exit a program by clicking its Close box in the upper right corner or by choosing Exit from the File menu.

- You can search for help instantly by typing a word or phrase in the Search box in the Getting Started task pane, the Help task pane, or the Ask-A-Question box.

- The seamless integration of Help with Office Online gives you a wide range of resources—you're sure to find the answer you need in there somewhere.

- Office Online has been redesigned to offer many new features, including improved customer feedback options and online training.

Working with Programs and Files

2

10-Second Summary

- ■ Work with multiple applications in the Microsoft Office System
- ■ Display, hide, and use the taskbar
- ■ Open application files
- ■ Print and fax files
- ■ Save files in a variety of formats

If you've spent any time at all working with the different applications in the Office System, you already know that there's a lot of similarity in their look and style. The menu bar is positioned in the upper left area of the screen (unless you've gotten fancy and changed it), and the Minimize, Restore, and Close buttons are always in the upper right.

The similarities extend beyond the look of the screen and the placement of the tools, however. The fact that the File menu is in the same place in every program means you always know where to find commands related to files—Open, Save, Print, Send To, and so on. Because the Help menu offers the same type of help from program to program, you're never far from stepping over your project's trouble spots.

The consistency among the Office System programs for the common tasks we'll discuss in this chapter will save you time you might otherwise spend learning how to print a report in Word, a spreadsheet section in Excel, and an invoice in Access. You can apply the time you save in more creative and productive activities. See? You're already saving time *and* getting more done.

This timesaving benefit only gets better as you become more comfortable working with multiple applications. You can have Word, Excel, and PowerPoint open at the same time while you copy text from an annual report and charts from Excel into the presentation you're creating. Knowing how to layer, arrange, select, and move among open programs takes a little practice and coordination, but soon it will be old hat. And as your experience grows, you'll find yourself getting more done in less time.

Using Multiple Applications

Even if you purchased the Office System to work primarily with one program (to create documents with Microsoft Office Word 2003, for example, or to create spreadsheets with Microsoft Office Excel 2003), as you discover the many things Office can do, you'll want to try the other programs as well. You can move data from one program to another almost effortlessly; sharing that data can save you hours you might otherwise spend retyping, re-entering, or reconfiguring data you already have.

You may wonder when you'd need or want to have more than one program open at a time. Here are a few scenarios:

- Someone sends you the latest sales figures and they are saved in a Word table. No problem—you can simply copy and paste them into your Excel spreadsheet to do the necessary calculations.

- You write the company newsletter in Word and want to send it out company-wide. You can send the file as an e-mail message in Outlook and then import it into FrontPage to add to your company's Web site.

- You've created an online survey with the survey features on your Microsoft SharePoint Team Services site and everyone in your division has completed their evaluations. Now you need to download the data to Microsoft Office Access 2003 and write a summary for your department managers using a Word template.

   Lingo A *survey* in this case is an online survey you can create easily using SharePoint Team Services. You create the type of questions you want (multiple choice, Yes/No, etc.) and team members go to the site to enter their answers online. The results are stored and tabulated on the site automatically, and you can download them to Excel or Access for analyzing and reporting.

- There's a policy change in your company's Human Resources handbook and you need to send the information to all HR personnel in your six offices worldwide. You write the change in a Word document, use your Access database to find the names and addresses of the HR personnel, and then mail merge and print the information from Word. If you want to send out e-mail messages about the upcoming change in the handbook, you can use Outlook to do that. And you can double-check the official name of the policy at the last minute by sending an instant message to your supervisor while she is online.

- You're applying for a small business loan and you want your application to look as professional as possible. Both your profit-and-loss statement and balance sheet are already saved in an Excel spreadsheet, and you have created charts that show your lenders at a glance that your business is a good investment. You create the final application in Word, inserting the Excel spreadsheet and chart at the appropriate places.

> **Aha!** Adding Quickly
>
> Of course, you might switch between programs for much less noble reasons than these. Sometimes when I'm feeling lazy and I need to add a column of numbers in a Word document that I'm working on, I simply drag and drop the numbers into an Excel spreadsheet, enter a function, and have Excel do the math. It saves me from having to open the Windows Calculator and clicking all the individual digits. (When you're trying to save work for yourself, every little bit helps.)

Working with the Taskbar

If you've worked with any of the last several incarnations of the Windows operating systems, you are familiar with the taskbar. It's that strip along the bottom of your screen that houses the Start button on the far left and a set of icons on the far right. In the middle is a blank area that fills with application names as you open them. Figure 2-1 shows how the taskbar appears when you have Word and Excel open.

Figure 2-1 The Windows taskbar is where the action begins in the Office System.

> **Lingo** The *taskbar* is a navigation device that enables you to start programs, move among open programs, and check system status easily.

There are four important areas on the taskbar—three of which you're likely to use regularly:

- The Start menu is the beginning point for many of the applications, utilities, and documents you work with in Windows.

- The Quick Launch bar lets you open programs quickly.

- The Program area shows the programs you have open.

- The notification area displays the icons for utilities and system controls on your computer. You won't use this area often, but you can refer to it to see which system utilities are running on your system.

> **Aha!** Launching Your Favorite Programs Quickly
>
> The Quick Launch bar shows Microsoft Internet Explorer and Microsoft Outlook Express as the default icons, but you can add your favorite Office System applications so that you can open them with a single click of the mouse (without the Office Shortcut Bar taking up space on your screen). To add an application, simply drag the program icon from your desktop to the Quick Launch bar. The program icon will stay on the desktop, but a smaller version will appear in the Quick Launch bar.
>
> If you don't have a program icon on the desktop, you can drag the icon from the All Programs menu. Click Start, point to All Programs, and then drag the program icon from the menu to the Quick Launch bar. The next time you want to start the program, just click it on the taskbar.

To switch from one open program to another, simply click the program name on the taskbar. Windows brings the program you selected to the forefront so that you can work in that application window.

> **Aha!**   Hiding Program Windows
>
> One of the great conveniences of the taskbar—besides the fact that you can switch among programs easily—is that you can temporarily "put away" programs you're not using to give yourself more room for on-screen work. When you want to reduce a program to a button on the taskbar, click the Minimize button in the window controls in the upper right corner of the program window. The program window shrinks to a button, clearing the way for other programs. When you want to redisplay the program window, click its button and you're back in business.

Hiding the Taskbar

The taskbar is a great navigation tool, but as you get more comfortable working with the Office System applications, you'll also notice that it takes up valuable room on the screen. You can set the taskbar so it disappears when you don't need it and reappears when you do. To make the change, position the pointer on the taskbar and right-click. Choose Properties from the menu that appears. In the Taskbar And Start Menu Properties dialog box, make sure the Taskbar tab is selected and then click Auto-Hide The Taskbar to instruct Windows XP to hide the taskbar when you're not using it. Click Apply, and then click OK.

The next time you move the mouse pointer off the taskbar, the taskbar disappears. When you want to use the taskbar again, simply point to the area of the screen where the taskbar *would* be if it weren't hidden. The bar reappears, ready for use.

Switching Among Applications

In addition to the point-and-click method of using the taskbar, there are four other ways you can move from program to program. Three of the methods involve the use of shortcut keys, and the third is a window procedure (which we'll cover in the next section).

- Pressing and releasing Alt+Tab takes you back to the previous application window you were most recently using. For example, if you are working in a Word document and switch to Excel, pressing Alt+Tab takes you back to Word; then pressing Alt+Tab a second time takes you back to Excel. If you have more than two programs running, you can use the Alt and Tab keys to move among them by holding down the Alt key and then pressing Tab. This action displays a pop-up window that displays the icons for your current open applications. To choose the application you want, continue to press and release Tab (while still holding down the Alt key) until the program icon you want is highlighted (a description of the item appears along the bottom of the pop-up window). When the program icon you want is highlighted, release both keys and that program window is displayed.

■ Pressing Alt+Esc cycles through all the applications you have open. This means that if you have Word, Excel, PowerPoint, and Outlook all open in your current work session, Windows will display each window in turn as you press Alt+Esc.

■ Just a few years ago, Ctrl+Alt+Del used to be the dreaded "reboot" key combination that dumped all your open files and restarted your computer. Now, however, Ctrl+Alt+Del brings up the Windows Task Manager, which lets you check the status of your programs (such as when you have a program that seems to be locking up). The Windows Task Manager also enables you to switch to a different program if you'd rather not use one of the other methods (see Figure 2-2). To change to a different open application, select the file in the Task list and click Switch To.

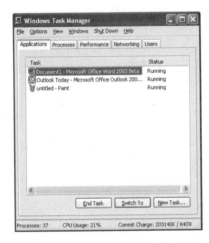

Figure 2-2 You can use the Windows Task Manager when you want to check the status of your programs or switch to a different one.

Arranging Application Windows

What happens when you have several programs running and you need to see more than one of them on the screen at once? You might be comparing the sales figures in that Word table with the ones you created in your Excel report to determine which ones are correct. To be certain, you need to see those sets of figures side by side, which means you need to resize and rearrange the application windows. Here are the steps to do this:

1 To reduce the window size, click the Restore Down button in the upper right corner of the application window (it's the middle one of the three window control buttons).

> **Note**   How much smaller the window gets depends on whether you've already reduced the size of the window. If you were previously working in the window at a smaller size, clicking Restore Down returns the window to that size.

2   To make the window smaller, position the mouse pointer at one corner of the reduced window and drag inward toward the center of the window. Release the mouse button when the window is the size you want.

Figure 2-3 shows the desktop with Word, Excel, and PowerPoint files all neatly arranged.

> **Note**   After you've worked with an application and closed it once, the program remembers the window size you used before. The next time you start the program, Office will open the application to the window size previously used. You can then resize it however you like.

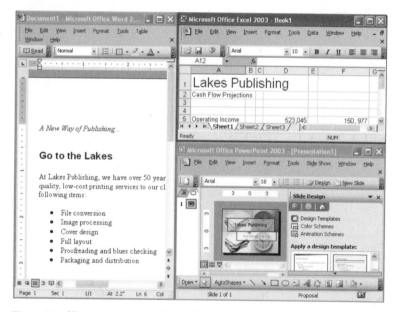

Figure 2-3   You can resize multiple windows so that you can see the necessary data for the work you're doing.

Aha!   Enlarging the Current Window

When you want to work in an application and give it the full desktop screen, click the Maximize button to enlarge the window. The other application windows are still open but they are hidden by the full-size window. To get back to those applications, use the taskbar or one of the shortcut key combinations.

Compare Side by Side

Sometimes it's helpful to see two copies of the same document at the same time so that you can easily review how they're different. To display two documents side by side, open the Window menu and choose Compare Side By Side. The currently open documents are positioned next to each other, with each getting 50 percent of the screen. If you want to scroll through the documents together (meaning you can press PgDn and both documents will scroll down simultaneously) by clicking the Synchronous Scrolling tool in the Compare Side By Side toolbar. When you're finished reviewing the documents, click Close Side By Side to return to normal view.

Tiling Windows

Windows also gives you a quick way to arrange two or more applications on your desktop: by tiling multiple windows. Begin by opening at least two programs, and then follow these steps:

1   Click the taskbar button of the first program you want to work with.

2   Press and hold the Ctrl key while clicking additional taskbar buttons (you can use this technique for as many windows as you like). This selects the windows you want to arrange.

3   While still holding down the Ctrl key, right-click one of the taskbar buttons you selected in step 2. A context-sensitive menu appears.

4   Choose Cascade, Tile Horizontally, or Tile Vertically to choose the type of arrangement you want. Cascade overlaps the windows so that each of the title bars is showing; Tile Horizontally places the windows one on top of another; and Tile Vertically positions the windows side by side.

Exiting Programs

When you find yourself stumbling over application windows you don't really need, it's time to close a few. Click the Close box in the upper right corner of the program window (marked with a red X).

> **Note**   The small X to the right of the Ask-A-Question box in the application window (just beneath the Close box) closes the file in which you're working but leaves the application open.

If you have made any modifications to the files in the program windows since the last time you saved the files, the Office application will display a warning message, asking whether you'd like to save the changes you made to the file. If you want to save your work, click Yes (and read on to the "Saving Files" section). If you want to let your changes go, click No or Cancel. The application discards your changes and closes the program window.

Now that you know the basic procedures for working with applications once you get into them, you're ready for some of the common tasks that all the Office System applications share. These operations include opening files, working with the Clipboard, saving files, and printing files.

Opening Files

You've already seen that when you start a program in the Office System, a new document opens on the screen. But not every file you work with will be a new file. When you want to work with an existing file, you have the option of opening the document as an Office document, or opening it within the specific application you'll be using. This section gives you the know-how for each of those situations.

Opening Files the Office Way

If you want to start right up with the Office document you plan to use, choose the Open Office Document option in the All Programs menu (or in the Office Shortcut Bar). This action brings up the Open Office Document dialog box, which shows all the different application files in the current folder, each with an icon showing which application it belongs to (as shown in Figure 2-4).

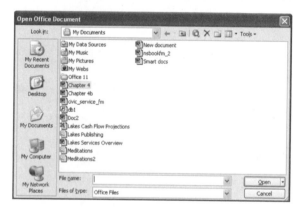

Figure 2-4   The Open Office Document dialog box lists all the Office files in the current folder and shows their program icons.

To open the file you want, navigate to the folder you want by clicking the Look In down arrow and choosing the folder you want from the list. Then select the file you want to open in the files list and click Open. The file appears in a program window on your screen.

Opening Files Within Applications

But suppose that you're working in Word and you want to look up the report you submitted last week—which you also created in Word. When you're using an application (any Office System application), you can open a file by clicking the Open tool on the toolbar.

> **Note**   You'll learn more about the different tools in the chapters on each of the individual programs. For now, just know that most common tools—New, Open, Save, and Print—are available on the toolbar of every Office System application.

In the Open dialog box, navigate to the folder you need, select the file from the list, and click Open. The document opens in the application window.

> **Aha!**   Options for Opening
>
> Office applications also give you a few more choices for opening documents. When you open a document in Word, for example, and click the small arrow to the right of the Open button, you see a submenu listing the Open As Copy and Open In Browser commands. Choose Open As Copy to create and open a copy of the selected document. Choose Open In Browser when you've selected a Web page file and want to see it in a browser window instead of the current Office applications.

Working with Stackable Documents

A convenient feature the taskbar offers is the ability to "stack" open documents. Now when you have several files open in Word, for example, you can see each of the file names in a pop-up list that appears when you click the Word button on the taskbar, as shown here:

To choose the one you want, simply click its button.

You can rearrange, tile, or cascade the documents in individual windows by right-clicking the Word taskbar button and choosing the look you want. You can also close all the documents at once by right-clicking and choosing Close Group.

Using the Clipboard

The Office System uses the Office Clipboard to help you move data, pictures, paragraphs, charts, and more from one document to another. The Clipboard functions like a 3-D clipboard—you take a document out of a file and put it on the Clipboard until you need it. When you're working with the file you want to add it to, you take it off the Clipboard and slip it in the file. You'll use two shortcut key combinations most often when you work with the Clipboard: Ctrl+C (for copying items) and Ctrl+V (for pasting). You'll also use Ctrl+X to cut (or remove) selected text, pictures, and objects from your documents.

Aha!   Viewing Clipboard Contents

For most tasks, you don't need to see what you've placed on the Clipboard. But if you cut an item you think you might want, for example, or you can't remember whether you've included an item or not, you can display the Clipboard contents by opening the Edit menu and choosing Office Clipboard. The Clipboard appears as a task pane and you can work with the items stored there as needed.

Printing Files

Every Office System application allows you to print—and although the different programs have different print options (we'll cover those in the specific program chapters), the process is by and large the same. Simply open the document, worksheet, presentation, or data table you want to print. Then choose one of the following:

- To get a quick print without setting any print options, click the Print tool in the Standard toolbar. The document is sent directly to your printer.

- To display the Print dialog box and choose options such as the selected printer, number of copies, and page range, press Ctrl+P. Set the options the way you want them and click OK to print.

Internet Fax Services in the Office System

Now you can use an Internet fax service to fax documents directly from the Office System applications. First make sure that you are connected to the Internet. Then display the document you want to fax, open the File menu, and choose Send To. Choose the Recipient using Internet Fax Service option, click OK in the message box that appears, and you are taken to a Web page offering various third-party fax services. The first time you use this option, you'll need to sign up for a service. On subsequent uses, your fax will be sent automatically.

Saving Files

The fastest way to save a file is to press Ctrl+S. You can also click the Save tool in the Standard toolbar if you prefer. The first time you save a file, the Save As dialog box appears so that you can enter a file name, choose the file format, select the folder in which you want to store the file, and click Save (see Figure 2-5).

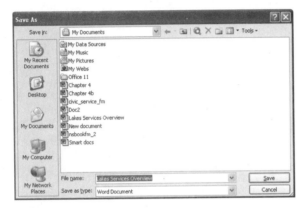

Figure 2-5 You save files using the Save As dialog box.

Aha!   A File by Another Name

If you want to save an existing file under another name (for example, creating a backup copy of the document for safekeeping), open the File menu and choose the Save As command. Enter a new file name in the File Name box (and choose a new folder if needed); then click Save. The newly created file is now your open document, and you have two copies of the file saved under two different names.

Extending Data Use with XML

The Professional Editions of Office System have added XML support in Word, Excel, and Access. XML is an industry-standard format that enables you to save the data itself—and the data's format—separately. This means that you can reuse the XML data in spreadsheets, data tables, documents, and an almost unlimited number of other applications. In the programs that support XML, you can choose XML format by clicking the Save As Type down arrow in the Save As dialog box. When you choose XML Document as the file format for the saved document, additional options appear that enable you to further control the way the data will be stored. For more about working with XML, see Chapter 3, "Creating and Viewing Documents."

Saving Office Documents as Web Pages

Everything's going to the Web these days. And you don't have to be handy with Hypertext Markup Language (HTML) or FrontPage in order to publish your Office documents online. In fact, you can save your Office documents as Web pages just by using the Save As command in the File menu. Here's the process:

1 Prepare your document as usual in Word, Excel, or PowerPoint.

2 From the File menu, choose Save As.

3 In the Save As dialog box, choose Web Page in the Save As Type box.

4 If you want to change the title for the page (the name displayed in the window's title bar), click Change Title, enter the name, and then click OK.

5 Enter the name for the file in the File name box and then click Save.

The program creates an HTML file along with the necessary folders, and you can then post the document to the Web using your File Transfer Protocol (FTP) or favorite upload utility. (If you are working on a network and are unsure how to upload documents to a Web server, check with your system administrator for more information.)

Fast Wrap-Up

- Having different Office System applications running at once gives you an easy way to share data among programs.

- Use the taskbar to switch among open applications and also to start programs and get system information.

- The shortcut keys Alt+Tab and Alt+Esc, as well as the Task Manager, give you alternate ways of switching among programs.

- Resize and rearrange program windows when you need to see more than one application on the screen.

- You minimize, resize, restore, maximize, and close windows using the window controls in the upper right corner of the program window.

- The procedures for opening, saving, and printing files are similar in all the Office System applications. Shortcut keys and tools on the Standard toolbar help you accomplish those tasks quickly.

Part 2
Microsoft Word Power: Create Professional Documents

Whether your daily work involves preparing memos, reports, chapters, or letters, Microsoft Word is the tool of choice for text document preparation. This part of the book helps you master Word features quickly as you create, edit, format, and check your documents. You'll also learn how to create and share team documents, work with revisions, and master long-document features, such as headers and footers, sections, and more.

Creating and Viewing Documents

3

10-Second Summary
- Start a new document
- Work with a template
- Enter text by typing, writing, or speaking
- Create a shared document
- Research while you work

When you work with information, you work with documents, in one form or another. Whether you're creating memos, reports, chapters, catalog copy, or press releases; filling in forms; writing evaluations; preparing newsletters; or drafting proposals, your tasks require knowing how to create new documents, enter text, and view the document in different forms. This chapter shows you the most efficient way to accomplish these basic document-building steps. Along the way, you'll learn new ways to enter and view the information you create.

New Features in Microsoft Office Word 2003

Word 2003 includes a number of new features that improve collaboration and make your work life generally easier. Here's an overview of the major additions and enhancements:

- **A New Look**   Word 2003 now adopts the Microsoft Office Windows XP design, adding color and depth to toolbars, menus, and task panes. New task panes also bring even more help to the Word window, enabling you to carry out tasks without digging through menus or searching for the command you need.

- **Reading Layout**   Word 2003 now includes a new view that can display the document in multipage view, hiding toolbars, and using ClearType technology to present the text as clearly as possible.

- **Sharing Documents**   Now with Word 2003 you can work collaboratively on documents using SharePoint Team Services. The Shared Workspace task pane is built right into Word, so you can track document versions, assign tasks, and contact other team members while you work on the shared document. A shared Web site enables you to share a common area for resource files, contacts, and more.

■ **Research Task Pane**   Now you can research topics while you're working on them by using the Research task pane. Enter a phrase and, if you're connected to the Internet, Office goes out and searches the sites and online databases you have set up as resources. The items found that are relevant to your search are displayed in the Search Results task pane.

■ **Open and Save Documents as XML**   Extensible Markup Language (XML) support is a big new feature in the Professional Editions of Office System. Now you can open, create, and save data in XML format, which enables you to reuse your data in a variety of ways with many different programs. If you are using a Standard or Small Business Edition of the Office System, you have the capacity to save documents in XML format but you won't be able to perform the higher level XML tasks that are available in the Professional Editions.

See Also For more about adding editing controls to your Word documents, see Chapter 4, "Using the Editing Tools In Microsoft Office Word 2003."

■ **Editing Controls**   Another big addition in the Office System is Windows Rights Management, which gives users running Windows Server 2003 the ability to control what's done to a document no matter where it goes or how long it lives. For example, you can disable the printing feature so that others can't print the document you send. Or you can make forwarding a document outside the company impossible. You also can limit the editing a person does to only the section he is responsible for. Pretty slick.

What Can You Do with Word?

Perhaps an easier question to answer would be, "What *can't* you do with Word?" If your project has anything to do with words—typing them, arranging them, enhancing them, or checking them—Word can take care of it. Here are just a few of the tasks you can accomplish with Word:

■ Compose the monthly sales letter to your field reps and pass it around to others for approval before you send it.

■ Pull together a team to collaboratively produce your company's annual report and house all important files in a shared site online.

■ Create the weekly lesson plan for your classroom.

■ Write, edit, and publish an entire book.

■ Compile your research on the behavior of army ants.

■ Design Web pages and post them on the Internet.

■ Publish a multicolumn newsletter.

■ Create, print, and send a mass e-mail campaign.

Individuals use Word for projects at work, school, and home. Companies use Word for just about everything imaginable. Word is used on stand-alone and networked systems alike;

it's a standard format for files sent hither and yon all over the Internet, worldwide. If you want to use a simple-but-powerful word-processing program that is compatible with the majority of programs on the globe, you're in the right place.

> **Aha!**   Word Your Way
>
> Don't like the way the toolbars are arranged? You can move them around on-screen any place you like. The toolbars are *dockable*, which means that you can remove them from their current place beneath the menu bar and put them someplace else. To do this, click the small column of horizontal lines at the left end of the toolbar and drag toward the center of the work area to release it; then place the toolbar wherever you want. You might want to put the toolbar along the right edge or just leave it, palette-style, in your document window. You can resize the toolbar by dragging an end of the toolbar toward its center.

Starting a New Document

When you start Word, a new document opens automatically on your screen. On the right, the Getting Started task pane offers you a number of choices, including searching online, opening an existing document, and creating a new document. To start a new document, click the Create A New Document link in the bottom of the task pane.

> **Aha!**   Display the Task Pane
>
> If for some reason you *don't* see the task pane along the right side of your Word window, you can display it by choosing Task Pane from the View menu.

The New Document task pane, shown in Figure 3-1 on the following page, offers you five choices for creating a new document:

- Clicking Blank Document closes the task pane and displays the blank document full-screen

- Choosing XML Document opens a blank document and shows the XML Structure task pane so that you can attach an XML schema

  Lingo An *XML schema* is a set of XML instructions that tells programs (like Word) how to recognize the XML data elements in the document you create.

- Selecting Web Page opens a new document in Web Layout View

- Choosing E-Mail Message displays an e-mail message window

- Clicking From Existing Document opens the New From Existing Document dialog box so that you can choose the file you want to open

Figure 3-1 In the New Document task pane, you choose the type of document you want to create.

> **Aha!**   Don't Forget Template Possibilities
>
> Additionally, in the Template area, you can choose to go to the Templates home page on Office Online to download new templates, choose a template on your computer, or go to one of your favorite Web sites to find a template you want to use.

Working with a Template

Word includes a huge selection of *templates* that can help you shortcut the process of creating a new document. In fact, you can use a template for everything from memos to Web pages to full-blown reports. Word 2003 comes with many different styles of templates, and a link to the Office Online Templates page is displayed first in the Templates area of the New Document window, so finding new templates is only a click away.

To use one of the templates on your computer, follow these steps:

1 In the Templates area of the New Document task pane, click On My Computer.

2 In the Templates dialog box, click the tab containing the type of document you want to create. (As Figure 3-2 shows, you have quite a variety to choose from.)

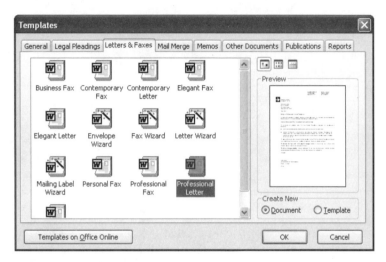

Figure 3-2 The Templates dialog box shows you all the types of documents you can create.

3 Select the template you want to use. The Preview window displays the template file you've chosen so that you can decide whether it's the one you want.

4 When you find the template you want to use, make sure the Document option is selected (this creates a new document, not a new template file), and click OK.

Once the document is open on your screen, you can simply click in the places it says [*Click here and type*] to add your own information. When you're finished making changes, press Ctrl+S to display the Save As dialog box so that you can name and save the file.

> **Lingo** A *template* is a ready-made file included with Word (and also in Microsoft Office Excel 2003, PowerPoint 2003, and FrontPage 2003) that enables you to build your document on what's already there. Templates include placeholder text that you replace with your own, and the formatting—such as headings, lists, body style, and so on—is already done, saving you time and trouble. You can use the templates built into Word or get more on the Web by clicking the template options in the task pane or the Templates On Office Online button in the Templates dialog box.

Entering Text

How many ways can you type a memo? The answer used to be, "One keystroke at a time." Today, however, Word has expanded our data-entry horizons by offering additional ways of getting text into our documents. You can enter text in a Word document in the following ways:

■ Use the good old-fashioned method and *type* text.

■ Use your Tablet PC, Pocket PC, or drawing tablet to *write* text.

■ Use the dictation feature in Word to *speak* text into the program.

■ *Import* text you've created in other programs.

> **Caution**   Be forewarned: Speech dictation and recognition was new with the previous version of Word, and although it's a great feature (and fun, too), you'll have to spend quite a bit of time "training" Word to recognize your speech patterns before it actually saves you time. The program needs to learn how you say things before it can enter your words and phrases accurately.

Typing Text

If you're familiar with computers at all, you know the basics of typing in a Word document. The flashing cursor shows you where the characters will appear as you type. Simply go to town entering your text. No need to press Enter at the end of a line; Word will automatically wrap the text to the next line for you. At the end of a paragraph, press Enter. It's that simple.

One important consideration when you're typing text in your document is whether you're working in Insert or Overtype mode. Insert mode *inserts* characters at the cursor position, pushing existing characters to the right. Overtype mode *types over* existing characters and can sometimes create a mess in your document if you're not paying attention. By default, your document is in Insert mode (which means characters won't be replaced). You can toggle Overtype mode on and off by pressing the Insert key on your keyboard. When Overtype mode is on, the symbol *OVR* appears in the status bar along the bottom of the screen.

Using AutoText

The AutoText feature in Word is great for helping you streamline the task of typing words you use often. The feature comes with a whole slew of choices already included—from headers and footers to mailing instructions to salutations and signature lines. You can add the text by using the dialog-box method or by displaying an AutoText toolbar in your work area (this is the best choice if you plan to use AutoText for a number of entries). Here's how to do it:

1 Choose AutoCorrect from the Tools menu.

2 Choose the AutoText tab in the AutoCorrect dialog box. Choose the AutoText entry you want to add by selecting it from the list.

3 Click Insert. The word or phrase is added at the cursor position in the document and the dialog box closes.

You can also use AutoText to add phrases you find yourself typing repeatedly. To do this, display the AutoText tab (if you're using the AutoText toolbar, you can simply click the AutoText tool to display it), type your phrase in the Enter AutoText Entries Here line, click Add, and then click OK. Now, when you want to insert the phrase, click the All Entries button on the AutoText toolbar, choose the Normal category (where customized entries are stored), and click the entry. Word inserts it at the cursor position.

Writing Text

Word now offers a number of "ink" options that enable you to enter text longhand in your Word documents. If you want to add a quick signature to a letter or invoice, you can use the Writing Pad or the Write Anywhere feature and your stylus to sign the document. If you want to take your Tablet PC to a meeting at a client's office, you can write your notes by hand and have Word convert them to text automatically. Here are the quick steps:

- To display and use the Writing Pad, click the Handwriting tool on the Language Bar and choose Writing Pad from the menu; then simply use your mouse or stylus to write the characters you want to add to your Word document.

- To use the Write Anywhere feature, choose Handwriting on the Language Bar and click Write Anywhere. A small palette of tools appears. Click the Ink tool and begin writing on the document.

- If you're using a Tablet PC with Word 2003 installed, you don't need to turn on any feature to begin writing on the screen. Handwriting is enabled by default, so you can simply write on the screen to enter text.

See Also If you're just getting started using your Tablet PC, check out Jeff Van West's book *Tablet PC Quick Reference* (Microsoft Press, 2003) for details on setting up, working with, and caring for your Tablet PC.

> **Caution**   You may not see the Language Bar when you first begin working with Word because it is most likely minimized in the system tray area of the taskbar. Display the taskbar and look for a small keyboard symbol. Click it to display a menu; then choose Show The Language Bar. If Handwriting does not appear as an option on the Language Bar, the feature may not be installed. Go to the Windows XP Control Panel and double-click the Regional And Language Options icon; then click the Languages tab and the Details button. Click Handwriting Recognition, and click Add to install the feature. (If you are on a network, be sure to check with your system administrator before making any change to your existing Office installation.)

Remote Word on the Pocket PC

If you have a Microsoft Windows-powered Pocket PC, you can use Pocket Word to write letters, create memos, work on your expense reports, and more. You can create documents on your Pocket PC and then upload them to your work computer or vice versa. For more information on Pocket Word, visit *http://www.microsoft.com/mobile/pocketpc.*

Speaking Text

Word also enables you to speak your text into being. Your applications for this feature may be somewhat limited, unless you are adding voice annotations to documents or recording notes you'll want to transcribe later.

> **Aha!**   Before you work with speech in Word, you must have set up the feature in Windows XP. To do this, click Speech Tools on the right side of the Language Bar, and then choose Options. This displays the Speech Properties dialog box, where you can create a training profile, test and adjust your microphone, and modify speech settings.

Simple Speech

To add text using the speech feature, follow these steps:

1 Position your cursor at the point in the document where you want to add the dictated text.

2 Choose Speech from the Tools menu. The Windows XP Language Bar appears across your document.

3 Make sure your microphone is turned on and positioned properly.

4 Speak clearly and slowly into the microphone. The text appears on the screen.

Using Voice Commands in addition to accepting dictation, Word's speech feature will also respond to your voice commands: "Open File" opens the File menu, "Print" displays the Print dialog box, and so on. To activate voice commands, click Voice Command on the Language Bar, and then speak clearly into the microphone.

> **Caution**   Depending on the power of your microphone, Word might pick up any little sound and interpret it as either a command or a word to be entered. While I was working on this section, for example, the telephone rang and I answered it. Somehow during that brief exchange, Word got the idea I was commanding it to print the document, so it opened the Print dialog box and tried sending the file to the printer. The moral: Turn the microphone off when you don't mean to speak into it.

Viewing Your Document

Word gives you a number of different ways to look at the same document. You'll discover that some views enable you to focus only on text; others let you see how the layout is shaping up (both for print and for the Web); and still others let you check the organization of your document. The following list explains what you can expect from each of the views in Word:

- Normal view is the view you work with when you are entering text and creating your document. This view does not show special formats or column layouts if you've applied them, but it allows you to enter text quickly now and fuss with formats later.

- Web Layout view shows the way the page will look after it's saved as a Web document. Any formats and images you've placed will appear here, but as you can see, the margins of the page are different (as they will be on the Web).

- Print Layout view is the view selected by default when you begin using Word. In this view you can see all formatting changes you make, as well as any added graphics, lines, and so on. You also get a realistic idea of how the page will look when printed.

- The new Reading Layout (see Figure 3-3) enables you to see full pages on the screen at one time. You can switch to Reading Layout easily by pressing Alt+R. The benefits of Reading Layout are that most of the toolbars are gone—only one navigation bar remains while you read—and ClearType technology is used to display the text so the characters are as easy on the eye as possible. You can choose different views—Thumbnails, Document Map, and Multiple Page view—to make reading easier.

- Outline view shows how the document looks when it's arranged according to heading levels. Working in Outline view is great when you are creating a long document that you (and perhaps your team) are building from an outline.

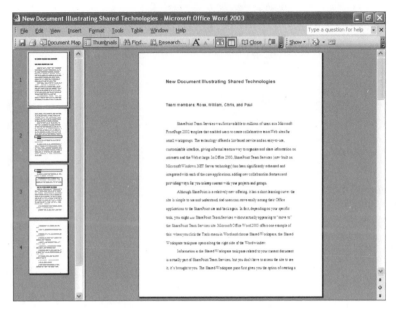

Figure 3-3 The new Reading Layout pane is designed to give you flexibility and clarity for viewing documents.

Other Looks for Other Tasks

The five views just described—Normal, Web Layout, Print Layout, Outline, and Reading Layout—are the primary ones available to you as you create your documents, but you have other options as well. While you're exploring the features of Word, be sure to check out these alternate looks:

- **Print Preview**   This mode enables you to see the document as it would be printed. You can zoom to different page sizes and display more than one page on the screen if you like. Try Print Preview by choosing the command from the File menu or by clicking the Preview tool on the Standard toolbar.

- **Document Map**   This divides your Word window into two panels. On the left you'll see all the headings in your document; and on the right you'll see the regular document, displayed in the view you were using. The Document Map feature is great for checking the headings you've used and for jumping to other sections in a long document. You can move directly to another section simply by clicking the heading in the panel on the left. To turn on the Document Map feature, choose Document Map from the View menu or click the Document Map tool on the Standard toolbar.

- **Show/Hide Paragraph Marks**   This tool on the Standard toolbar displays your document in the selected view but adds paragraph and tab characters wherever you have pressed Enter, Tab, or the spacebar in your document. This can be helpful if you are looking for an errant tab code that's knocking a list out of alignment, but otherwise it can make you cross-eyed. Leave this feature off until you need it.

- **Zoom**   This tool on the Standard toolbar allows you to enlarge or shrink the display until the page is a size you're comfortable working with. Yes, it's true—you can put away those bifocals and work with your text zoomed to 150 percent if you choose! (Of course, that means you'll have to scroll the page back and forth to read your entire document, which can be a pain.)

- **Full Screen**   This view is what Word enthusiasts who can't stand to have the screen cluttered with toolbars prefer. When you choose Full Screen view (by choosing Full Screen from the View menu), Word removes *all* the menus and toolbars and displays a Close Full Screen button floating over the work area. When you're ready to return to the menu/toolbar system, click the button and you're back.

Working with Shared Documents

Word 2003 makes collaborating simpler than ever by providing an easy way for you to organize, track, and share documents and supporting files online. This feature uses SharePoint Team Services to create a Web site that enables you to store, organize, and work with all files related to your shared project. To create a shared workspace, follow these steps:

1   Open the document you want to share, and choose Shared Workspace from the Tools menu.

2   In the Shared Workspace task pane, choose or enter a location where you want to store the shared documents. This location might be a folder on your company network or space on the Web you or your administrator have set up for this purpose. Click Create to create the shared workspace.

> **Note**   If the Shared Workspace option is not available in your Tools menu, SharePoint Team Services are not available on your system. If you are working on a network, check with your system administrator to find out more. To find out more about installing SharePoint Team Services on your stand-alone system, go to *www.microsoft.com/sharepoint/teamservices*.

The Shared Workspace task pane gives you a number of tools for organizing and working on your team project (see Figure 3-4). The following list describes the different tabs available when you're sharing documents:

Status   Tasks

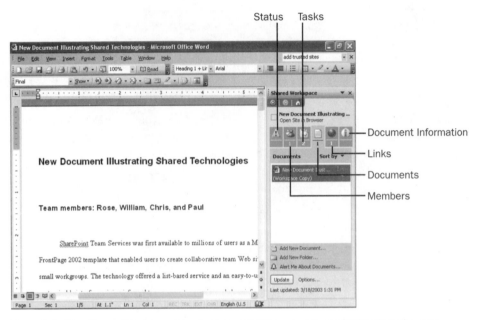

Figure 3-4   The Shared Document task pane provides a number of tabs that give you different types of information about the shared file.

- ■ **Status**   This tool gives you information about the shared file. If there are errors or restrictions on the file, you will be alerted here.

- ■ **Members**   This tool shows you which of your teammates are currently online and enables you to invite others to collaborate.

- ■ **Tasks**   This tool allows you to assign and organize tasks for each team member.

- ■ **Documents**   This tool lists files you've stored in the site for the team to share.

- ■ **Links**   This tool provides helpful sites that can help team members find the resources they need.

- ■ **Document Information**   This tool gives you information about the data currently stored in the workspace, including notifications of any changes made to critical documents.

> **Aha!**   Managing Shared Documents
>
> You'll use the features in the Document Information tab of the Shared Workspace task pane to allow (and restrict) permissions you give to others to modify the file. You can also set up alerts so that you receive an e-mail message when a document has been modified. Finally, the Version History option in Document Information enables you to see how many times the document has been changed—and by whom.

Although you must be using the Office System in order to use the shared workspace task pane, team members can access the shared site using any Web browser. This means you can share documents with someone down the hall or around the world, as long as they work with Office applications and have Web access.

Researching While You Work

How many times during a typical workday do you stop and look up something you need in order to continue? It might be a product number, the spelling of a name, or the date and time of an important event. Now you can do your research without leaving your Word application (this feature is available in Excel and PowerPoint, too). Here are the steps:

1 Choose Research from the Tools menu.

2 In the Research task pane (see Figure 3-5), type your word in the Search box and click the green Start Searching button.

Figure 3-5 The Research task pane makes it possible for you to find what you need without interrupting your work.

Aha!   Fast Research

You can research a word even faster by pressing Alt and clicking the word in your document. Word will open the Research task pane automatically and display the results of the search.

See Also You also can use shared attachments to send a copy of your shared document to other team members. For more about sending shared attachments, see Chapter 13, "E-Mailing with Outlook."

The Research task pane then displays the results of the nearly instant search of both online and offline resources. When you're offline, Word searches the available thesaurus and dictionary information; but when you're online, your search will produce results from a wide variety of online information services (click the All Other Services down arrow to see a list of resources). You can customize the research sites list by clicking Research options and adding, updating, removing, or specifying parental controls for different sources.

Fast Wrap-Up

- You can create all kinds of documents—from simple memos to invoices and travel reports to complicated reports—in Word.

- You can create five different types of new documents by simply clicking a link in the New Document task pane.

- Use one of the many templates in Word to start right off with a document that has been designed and formatted in advance.

- You can enter text a number of different ways in Word: by typing it, writing it by hand, or speaking it. Word 2003 now fully supports the Tablet PC and makes it easy to convert handwriting to typed text.

- Word offers five views that enable you to see your document in different perspectives: Normal, Web Page Layout, Print Layout, Outline, and Reading Layout views.

- Now you can use the Shared Workspace to work collaboratively on documents and store documents, support files, links, and more in a common Web space.

- Word includes a Research task pane that enables you to research what you need instantly without interrupting the work you're doing.

Using the Editing Tools in Microsoft Office Word 2003

4

10-Second Summary
- Correct your document
- Use Find and Replace
- Check spelling and grammar
- Use the thesaurus
- Track changes and adding comments

So now that you know how to create documents easily in Word, you've probably been up half the night typing, right? Most likely, you've got a report full of typos and an oddly organized cover letter that you need to fix before you hand them out for review at the meeting this afternoon. This chapter focuses on the best features for cleanup detail in Word: the editing toolset.

What Kind of Editing Can You Do with Word?

Because there are different kinds of errors in a document, Word gives you different ways to correct those errors:

- **Line-by-line corrections** The common typo is the kind of correction for which you must position the mouse pointer where the error occurs, erase the errant character, and type the correct one. Other line-by-line corrections are simple text editing, deleting and adding words, and revising phrases. This kind of correction always involves positioning the cursor and then deleting text, retyping text, or both.

- **Block corrections** When you need to move a paragraph, change the location of a heading, or change the order of sections in your document, you first select the text you need to work with, which highlights it as a block. Word has a number of shortcut keys and tools that make working with blocks of text easier.

- **Automatic corrections**   Word includes several features that make corrections without your doing anything at all. AutoCorrect is a feature that corrects common errors as you type. The Spelling And Grammar checker scans through your document, evaluates the words you've used, and the way you've used them.

> **Aha!**   What's another word for ...
>
> The Thesaurus has been expanded in Word 2003. Now you can use customized dictionaries to find alternate words and phrases by selecting them in the Research task pane. You can also use the translation feature to translate words and phrases.

- **Collaborative editing**   Word also makes it easy for a number of people to leave their mark on a team document. Using the Track Changes feature, one person can write the document, another can edit, a third can review it, and all three people can see the comments and changes that others have made. In addition, the Shared Workspace feature enables you to create a shared workspace online where you can discuss, review, and share resources related to the developing document.

AutoCorrecting Your Document

The first kind of editing you're likely to notice with Word is the kind that happens right before your eyes as you type. The AutoCorrect feature fixes such things as month names you forgot to capitalize or repeated letters in a common word. AutoCorrect is turned on by default; you've probably already seen it in action. You can tailor the types of corrections AutoCorrect makes so that it finds and changes only those you want made.

Changing AutoCorrect Options

The fastest way to view your current AutoCorrect settings is to right-click a red-underlined word in your document (that red line is Word telling you there's something wrong). When the shortcut menu appears, click AutoCorrect and then choose AutoCorrect Options, as shown in Figure 4-1 on the following page.

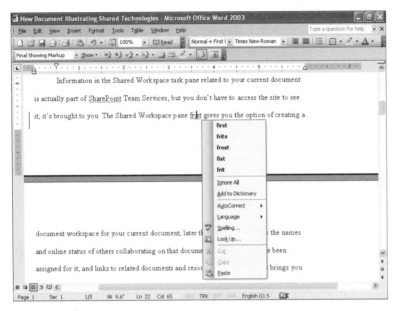

Figure 4-1   Click a red-underlined word or phrase in your document to display the short-cut menu.

> **Lingo**   A *shortcut menu* is a pop-up menu that displays options that relate to the task you are trying to perform. Right-clicking always makes the shortcut menu appear.

Caution   If you don't see a wavy red line, chances are that someone has changed a setting in your spelling options. To find out, choose Options from the Tools menu and click the Spelling And Grammar tab. If the Hide Spelling Errors In This Document check box shows a check mark, click it to clear the mark, and then click OK. Now any spelling errors should appear with those funky wavy lines.

The AutoCorrect dialog box lists the various changes Word automatically makes for you (as shown in Figure 4-2). Many of the options have to do with capitalization, but in the Replace and With boxes, you have the opportunity to enter words, symbols, or phrases you want Word to catch for you. This is great for those times when you just *know* you are going to spell your new supervisor's name wrong, or when you have a long product name you'd rather abbreviate as you type, knowing that Word will fill in all the missing characters using AutoCorrect.

To enter your own AutoCorrect entries, click in the Replace box and type the word or phrase you want Word to find. For example, if your company name is Consolidated Financial Publishing Group, Ltd., you could enter CFPG in the Replace box and the full name of the company in the With box. Then click Add and AutoCorrect adds the entry to the list. Now the next time you type CFPG in your document, AutoCorrect will substitute the full name of the company for the characters you entered, saving you time and keystrokes.

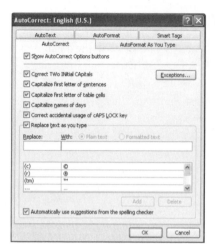

Figure 4-2 AutoCorrect checks for a number of errors automatically, but you can always add your own.

Turning AutoCorrect Off

AutoCorrect is a nice feature, but you may find that some of the "help" you receive isn't exactly what you'd hoped for. In some documents you may want to type (c) and have it stay (c) instead of automatically substituting the copyright symbol, ©, which is one of the changes AutoCorrect makes by default. When you want to turn AutoCorrect off, you do so by choosing AutoCorrect Options from the Tools menu, clearing all the check boxes on the AutoCorrect tab, and then clicking OK.

For the best results, you may want to simply clear the check boxes of those items that interfere with the tasks you are trying to perform. For example, if you are writing a review of a new band called *tuesday* (which is meant to appear in all lowercase letters), you could simply clear the Capitalize Names Of Days check box and leave the others selected.

> **Aha!**   Reversing AutoCorrect
>
> If AutoCorrect makes a change you don't like, you can use the Undo function (either by choosing Undo from the Edit menu or by pressing Ctrl+Z) to remove that change while still leaving AutoCorrect fully functioning. AutoCorrect learns from your correction and won't make the correction again in that document.

Starting Simple: Correcting Typos

As you edit your documents, you will likely use different editing techniques for different things. Some words you'll let Word correct for you; others you'll retype. Or perhaps you'll select the word and delete it by pressing Delete. This section shows you how to complete simple editing tasks.

Common Editing and Navigation Keys

Simple line-by-line editing really involves two steps: detecting the error in the document and correcting it. This means you'll use a combination of navigation keys and editing keys to make the changes you need to make. Table 4-1 lists the keys you'll use to get around within the document, and Table 4-2 highlights the most common editing keys.

Table 4-1 Keys for Moving Around Within the Document

Pressing This Key	Performs This Action
PageUp	Scrolls the document up one screen
PageDown	Scrolls the document down one screen
Home	Moves the cursor quickly to the left end of a line of text
Ctrl+Home	Moves the cursor to the beginning of the document
End	Moves the cursor quickly to the end of the current line
Ctrl+End	Moves the cursor to the end of the document
Right arrow	Moves the cursor to the right one character or space
Ctrl+Right arrow	Moves the cursor to the right one word at a time
Left arrow	Moves the cursor to the left one character or space
Ctrl+Left arrow	Moves the cursor to the left one word at a time
Up arrow	Moves the cursor one line up
Down arrow	Moves the cursor one line down
F5	Displays the Find And Replace dialog box with the GoTo tab selected so that you can enter the number of the page you want to go to

Table 4-2 Keys for Simple Line Editing

Pressing This Key	Performs This Action
Backspace	Erases the character to the left of the cursor
Enter	Completes a paragraph and moves the cursor to the next line in the document
Delete	Deletes the character immediately to the right of the cursor
Insert	Toggles the typing mode from Insert to Overtype mode

Browsing by Object

Word gives you another handy way to move through your document, but it's so small you might miss it. In the bottom of the vertical scroll bar in the Word window, you'll see a small circle with two double-arrows above and below it. That's the Browse Object feature. When you click the circle, a palette of objects appears. You can click the object you want (your choices are Field, End-note, Footnote, Comment, Section, Page, Go To, Find, Edits, Heading, Graphic, and Table), and then click the up arrows or down arrows to search back or forward through the document. Clicking Go To displays the Go To dialog box, and Find displays the Search dialog box.

For example, suppose that you have been working on a document with two other team members and you want to review the document to see what others have said about it. You can choose Browse By Comment to move from comment to comment and read the comments your teammates have inserted. Or if you're double-clicking the tables in a report, you can choose Browse By Tables to move from one table to another.

Using Smart Tags

AutoCorrect is a customizable editing tool that lets you know when something is amiss in your document by underlining the word or phrase. This is an example of a smart tag, a feature that can offer you a menu of additional choices as you are writing or revising your documents. For example, smart tags can highlight the names of people who are in your contact list and give you instant messaging access to them if they are currently online. Smart tags were new in Microsoft Office XP, and they have been greatly enhanced in the Microsoft Office System.

Some smart tags are enabled by default in your Word documents. You can see which tags are turned on by displaying the AutoCorrect dialog box and clicking the Smart Tags tab (see Figure 4-3). If you want to turn off smart tags entirely, click the Label Text With Smart Tags check box to turn off the feature. If you want select additional recognizers, click the items you want to include.

Figure 4-3   You can control the smart tags you want to use in your documents.

> **Lingo** A *recognizer* is a text element Word will use as a smart tag. For example, if you want Word to "recognize" and display smart tag choices for phone numbers included in your document, click the Telephone Number recognizer.

The Office System includes tools for developers that make creating smart tags easier than ever. This means that expert users can create custom smart tags that relate to specific industry areas or applications. For example, a custom smart tag might recognize a particular order number and offer menu choices such as displaying the customer or vendor information, or showing when the order is scheduled to go out.

Aha!   Get More SmartTags

The Smart Tag tab in the AutoCorrect dialog box includes a More Smart Tags you can use to search Office Online for additional smart tags. This is worth checking periodically—you just might find something that will make your life easier.

Smart Documents and Microsoft Office InfoPath Possibilities

Two additional new tools in the Office System extend the idea of data reusability in exciting ways. Smart documents take the smart tag idea and expand it to a larger scale. A developer might create a smart document, for example, to be sensitive to the kinds of data a user is entering and provide related tips, links, or data in a customized task pane. Using the "order number" smart tag example, a smart document might recognize the order number and display a custom task pane offering options that enable the user to click and fill the entire document with the details of that order. Smart documents can also build in additional help resources or prompts for readers filling out common business documents.

InfoPath is a new forms technology built on Extensible Markup Language (XML), which means that data entered in InfoPath forms is saved in such a way that it can be stored in a database and repurposed for use in any number of applications. InfoPath is a new application from Microsoft that uses the familiar Office interface to enable businesses to create electronic forms based on traditional office documents.

Working with Paragraphs

Making line-by-line corrections may be the biggest part of your editing task, but you'll also be moving paragraphs around if you need to restructure documents or reorganize sections. The first step in working with paragraphs involves marking that paragraph (or section) as a block. Table 4-3 provides block selection methods.

> **Lingo** A *block* of text is any text (including a character, a word, a line, a paragraph, a section, or an entire document) that you highlight.

Table 4-3   Selecting Text Blocks

Action	Description
Double-click	Selects the word at the cursor position
Ctrl+click	Selects a sentence
Triple-click	Selects the current paragraph
Double-click in the left margin	Selects the paragraph at the cursor position
Click, drag, and release	Selects a phrase
Ctrl+Shift+Home	Selects all text from the cursor position to the beginning of the document
Ctrl+Shift+End	Selects all text from the cursor position to the end of the document
Ctrl+A	Selects the entire document

Aha!   Selecting Multiple Paragraphs

You can select multiple blocks of text in different parts of the document (called *non-contiguous* blocks because they are not positioned next to each other). You might do this, for example, when you want to change the format of several headings in your document. You could select the first heading normally (triple-click the text to select it); then press and hold Ctrl. Scroll to the next heading and triple-click it; this text is selected too. Finally, still holding Ctrl, scroll to the additional headings and select them. Once the text blocks are selected, you can make whatever changes you were going to make and the edits are applied to all the selected blocks.

Once you select the text you want to work with, you need to specify what you want to do with it. Some of the more common block edits involve copying, pasting, moving, or deleting text. Here are the fastest ways to get the jobs done:

- To cut selected text, click Cut on the Standard toolbar or press Ctrl+X.

- To copy selected text, click Copy on the Standard toolbar or press Ctrl+C.

- To paste selected text into the document, position the cursor where you want to paste the text and click Paste on the Standard toolbar or press Ctrl+V.

- (If you accidentally paste text in the wrong place, simply press Ctrl+Z to undo the change.)

- To delete selected text, press Delete.

Aha!   Display Clipboard Contents

Remember that you can also display and work with the contents of the Office Clipboard by choosing Office Clipboard from the Edit menu.

Understanding Paste Special

Word also enables you to do a special kind of paste with some items you'll paste from the Office Clipboard. Choose the Paste Special command from the Edit menu when you are adding information such as text, graphics, a chart, or an HTML document and you want to preserve the format of file from which you originally copied the data. In the Paste Special dialog box, you can choose whether you want to embed the file or create a link that allows users to move to the application that created it.

Using Find and Replace

The Find and Replace features are tools you can't do without. They enable you to search for a particular word, phrase, or format and replace it with something else. For example, suppose that your company's new product was referred to as RatPackX during its development stage. Now that the product is getting close to its release date, the official name, Mouse Manager, needs to be printed on all product specification sheets and documentation. It's your job to make the change. This is an ideal candidate for find and replace. Here's what you do:

1 Open the document you want to edit.

2 Press Ctrl+H to display the Find And Replace dialog box, shown in Figure 4-4.

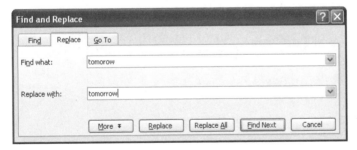

Figure 4-4 The Find And Replace dialog box enables you to make changes quickly throughout your document.

3 In the Find What box, type the word or phrase you're looking for.

4 In the Replace With box, type the word or phrase you want to replace it with.

5 Click Replace All to replace all instances of the original word or phrase with the new entry.

If you want to check each occurrence before you replace it, you can click Find in the Find And Replace dialog box to locate the next item so you can read its context before you change it; then click Replace to change the found item.

Aha!   Just Find, Please

To use Find by itself, press Ctrl+F. (You also can display the Find dialog box by choosing Find from the Edit menu, or by clicking Find in the Select Browse Objects palette.) You will see that Find is just another tab in the Find And Replace dialog box. The options are similar, with one exception: the Highlight All Items Found In option enables you to highlight all found words or phrases at once. You can then change the format or make a different editing change (click the Replace tab if you want to replace the highlighted words with something else).

Special Find and Replace Considerations

When you click More in the Find And Replace dialog box, a number of additional options appear to help you get more specific about the text you're searching for. Here's a quick rundown:

- **Match Case**   Looks for words and phrases that are capitalized exactly the way you entered them.

- **Find Whole Words Only**   Locates only those words that stand alone, not the ones that include the entered phrase as a part of the word. If you were going through the document to replace the word *if* with *whether*, for example (an old editing pet peeve), selecting this option ensures that only the word *if* is highlighted—not *life*, or *miffed* or *cliff*.

- **Use Wildcards**   Enables you to enter a partial phrase and wildcard characters to narrow your search.

- **Sounds Like (English)**   Locates words that sound the same but are spelled differently (there and their, scene and seen, and so on).

- **Find All Word Forms (English)**   Lets you find words that have the basic root in common. The word *light*, for example, would find *highlight*, *stoplight*, and *lightly*.

- **Format**   Allows you to search for text formatted a certain way, perhaps in a font, size, or style you want to edit.

- **Special**   Enables you to find special characters such as line spaces, em dashes, ellipses, or blank spaces.

Checking Your Spelling and Grammar

Even if you were the champion in your fifth-grade spelling bee, chances are that, sooner or later, you're going to spell a word incorrectly. The Spelling And Grammar Checker is a simple but robust utility that runs mostly behind the scenes as you work in Word. Along the way, if you type something that Word doesn't recognize, it will alert you with a wavy red underline that the spelling looks strange (grammar errors get a green line). You can see what Word's trying to tell you by right-clicking the word (here's that smart tag functionality again). A shortcut menu of spelling alternatives appears, and you can choose one of the words displayed if you find that it offers the correct spelling.

When you want to run the spelling checker on the entire document, move the cursor to the beginning of the document by pressing Ctrl+Home and press F7 to start the Spelling Checker (see Figure 4-5).

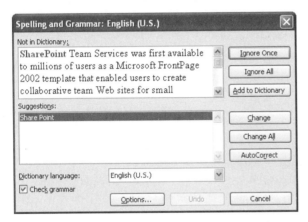

Figure 4-5   Word takes care of the spelling and grammar check in the same procedure.

When the first thing Word considers odd is found in your document the Spelling And Grammar dialog box appears. In the Not In Dictionary window in the top of the dialog box, you see what's stumping Word. In the Suggestions box in the bottom of the dialog box, you see what Word holds out as possible alternatives. To select one of these suggestions, click it and choose Change. If you want to make this change for all occurrences in the document, click Change All. If you want to add the edit to your AutoCorrect list, click AutoCorrect.

If you don't need to change the phrase or word, you can click Ignore Once to skip this occurrence of this word. If you want to skip every occurrence of the word in the document, click Ignore All. If you want to add the word to the dictionary so that Word won't keep catching it in the Spelling And Grammar Checker, click Add To Dictionary.

Word will continue checking the document. When Word has finished, you'll receive the message: *The spelling and grammar check is complete.* Click OK to return to your document.

Spelling and Grammar Options

This only skims the surface of what the Spelling And Grammar Checker has to offer. You can set up the checker to do a number of other things by selecting the options you want in the Spelling And Grammar tab of the Options dialog box. (When you are working in the Spelling And Grammar dialog box, you can also display this dialog box by clicking Options.) Here are some additional features you might want to try:

- Add your own custom dictionary by clicking Custom Dictionaries, selecting Add, and choosing the dictionary file from the displayed list.

- Check the Show Readability Statistics box to display a report of your document that gives you data such as word count, sentence length, and readability level.

- Click the Settings tool in the Grammar area to customize the types of grammar issues that are found by the checker.

- In the Writing Style box, choose Grammar And Style to add a style checker that catches clichés and jargon, passive voice, sentence fragments, split infinitives, and more.

- Turn off the grammar checker so that it does not run at the same time the spelling checker runs by clearing the Check Grammar With Spelling check box.

Using the Thesaurus

The Thesaurus in Word 2003 has been enhanced and tied in with the Research task pane. To use the Thesaurus, select the word you want to look up and then press Shift+F7. The Research task pane appears, showing you options from several different language dictionaries, as well as a Translation selection. To display the synonyms for the word you selected, click the resource you want to view. A list of alternative words is displayed from that reference. To use one of the displayed words, click it and click the down arrow that appears to the right of the word. Click the action you want to take; Insert, Copy, or Look Up the word to see whether it will fit what you're trying to say (see Figure 4-6).

Figure 4-6   The Thesaurus gives you the option of choosing the dictionary you want to use and inserting, copying, or looking up selected words.

Tracking Changes

When you are working with a team to prepare a document, it's imperative that you be able to see what each of the team members has contributed and know what you want to keep and what you want to discard. The fastest way to turn on tracking is to press Ctrl+Shift+E (you can choose Track Changes from the Tools menu if you prefer).

Tracking is now on, and any changes you make in the document will appear in a different color and underlined. A bar along the left side of the document also points out places in the document that have been edited (see Figure 4-7).

Controlling Editable Areas

Now in Word 2003 you can protect your documents by controlling the things team members can and can't do with them. When you display the Protect Document task pane (choose Protect Document from the Tools menu), you can limit the formatting so that others can choose only assigned styles in the document or add editing restrictions so that only certain types of changes can be made.

In the Exceptions area of the task pane, you can change the permissions of individual users or apply permissions to the entire group. Select the name of the team member in the displayed list; then click the down arrow to show a menu of choices that let you find editable regions for that user, display all editable regions for that user, or remove all editing permissions for that user. To put the restrictions into effect, click the Yes Start Enforcing Protection button.

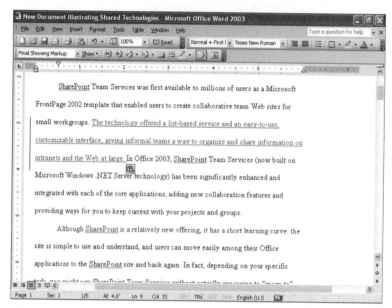

Figure 4-7 Tracking enables you to see what has been done to a document during the editing process.

Using the Reviewing Toolbar

When you turn on change tracking, the Reviewing toolbar appears by default. You use the Reviewing toolbar for tracking comments and adding, reviewing, and resolving comments. Table 4-4 tells you a little about each of the tools.

Table 4-4   Using Reviewing Tools

Tool	Description
Display For Review	Click the down arrow to choose the version of the document you want to see: Original, Original Showing Markup, Final, or Final Showing Markup.
Show	Click the down arrow to choose what you want to display in the document (Comments, Insertions and Deletions, Formatting, Reviewers, and Reviewing Pane).
Previous	Jumps to the previous change.
Next	Jumps to the next change.
Accept Change	Adds the selected change to the document.
Reject Change/Delete Comment	Discards the current change and returns the document to its original state at that point. If a comment is selected, this tool removes the comment.
Insert Comment	In Normal view, displays the Reviewing Pane; in Web Layout and Print Layout views, displays a comment balloon. Either way, simply type in the comment you want to add.

Table 4-4 Using Reviewing Tools

Tool	Description
Insert Voice	Enables you to record a note and link the sound object to a specific place in the document.
Highlight	Highlights an area you select.
Track Changes	Toggles tracking on and off.
Reviewing Pane	Displays the Reviewing Pane along the bottom of the document so that you can scroll through the changes and comments added to the document.

Setting Tracking Options

Especially if you are working with several people on a project, it is helpful for each to choose a color or style for his or her changes. That way the person compiling the final document can easily see which changes were made by which team member. You can set these colors and more options in the Track Changes dialog box (shown in Figure 4-8), which you display by clicking the Show down arrow on the Reviewing toolbar and choosing Options.

Figure 4-8 You can change the color and style of your changes, as well as the way in which changes appear, in the Track Changes dialog box.

These are the tracking options you can change:

- You can change the way your inserted, deleted, and formatted text is displayed by clicking the element's down arrow and choosing a different style.

- Choose a different color for your changes by clicking the Color down arrow and making your choice.

- If you want to change the indicator used to show formatting changes, click the Formatting down arrow and choose the style you want.

> **Aha!**   Keep It Simple
>
> You may prefer to leave Formatting set to None because tracked changes can eas-
> ily pile up if you have several people making changes on a document—and adding
> formatting changes can magnify the swirl of color in the document in progress. For-
> matting changes are typically secondary to added or deleted text, so you might
> want to leave this option disabled, enabling you to focus on the content.

- You can do away with the balloons used to display tracked changes in Print and Web Layout views by changing the Use Balloons setting from Always to Never. (In addition, you can change the balloon width and placement using the options in this section.)

- You can set up the way you want documents to print with tracked changes by selecting Auto, Preserve (the default, which keeps the document's current set-ting), and Force Landscape.

- You can alter the Changed Lines setting to change the bar indicator along the left edge of the page that shows changes have been made.

Accepting or Rejecting Changes

When you have received a document and are reviewing and evaluating the changes and additions, you need to be able to accept or reject the changes and suggestions everybody made. Two tools on the Reviewing toolbar make that a simple matter: Accept Changes and Reject Changes. The process goes like this:

1 Click Next to move to the next change in the document.

2 Review the change and decide whether you want to keep or discard it.

3 Click Accept Change to keep the change or Reject Change to discard it.

4 Click Next to move to the next change.

> **Note**   Instead of working through the changes one by one, you may prefer to
> accept or reject all the changes in the document at once. To choose those
> options, click the down arrow to the right of either the Accept Changes or Reject
> Changes tool. Then choose Accept All Changes In Document or Reject All
> Changes In Document to complete the task.

Replying with Changes

If you are working on a document that was sent to you via e-mail, the Reviewing toolbar will include a tool called Reply With Changes. It works like this: when you're finished reviewing the document you received, press Ctrl+S to save the document and then click Reply With Changes. Word creates a new e-mail message addressed to the person who sent you the document, attaches the file, and even adds some text for you. The Attachment Options task pane appears, enabling you to choose whether you want to send the file as a regular attachment or as a shared attachment.

> **Lingo** A *shared attachment* sends all team members a copy of the document and places a copy in the Shared Document Workspace so all changes can be automatically added to the master document on the site.

Adding Comments

As part of the review process, team members may be more interested in adding their suggestions than in making actual changes. Comments are perfect for that. When you position the pointer over each comment, a pop-up box displays the reviewer's name and the date and time the comment was added. Comments appear in balloons on the right of the document in Print and Web Layout views. (In Normal view, you must have the Reviewing Pane open to view the comments.)

> **Aha!**   Choosing Your Balloons
>
> Word 2003 now enables you to turn balloon display on and off easily. If balloons are displayed and you want to hide them, click the Show down arrow on the Reviewing toolbar, point to Balloons, and click Never. If you want balloons displayed only for comments and formatting changes (this can greatly reduce the number of balloons you see because all insertions and deletions are automatically displayed in balloons by default), choose Only For Comments/Formatting.

Resolving Comments

You can move from comment to comment in a document by simply scrolling through and reading the balloons, by clicking Next on the Reviewing toolbar, or by clicking Browse By Comment using the Browse Object feature.

After you review a comment, you can discard it by right-clicking the comment and choosing Delete Comment from the shortcut menu. If you want to delete all comments at once, click the down arrow to the right of the Reject Change/Delete Comment tool on the Reviewing toolbar and click Delete All Comments In Document from the menu that appears. All comments are removed and your document is ready for a final review.

> **Note**   The Reviewing Pane is a scrollable area of the document window that you can open to display the comments and changes in your document. This is a log of all of the changes and comments that appear in balloons in Print and Web Layout views. To display the Reviewing Pane, click the Reviewing Pane tool on the Reviewing toolbar. To hide the pane, click the tool a second time.

> **Aha!**   Grant Permission to Specific Users
>
> Now Word 2003 helps you make sure that only those people you want to see your document will have access to it. You can grant varying levels of access to documents by opening the File menu, choosing Permission, and then selecting Do Not Forward (which blocks the document from being e-mailed to another person) or Restrict Permission As (which displays a dialog box in which you can choose the permission settings you want). By default, Permission is set to Unrestricted Access, which means anyone who receives your document can forward it at will.

Adding Audio Comments

When you are editing or revising a document, you can click the Insert Voice tool to record a voice note that is inserted in the document. The Sound Object dialog box appears so that you can record your note; Word links the note to the cursor position in the document (see Figure 4-9). After the sound object is recorded, you can play it back by double-clicking the sound object in the comment.

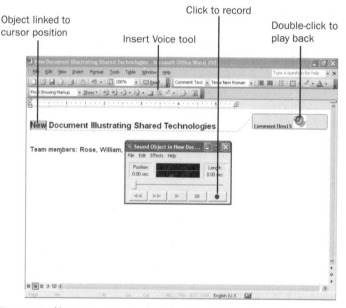

Figure 4-9   Now you can use the speech features to insert a voice comment directly into a document.

Fast Wrap-Up

- AutoCorrect does on-the-spot corrections as you type. You can customize this feature to fit your own style and typing foibles.

- When you copy, move, cut, paste, delete, and format text, you first mark it as a block.

- The Find And Replace feature enables you to search for specific words or phrases in your document and replace the found items with other text.

- The Thesaurus now allows you to search multiple dictionaries and insert, copy, or look up alternate words.

- The Spelling And Grammar Checker is a full-featured utility that checks not only spelling and simple grammar but style and usage as well.

- You can use Word in a workgroup to develop a document and track changes so that you can see what each team member has added. New features enable you to set editing controls and send shared attachments to the group.

- Comments allow you to insert notes and suggestions in a collaborative document. You now can record voice comments and link them to specific words or sections in your document.

Formatting in Microsoft Word

5

10-Second Summary
- ■ AutoFormat your document
- ■ Change fonts
- ■ Adjust document spacing and setting tabs
- ■ Create and format tables
- ■ Add columns and apply styles

You can write the best document in the world, but if it appears cramped and crowded and readers have to work to decipher it, chances are that it won't be read. This chapter shows you how to use the formatting features of Microsoft Office Word 2003 to make your document look like something that people will want to read. Word includes some automatic features (such as AutoFormat and themes) that can make formatting less of a chore and gives you a wide range of options you can use to tailor your documents to look just the way you want them to look.

Aha! Don't Forget Templates

For a simple, quick format with a professional look, try creating your document based on Word's ready-to-use templates. You'll find templates for memos, fax cover sheets, reports, Web pages, and more. To see which templates are available in Word, choose New from the File menu, and then click the link you want in the Templates area of the New Document task pane. Remember, too, that you can make your own templates from favorite documents you create.

Letting AutoFormat Do the Work

AutoFormat is a great feature that sometimes gets a bad rap. AutoFormat can help you by automatically adding bullets to your lists as you type, changing heading styles, numbering steps, changing quotes and dashes, and more. But because AutoFormat is occasionally over-eager, changing what you'd rather not have changed, some people prefer to turn off the feature completely and format things by hand. I think the best way to handle Auto-Format is to teach it to do what you want it to do. You do this by setting the AutoFormat options you prefer.

AutoFormat is turned on by default when you begin working with Word. To display the AutoFormat dialog box (shown in Figure 5-1), choose AutoFormat from the Format menu.

Figure 5-1   You can have Word do a quick AutoFormat based on the document style you select.

The two primary choices in the AutoFormat dialog box allow you to determine how you want the formatting to be done. If you want Word to go through the whole document and make any changes that are needed, leave AutoFormat Now selected. If you want Word to alert you about each formatting change before it is made and give you the option of accepting or rejecting the change, click AutoFormat And Review Each Change. When you click OK, AutoFormatting begins.

> **Note**   Word gives you the option of applying AutoFormat choices based on the kind of document you are creating. The General Document option is selected by default, but you can click the down arrow and choose Letter or E-mail instead.

Controlling AutoFormat

Depending on the nature of your document and how specialized your formats need to be, you may want to turn off some of the AutoFormat features so they aren't carried out automatically. Here's how to do that:

1   Click Options in the AutoFormat dialog box.

2   On the AutoFormat tab, click the check box of any AutoFormat option you want to turn off to clear it. Table 5-1 presents the different AutoFormat options.

3   Click OK to accept your change, and then click OK again in the AutoFormat dialog box to return to your document.

Table 5-1 AutoFormat Options

Option	Description
Built-In Heading Styles	Applies the default headline styles for the current document
Automatic Bulleted Lists	Turns a list into a bulleted list automatically
List Styles	Applies list styles used in the current document
Other Paragraph Styles	Formats the paragraphs in your document according to styles in your current document
"Straight Quotes" With "Smart Quotes"	Replaces double-prime characters (quotation marks that are vertical) with open and close quotation marks, which are curly
Ordinals With Superscript	Formats ordinals to be superscript above and to the right of the number (1st, 2nd, 3rd)
Fractions (1/2) With Fraction Character (½)	Formats full-size fractions (2/3) to single-character size ($^2/_3$)
Hyphens (–) With Dash (—)	Replaces two hyphens in a row typed from the keyboard with a longer dash character
Bold And _Italic_ With Real Formatting	Boldfaces text you type surrounded by asterisks and italicizes text you enclose in underscores
Internet And Network Paths With Hyperlinks	Recognizes URLs and network paths and creates hyperlinks automatically
Preserve Styles	When the autoformat is done, keeps any styles applied in the current document
Plain Text Wordmail Documents	Causes any e-mail messages you open in Word to be displayed in an e-mail format

Disabling AutoFormat

If you decide that you're really a do-it-yourself kind of person and you'd rather have Auto-Format turned off completely, you can disable the feature. Just display the AutoFormat tab (click Options in the AutoFormat dialog box) and clear all the check boxes by clicking the ones displaying check marks. Additionally, click the AutoFormat As You Type tab and clear those check boxes as well. When you click OK to return to your document, AutoFormat features will be turned off and all the formatting will be left up to you. Even if you disable AutoFormat, there is another kind of AutoFormat that is available to you: Table AutoFormat. You'll learn more about that feature in the section entitled "Using Table AutoFormat," later in this chapter.

A Return to Themes

You can apply themes to your documents (either before or after you create them) to create a consistent look and feel. Word 2003 adds many new themes to the collection. Here are the steps:

> **Lingo** A *theme* in Word is a design that is carried through your document and can be applied to other documents, your Web page, e-mail messages, and more. A theme applies design choices such as color selection, border style, list styles, text font and size, and line styles.

1 Open the document to which you want to apply the theme (or begin a new document).

2 Choose Theme from the Format menu. In the Theme dialog box, click the theme style you'd like to see (see Figure 5-2).

Figure 5-2 Word includes themes that coordinate the heading, text, link, and list styles used in your documents.

3 Click OK to apply the theme to your document.

Changing Fonts, Font Styles, and Point Sizes

The font you choose for your document plays a major role in how well your document is received. Most traditional business documents use fonts similar to Times Roman; many documents displayed on the Web use Arial or Verdana. In addition to these commonly-used fonts, you have dozens of different fonts from which to choose. Some are fancy, some are plain, and some contain symbols instead of alphanumeric characters.

> **Lingo** A *font* is the term used to refer to typeface in one particular size and style. Times Roman, 12-point bold text is an example of one font; Arial 10-point normal is another.

You can use the tools on the Formatting toolbar to change the font style and size quickly. Here's how:

■ **Change a font**   To change the font of existing text, select the text and click the Font down arrow in the Formatting toolbar. Choose the font you want from the displayed list.

- **Change font size**   Select the text you want to resize and click the Font Size down arrow. Click your choice.

- **Change font style**   To boldface, italicize, or underline existing text, select the text and then click the Bold, Italic, or Underline tool in the Formatting toolbar.

More Changes in the Font Dialog Box

Although the Formatting toolbar contains most of the tools you need for common formatting operations, you may also want to change font color or apply other font styles, such as super- or subscript, strikethrough, embossed, outline, or small or large caps. You can display the Font dialog box two different ways:

- Choose Font from the Formatting menu.

- Right-click selected text and choose Font.

You can select the font, size, color, and style as needed; then click OK to apply the settings to selected text.

Aha!   Adding Fonts

You can easily add new fonts to the Office System and make them available to all the programs in the system. You'll find many font companies online (one I particularly like is Fonts.com). You can purchase and download fonts from the Web or arrange to have a CD sent to you—either way, the font manufacturer provides simple instructions on how to install the fonts in Windows XP and make them available to all your Office System applications.

Changing Spacing

If the spacing in your document is done well, your readers will never notice it. If the spacing is too tight, your readers will have to struggle to read the page and may just give up. If the spacing is too wide, your readers may get distracted and stop reading. Spacing done well gives readers' eyes a break, shows them at a glance where they need to begin reading on a page, and what the most important points are. Word enables you to control spacing by setting indents, changing paragraph spacing, and altering spacing between lines.

Changing Indents

Many people rely simply on the paragraph indent to let readers know where one paragraph stops and another starts. For many documents this works fine. This is called setting a *first-line indent*, and here's how to do it:

1 Choose Paragraph from the Format menu.

2 In the Indentation area of the Paragraph dialog box, click the Special down arrow and choose First Line. The value .5 appears in the By box (see Figure 5-3). This tells Word to begin each new paragraph with an indent of one-half inch.

3 If you want to make the indent smaller or larger, decrease or increase the value shown. (*Note:* One-half inch is considered a standard indent for typical business formats.)

4 Click OK to save the changes.

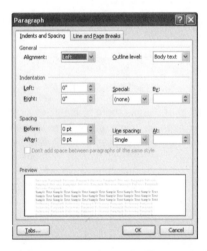

Figure 5-3 You can use the Paragraph dialog box to change spacing.

Aha!   Changing Indents on the Ruler

You also can change the indents in your document by dragging the left and right indent markers inward on the horizontal ruler. If you want to change the indents for existing text, select the text before you move the indent markers. Selected text—and any text you enter after that point in the document—will take on the indent settings you modified.

Page Margins: A Different Matter

The indents you enter are added to the existing page margins for your document, which means that the text may be indented more than you expect. *Page margins* are the amount of white space around the edges of each page. You set the page margins for your document by choosing Page Setup from the File menu. By default, Word creates 1-inch margins for the top and bottom, and a 1.25-inch margin for the left and right edges. When you enter Left and Right indent values in the Paragraph dialog box, those values are added to the page margins displayed in the Page Setup dialog box.

Before and After Paragraphs

If you prefer not to use first-line indents to show the reader where your paragraphs begin and end, you can simply add extra space before and after paragraphs instead. In the Paragraph dialog box, click the Before box in the Spacing area and increase the value to add space preceding the paragraph. Decrease the value if you want to lessen the space before the first line of the paragraph. Click the After box and change that value as needed. Click OK to accept the changes and return to the document.

> **Note**   The values entered in the Before and After boxes show the characters pt. This is an abbreviation for points, which is a type measurement. To give you an idea of how much space 6 and 12 points really is, there are 72 points to an inch, and 12-point text is typically used for body text in a document.

Changing Line Spacing

Another important setting in the Paragraph dialog box you might want to use is the amount of vertical space between lines in your document. Word gives you the option of choosing Single, 1.5, Double, At Least, Exactly, or Multiple line spacing. The first three choices are standard—your document is single-spaced by default. The last three choices enable you to precisely control the line height, known as *leading*, by entering a specific value in the At box to cause the text to be placed at a desired measurement. To change the line spacing, click the Line Spacing down arrow and choose your selection from the list. If you select Exactly, At Least, or Multiple, enter the value for the line height in the At box.

> **Aha!**   Changing Line Spacing Quickly
>
> You can change line spacing quickly by selecting the text you want to change and clicking the down arrow to the left of the Line Spacing tool in the Formatting toolbar. Click the spacing setting you want.

Setting Tabs

Tabs control where and how your text lines up on the page. You set tabs using the horizontal ruler along the top edge of the Word window. If your ruler isn't visible, display it by choosing Rulers from the View menu. The following graphic shows you the important elements of the ruler, as far as tabs are concerned:

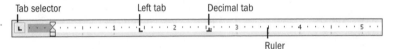

You can set tabs in two ways: by using the ruler or by working in the Tabs dialog box. Generally, for documents in which precise measurement isn't important, I like to use the click-and-drag method in the ruler. Just click the tab selector on the far left side of the ruler until you see the tab you want (use Table 5-2 as a key). Then drag the tab to the place on the ruler bar where you want it to appear. It's that simple.

Table 5-2   Word Tab Styles

Icon	Tab Name	Description
L	Left tab	Left-aligns text at this tab stop
⌐	Right tab	Right-aligns text at this tab stop
⊥	Center	Centers text at this tab stop
⊥	Decimal tab	Creates a decimal tab so that numbers are aligned at their decimal points
I	Bar tab	Allows you to set a tab for bar characters

For more complicated tab-setting, you need the Tabs dialog box (shown in Figure 5-4). Display it by choosing Format and selecting Tabs. Here you have additional options, such as adding leaders, clearing all tabs, changing tab alignment, and more.

> **Lingo** A *leader* is a line (which could be solid, dashed, or dotted) leading from one tab to the next. This is a technique often used in creating a table of contents to help lead the reader's eye from the text to the page number.

To set tabs using the Tabs dialog box, click in the Tab Stop Position list box; type the location where you want to add the tab; choose the Alignment style (Left, Right, Center, or Decimal); click a Leader style if you want one, and then click OK. The tab is added in your document and applied to your text the next time you press Tab.

Figure 5-4   You can use the Tabs dialog box to set tabs at specific points in your document and add leaders.

> **Aha!**   Setting Global Tabs
>
> Tabs aren't retroactive, so they affect only the text in the current paragraph, or the paragraphs you create after the current paragraph (when you press Enter, the tab entry travels with the cursor to the next paragraph). If you want to apply a tab to an entire existing document, press Ctrl+A to select all text before you display the Tabs dialog box or add a tab to the ruler.

When you want to clear tabs, you can do it two ways: Drag the tab off the ruler, or select the tab in the Tabs dialog box and click the Clear button. If you want to remove all tabs in the selected text, click Clear All.

Creating Bulleted and Numbered Lists

Bulleted and numbered lists give your readers' eyes a break; they help you make your points more clearly; they lead students through processes and confused gadget-builders through instruction manuals. The easiest way to create a numbered or bulleted list is to use the Numbering or Bullets tools on the Formatting toolbar. Simply position the cursor at the point you want to begin the list, and click one of those two tools. If you click Numbering, a number 1 is inserted in your document. If you click Bullets, a bullet character appears. Create your list by typing an item and pressing Enter; Word moves the cursor to the next line and adds another bullet or the next number, depending on what you have selected.

You can change the way Word handles bullets and numbers by choosing Bullets And Numbering from the Format menu. This displays the Bullets And Numbering dialog box, shown in Figure 5-5 on the following page. To choose a different bullet or number style, click the tab you want and then click the example you like in the preview window. When you click

OK, the new style is applied to your list and will be automatically used the next time you create a bulleted or numbered list.

You also can customize the bullet and number styles used in lists by clicking Customize in the Bullets And Numbering dialog box. This allows you to change the look, size, and position of the character, as well as the spacing of the text and the color and style attributes.

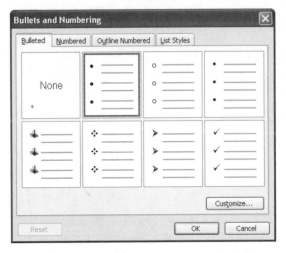

Figure 5-5 You can change the style of bullets and numbers Word uses in the lists you create.

Aha!   Add a Picture Bullet

If you want a different kind of look for your list, you can use one of Word's picture bullets. When the Bullets And Numbering dialog box is displayed, click a bullet style and click the Customize button. In the Customize Bullet Style dialog box, click the Picture button. The Picture Bullet palette appears. Click the bullet style you want to use, or click Import to import a picture of your own you'd like to use. Click OK twice to add the new bullet to your document.

Adding Tables

Tables, like bulleted and numbered lists, are another great quick-look feature that break up the long sections of text in your document and add visual interest to the page. A table can also be very useful in helping readers understand information quickly. Reading a detailed, four-page description about the new products in your spring catalog might be helpful for salespeople who have lots of time to kill and want to learn every subtle nuance of your latest line additions, but a table highlighting the key sales features, costs, and specifications of each of those items is a great way to help people grasp the information at a glance.

Word makes it easy for you to create, format, and modify tables in your document. You begin in one of two ways: by using the Insert Table tool, or by choosing Insert from the Table menu. The Insert Table tool is the fastest method, so that's the one I'm going with here. If you prefer, however, you can use the Table dialog box (choose Insert, Table from the Table menu) to do the same thing.

Creating a Table with the Insert Table Tool

You'll find the Insert Table tool on the Formatting toolbar. When you click it, a drop-down grid appears, enabling you to select the number of rows and columns you want to create (as shown in Figure 5-6). Just drag the mouse to highlight the rows and columns you want, and then click the mouse button. Word adds the new blank table at the cursor position in your document.

Figure 5-6   You can use the Insert Table tool to create a simple table quickly.

Adding Table Data

Okay, you've added the table; now you need to enter data. The cells across the top of the table will most likely be your column headings—that is, the text labels that identify the values in the columns. You may also want to add row labels in the first column to identify the data being tracked. To enter your data, simply click in the *cell* to which you want to add data, type the information, and press Tab. The cursor moves to the next cell, and you can continue entering data as needed.

> **Lingo**   A *cell* is the rectangular area where you enter data in a table or spreadsheet. Each cell is the intersection of a column and a row.

Using Table AutoFormat

You can format the table by changing the lines, colors, and more, but did you know Word provides an automatic feature that can take care of the format for you? The Table Auto-Format command in the Table menu provides you with dozens of formats to apply to your new table (see Figure 5-7). Simply scroll through the list, click the one you want, and then click OK to apply the format.

Figure 5-7 In the Table AutoFormat dialog box, you can choose the table style you want and add your own enhancements, if necessary.

> **Aha!**   Create Your Own Table Formats
>
> You can customize the table format you've selected by clicking Modify in the Table AutoFormat dialog box. The Modify Table dialog box gives you all kinds of options, including changing the border style and width, content alignment, shading, and more. You can also save the modified table style as a new style if you choose.

Inserting and Deleting Table Columns and Rows

As your table grows, you will undoubtedly need to add rows and columns to accommodate the information. Here are the procedures for each of these simple tasks:

- To add a row at the end of an existing table, click in the cell in the bottom right corner of the table and press Tab. A new row is added.

- To add a row in the middle of an existing table, click just to the left of the first cell in the row above which you want to add the new row. The entire row should be selected. (If the row doesn't highlight automatically, drag to select the whole row.) Now choose Insert from the Table menu and select Rows Above to add the row. (As you can see, you can also add rows below the selected row if you choose.) If you want to add multiple rows, highlight however many rows you want to add before you select Insert Rows. When Word adds the rows, the number of rows you highlighted will be the number of rows inserted.

- To add a column, position the pointer at the top edge of the column beside which you want to add the new column. When the pointer changes to an arrow, click to select the entire column. Now choose Insert from the Table menu, and choose Columns To The Right or Columns To The Left, depending on where in the table you want to add the column. Word then inserts the column and the other columns are resized accordingly.

- To delete columns and rows, begin by highlighting the columns or rows you want to delete. Then choose Delete from the Table menu and point to either Columns or Rows. Additionally, you can select and delete the entire table if you're ready to see it go.

> **Note** Tables are a powerful Word feature and there are many, many things you can do with tables beyond these basics. You can use functions in your tables, sort data, use macros, create nested tables, and much more. For a fuller discussion on tables and the many things you can do with them, see *Microsoft Office Word 2003 Inside Out*, by Mary Millhollon and Katherine Murray, published by Microsoft Press.

Specifying Columns

Not all documents are made up of margin-to-margin text. Some have multiple columns, newsletter-style. Word lets you easily create multiple columns in your documents. To start the process, choose Columns from the Format menu, and the Columns dialog box appears (as shown in Figure 5-8).

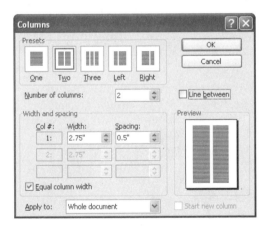

Figure 5-8 You can easily create multiple columns in your Word documents.

Where Do You Want Columns?

You can create multiple columns for the entire document or you can choose columns for only a specific section, whichever you prefer. By default, Word applies the column change to the whole document. If you want to create columns in a section of your document, first highlight the text you want to format in columns. Next, display the Columns dialog box, click the Apply To down arrow, and choose Selected Text. If you want to create columns from the current cursor position onward, select This Point Forward. Click OK to save your changes and close the Columns dialog box.

You use the settings in the Columns dialog box to control how many columns you have, how they are positioned, how much space you place between them, and whether they have a vertical line to separate them. Here are the specifics you can use to set up the columns in your document:

- In the Presets area, click the column style you want to create.

- In Number Of Columns, enter the number of columns.

- If you want a line to appear vertically between the columns, select the Line Between check box.

- In Width And Spacing, you can customize the widths of individual columns and control the amount of spacing between them. As you make these changes, Word displays the columns in the Preview window.

> **Aha!**   Columns of Unequal Widths
>
> If you want the columns in your documents to be different sizes, click the Equal Column Width check box to clear it. You can then change the Width setting for each column to set individual values.

When you've got the column settings the way you want them, click OK to save the entries and create the columns. At first the only change you'll see in your document (unless you are applying the column change to selected text) is the addition of column markers in the horizontal ruler along the top of the document. As you enter text, you will see the text flow into the next column after the first column is filled.

> **Note**   When you are working in Normal view, the columns you've created aren't visible. This can be confusing, so it's best to work in Print Layout view when you have a multicolumn document open on the screen. You'll also want to use Print Preview regularly to keep an eye on how your document will look when it is printed.

Applying Styles and Templates

All the formatting talk in this chapter has shown you how to control the look and feel of the text in your document. Wouldn't it be nice to be able to save all these settings for future use? That's what styles allow you to do. A *style* in Word is a preset format you apply to text in your document. By default, Word documents have the Normal template attached (this template includes the default styles for Heading 1, Heading 2, and so on). But you also can choose different styles, modify existing styles, or create your own styles, based on all the formatting changes you've learned to make in this chapter. And once you've created those styles, you may want to save them in your own template, or add them to a template you already use. This section provides you with quick steps for working with styles and templates.

- To display the Styles And Formatting task pane, click the tool that looks like a double-A. You do most of your work with styles in this task pane (see Figure 5-9).

Figure 5-9 You'll use the Styles And Formatting task pane to work with styles in your document.

- To choose a style for selected text, click the style name in the Styles And Formatting task pane.

- To create a new style, format the text in the document the way you want it; then highlight the text and click the New Style button in the Styles And Formatting task pane. Enter a name for the style, and make any other necessary changes; click OK to save the style.

> **Aha!**   Replacing Styles Globally
>
> If you decide that you *really* like this new style you created and you want to use it instead of other styles in your document, you can make the change easily. In the Styles And Formatting task pane, click the down arrow to the right of the style you want to change, and then click Select All *x* Instances (where *x* is the number of times that style appears in your document). Word highlights every occurrence of the style you want to change in your document. Now scroll through the style list and click the style you want to use. Word automatically formats all the selected text using the style you selected.

- To save the file as a template, choose Save As from the File menu and enter a name for the template. Click the Save As Type down arrow and choose Document Template; then click Save.

> **Caution** If you are creating this template based on a real document you are using for something else, don't forget to save the document as a regular document, too. If you close the document now without saving, any text changes you made during this work session will be lost.

- To attach a template to a document, choose Templates And Add-Ins from the Tools menu. In the Templates And Add-Ins dialog box, click Attach. Navigate to the folder in which you saved the template file. When you find it, click the file and then click Open. In the Templates And Add-Ins dialog box, click the Automatically Update check box, and click OK.

Fast Wrap-Up

- Word includes many different formatting features to help you control the way your text looks and feels.

- AutoFormat can help you format as you work and can help you automate lists, headings, and more.

- Themes give you a coordinated effect for your printed and electronic documents by establishing preset selections for colors, headings, links, and more.

- Changing the font, size, and font style is a simple matter of point-and-click on the Formatting toolbar.

- You adjust paragraph, line spacing, and indents by using the features in the Paragraph dialog box.

- You can add tabs either by using the horizontal ruler or the Tabs dialog box.

- Tables enable you to show readers information quickly in a compare-and-contrast fashion. Word helps you add a professional touch to your table design with AutoFormat.

- Word allows you to create up to 11 columns in your document; you control the spacing, width, and flow of text in those columns.

- You can save your formatting choices as styles and use them again in other documents.

- The styles are saved in templates, and you can apply those templates to new or existing documents, which saves you time and formatting effort later.

Special Tasks in Microsoft Office Word 2003

6

10-Second Summary
- ■ Work with sections
- ■ Add headers and footers
- ■ Insert pictures and draw diagrams
- ■ Work with XML
- ■ Create a table of contents
- ■ Record and run macros

Now that you're comfortable with the basics of creating and formatting Word documents, you're ready to tackle more specialized tasks. This chapter explains the basics of working with sections, adding art, drawing diagrams, inserting bookmarks, and creating hyperlinks. You'll also learn here about working with XML in Word, and you'll find out how to add a table of contents, an index, and macros to your documents.

Working with Sections

It's possible to have a long document and never need to work with sections. But if you want variety and flexibility in your formats, page orientation, and headers and footers, you'll need to learn how to create and work with sections.

> **Lingo** A *section* serves as a kind of document within a document, allowing you to set formats for the different sections that do not affect the whole.

- ■ To add a section break, position the cursor where you want to add the section break. Choose Break from the Insert menu. Select the type of section break you want to add (see Table 6-1 for an overview of the different types).

- ■ To remove a section break, highlight the section break line (you need to be in Normal view or have paragraph marks turned on in other views to see it) and press Delete. The format of the section that follows the break will be applied to the section that precedes the break.

Table 6-1   Section Break Types

Break Type	Description
Next Page	Creates a section break that ends the current page and begins the next section on a fresh page
Continuous	Begins a new section but does not advance to the next page
Even Page	Begins the new section on the next even-numbered page
Odd Page	Starts the new section on the next odd-numbered page

> **Aha!**   Viewing Section Breaks
>
> Depending on the view you are working in, you may not see anything at all after you add the section break. In Web Layout view and Print Layout view, no insert line is visible. If you are working in Normal view, you see a double dotted line with the name of the break type in the center.

Adding Headers and Footers

Almost all books have headers and footers. Reading them is one thing, but you might think that *creating* them is a tougher deal. Actually, creating headers and footers is pretty simple in Word, even if you decide to use sections and want to vary the text from page to page. Here is the process:

- To insert a header or footer in your document, choose Header And Footer from the View menu. Type your text in the window that appears, and use the Header and Footer tools shown in Table 6-2 to customize the text as needed. Click outside the text area to return to the document.

- To remove a header or footer, display it by choosing Header And Footer from the View menu. Click in the item and press Ctrl+A; then press Delete.

- To insert a page number in a header or footer, position the cursor and click the Insert Page Number tool. To format the page number, use the Format Page Number tool.

Table 6-2   Header and Footer Tools

Tool Icon	Name	Description
Insert AutoText ▾	Insert AutoText	Displays a drop-down list of items you can have Word insert in the header or footer
⟦#⟧	Insert Page Number	Inserts the current page number at the cursor position
⟦⊞⟧	Insert Number Of Pages	Displays at the cursor position the total number of pages

Table 6-2 Header and Footer Tools

Tool Icon	Name	Description
	Format Page Number	Displays the Page Number Format dialog box so that you can enter page-numbering options
	Insert Date	Inserts the current date in the form MM/DD/YYYY
	Insert Time	Adds the current time
	Page Setup	Displays the Page Setup dialog box so that you can change header and footer options
	Show/Hide Document Text	Alternately hides and displays document text
	Same As Previous	Makes the selected header or footer the same as the previous one
	Switch Between Header And Footer	Moves the display from the header to the footer and back again
	Show Previous	If the header is selected, jumps to the previous header; if the footer is selected, jumps to previous footer
	Show Next	If the header is selected, jumps to the next header; if the footer is selected, jumps to next footer
Close	Close	Closes the Header and Footer toolbar

Aha!   Expanding and Viewing Headers

You can create multiline headers and footers by pressing Enter at the end of the first line. This gives you room for more text. To see how the page will look when printed (headers, footers, and all), click the Print Preview tool on the Standard toolbar.

Inserting Pictures

Not long ago, adding a photo to a document was a big deal. Cutting and pasting and rubber cement were part of the process. Today, you can add photos, charts, clip art, and diagrams easily to just about any document you create. If you have a digital camera or a scanner, you can import your own images directly into Word. And, using the Internet, you can download thousands of pictures to help you add visual appeal to the words on your pages. There are three different ways you can add artwork to your Word documents:

■ To insert clip art, choose Picture and then Clip Art from the Insert menu. Enter a word or phrase describing the art you want to use; then click Go. Click the clip art image you want to use to add it to your document (see Figure 6-1). You also can click the down arrow on the right side of the image to display a menu of options.

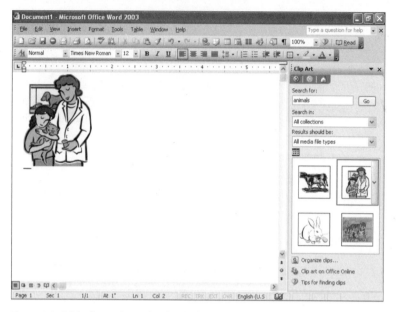

Figure 6-1 Add clip art by selecting it from the Clip Art task pane.

■ To add an image from a file, choose Picture from the Insert menu, and then select From File. In the Insert Picture dialog box, navigate to the file you want to add, click it, and click the Insert button.

■ To scan an image directly into your document, place the photo or drawing in your scanner; then choose From Scanner Or Camera from the Picture submenu. In the Insert Picture From Scanner Or Camera dialog box, choose the device and click Insert. If you want to add the scanned image to the Clip Organizer, make sure the check box is selected.

> **Caution**   Art abounds on the Internet, but you can't use it unless you are downloading clips from a freeware or shareware Web site, or you have the permission of the artist to use the image you're copying. Copyright laws apply, even for pictures comprised only of colored electronic dots. To be safe, be sure to get the necessary permission before you use someone else's images in your documents.

A Quick Look at the Microsoft Clip Organizer

When you work with clip art in any Microsoft Office System application, you're using the Microsoft Clip Organizer, a media library that enables you to save, organize, and access picture, sound, and video files from a variety of sources. Display the Clip Organizer by clicking the Organize Clips link at the bottom of the Clip Art task pane. The first time you click this link, the Add Clips To Organizer dialog box tells you that it will scan your hard drive to collect and catalog all the image, sound, and video files already stored on your computer. Click Now to continue the cataloging. After a few moments, the Clip Organizer creates a Collection List and displays all the found media items in their various folders. To check out all the clip art included with the Office System, click the Office Collections folder and explore the subfolders.

Aha!   Getting More Clips Online

If you don't find the pictures you were hoping for, you can continue your search online. To begin the process, click Clip Art On Office Online in the bottom of the Clip Art task pane. If you are not currently connected to the Internet, the Connect dialog box appears so that you can establish the connection. Click Connect and you are taken to the Microsoft Office Design Gallery Live. The first time you visit, you are asked to review the end-user license agreement. After you click Accept, you are taken to a site that gives you a powerful search feature, articles on finding and using clips, and a wide selection of clips and tips-of-the-month that can help you in your work. It's a great resource! Check back often.

Working with Pictures

When you insert and select a picture in your document, the Picture toolbar appears. These tools give you many options for working with pictures (see Table 6-3).

Table 6-3 Tools on the Picture Toolbar

Tools	Name	Description
	Insert Picture	Insert an image into a document
	Color	Change the color of the image
	More Contrast	Increase the contrast
	Less Contrast	Decrease the contrast
	More Brightness	Increase the brightness
	Less Brightness	Decrease the brightness

Table 6-3   Tools on the Picture Toolbar

Tools	Name	Description
	Crop	Crop the image
	Rotate Left	Rotate the image to the left
	Line Style	Change the line style used to border the picture
	Compress Pictures	Compress the image to reduce its file size
	Text Wrapping	Control the way text wraps around the image
	Format Picture	Change the format of the picture
	Set Transparent Color	Makes the color you select transparent
	Reset Picture	Reset the picture to its original settings

Introducing the Picture Manager

The Microsoft Picture Manager is a new image-editing tool in the Office System that enables you to find, edit, and share images. Start the Picture Manager by choosing Start, All Programs, Microsoft Office System and selecting Microsoft Picture Manager. You can then use the program to do the following things:

■ Find new images

■ Change brightness and contrast

■ Alter the color of the picture

■ Crop the image

■ Rotate and flip the image

■ Remove red eye in the photo

■ Resize the picture

Picture Manager includes an AutoCorrect feature that can make image corrections for you automatically. In addition, you can use the Picture Manager to print pictures, export images to other file formats, e-mail pictures to friends and coworkers, compress images, and work with images in groups for export, conversion, or print processes.

Drawing Diagrams

If your job involves using Word to write procedures and create flowcharts, you'll love the diagramming feature in Word 2003. The built-in diagram tool enables you to create hierarchical diagrams in your document without ever leaving Word. Here are the steps:

1 Choose Diagram from the Insert menu.

2 In the Diagram Gallery (shown in Figure 6-2), click the type of chart you want to create. (If you're not sure which chart you need, click the different chart types to see a basic description of each.) After you've selected the diagram you want, click OK.

Figure 6-2 Word includes six types of diagrams you can create on the fly.

3 Click the prompt *Click to add text* to show you where to add your own information as needed.

4 Use the tools on the Diagram toolbar to add shapes, move diagram elements, apply formatting settings, or change to a different type of diagram.

5 Click outside the diagram to add it to your document.

> **Aha!**   Choosing Styles for Diagrams
>
> The Diagram feature includes a Diagram Style Gallery that lets you change the look of the shapes and colors in the diagram. To display the Style Gallery, click AutoFormat on the Diagram toolbar. Scroll through the Diagram Style list to find the look you want; then click Apply to apply the change to the diagram.

Adding and Using Bookmarks

If you are working in a long document and want to be able to return to your place easily later, you can add a bookmark.

■ To add a bookmark, choose Bookmark from the Insert menu. Enter a name for the bookmark and click Add.

■ To move to a bookmark in your document, choose Bookmark from the Insert menu, and click the name of the bookmark you want to find. Click Go To, and you're brought to that bookmark.

■ To display bookmarks in a document, choose Options from the Tools menu; then click the View tab. Click the Bookmarks check box to display the bookmarks within your document.

■ To remove a bookmark, display the Bookmark dialog box, select the bookmark you want to remove, and click Delete (or press Del).

Creating a Hyperlink

You can create links in your Word document so that readers who are viewing your document on the screen can move right to the sites and files you mention. In addition to linking to other Web pages and files, you can create e-mail links so that interested readers can e-mail you directly in response to your document.

To create a hyperlink in your document, select the item you want to link (this could be text or an image); then press Ctrl+K. In the Insert Hyperlink dialog box (see Figure 6-3), click your selection in the Link To column on the left. Click OK to create the link.

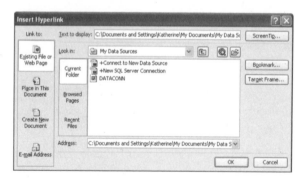

Figure 6-3   You add hyperlinks for text and images in your Word documents using the Insert Hyperlink dialog box.

Aha!   Hyperlink Options

The Hyperlink dialog box changes depending on which item you select in the Link To column. If you are creating an e-mail link, the Insert Hyperlink dialog box changes to allow you to enter the e-mail address and any subject you want displayed in the Subject line. When a reader clicks the text you've used for the hyperlink, a new e-mail message will open in his or her e-mail program with your e-mail address and the Subject line filled in.

You can later remove hyperlinks by pressing Ctrl+K to display the Edit Hyperlink dialog box, clicking Remove Link, and clicking OK.

Preparing and Using XML Documents

XML (Extensible Markup Language) is a relatively new data standard that allows for the easy exchange of data across formats. You may hear it called a *markup language*, similar to HTML, because that's what its name implies. But XML is more than a language of tags; XML actually allows users to create their own markup languages specific to their data needs, based on a collection of set standards.

With XML, you use specific rules to create your own tags and style sheets; the individual tags describe the content and meaning of the data rather than the display format of the data (which is what HTML controls). XML is ordinarily logical and pretty easy to read, which makes it easy—even for users unfamiliar with XML—to see what's going on in an XML data file. All these possibilities and more make working with XML in Word a simple but powerful feature for changing the way data is prepared, used, shared, and saved for the future.

> **Note**   Different levels of XML support are available in different versions of Office System. If you are using Professional Enterprise or Professional Editions, you have full XML support and can attach schemas, use transforms, and more. If you have the Standard or Basic Editions of Office System, you can save documents in XML format but do not have access to the higher-end XML features.

Introduction to XML in Word

The new XML features in Word 2003 enable you to view, work with, and save XML files easily. Here's the process in a nutshell:

1 Attach an XML schema using the XML Structure task pane.

> **Lingo** An *XML Schema* is document that defines the elements, entities, and content allowed in the document.

2 Identify the data by adding XML tags. You can tag document information to identify its content (such as <HEADING>, <BODYTEXT>, or <GRAPHIC>). You use tag view to add tags to your data easily.

3 Save the document as XML. Word gives you the option of saving the document as data only or applying a transform (format specification for the data).

> **Lingo** *XSL Transforms* save the document in different forms for different views and are available whenever a Word file is opened and/or saved.

Attaching an XML Schema

The first step in working with XML in your document is attaching the XML schema, the file that defines and describes the tags used and recognized in your XML document. To attach a schema, display the XML Structure task pane (click the down arrow in the task pane title bar), and click the Templates And Add-Ins link in the XML Structure task pane (see Figure 6-4). Click the Add Schema button to display a dialog box in which you can select the schema you want to attach to your document.

Aha!   Where Do You Get a Schema?

In some circumstances, you will be applying a schema others have created to go along with your data. In other cases, you may be creating a schema yourself for a specific use. Industry-standard schemas are now being developed to allow for common data exchange among various industry areas.

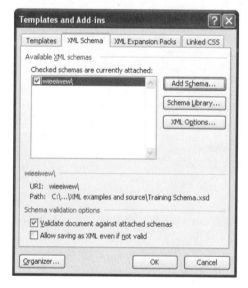

Figure 6-4   You can select and add a schema to your current document in the XML Schema tab of the Templates And Add-Ins dialog box.

Note   You can add more than one schema to a single document if you like. Word will apply both sets of definitions and rules, and alert you if there is a conflict.

After you attach a schema and click OK, Word evaluates the incoming schema to see whether it's properly formed. If there are errors in the code, Word will alert you and stop the attachment until the code is corrected.

Adding XML Tags

You use the XML task pane to view the structure of your XML document so that you can navigate easily through the document and add XML tags as needed. By using the features in this task pane, you can easily add XML tags in your document while you work (see Figure 6-5). Word checks tags against the applied schema to make sure that you are entering tags the XML schema will recognize.

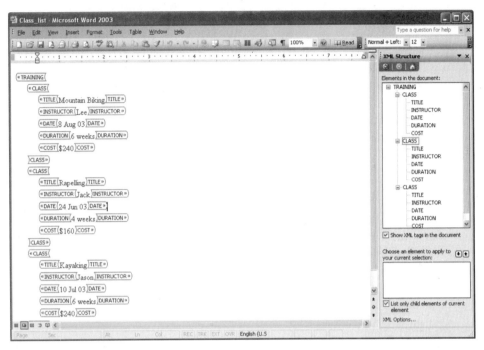

Figure 6-5 The task pane displays the tree structure of the current XML document and enables you to click and add tags while you work.

> **Note** You can turn tag view off and on by clicking the Show XML tags in the document check box in the task pane.

Saving the XML Document

When you open an XML file in Word and choose XML files from the Files Of Type list in the Open dialog box, you also have the option of applying an XSL Transform as you open the file. Display the shortcut menu by clicking the small arrow to the right of the Open tool to find the Open With Transform option.

> **Lingo** An *XSL Transform* allows you to display an XML document in different views; for example, perhaps you are opening a report file that you also want to display on the Web. Applying a Transform allows you to see the file in a Web-based format without making modifications to the file itself.

When you choose XML Document in the Save As Type field of the Save As dialog box, two XML-specific options appear to the left of the Save button. You can click the Apply Transform check box to enable the Transform button; then click that button to choose the transform you want to apply.

Creating a Table of Contents

A table of contents is crucial when you are creating a document that people need to navigate easily. Word creates the table of contents based on the headings you've entered in the document that use (or are based on) the default heading styles. To create a table of contents, follow these steps:

1 Position the cursor at the point in the document at which you want to create the table of contents.

2 Choose Reference from the Insert menu; then choose Index And Tables from the submenu.

3 In the Index And Tables dialog box, select the Table Of Contents tab.

4 Review the format settings (the page numbers are right-aligned, with a dot tab leader). Change the settings to fit the needs of your project.

5 Click OK to generate the table of contents. The table is placed at the cursor position in your document.

If you change the headings later, you can easily update the table of contents by clicking in the table and pressing F9. A dialog box will appear, asking whether you want to update the page numbers only, or the entire table. To make sure that you've got the most up-to-date TOC possible, select Update Entire Table and click OK.

Adding an Index

Indexes are a bit more complicated than tables of contents because you need to go through your document and mark the entries you want to include in your index; then you have Word compile the index into the traditional form that appears at the end of your favorite books. If you're a word-puzzle person and love crosswords and search-a-words, you'll enjoy creating indexes. Here's a quick overview of the process:

1 Beginning at the start of the document (so that you can review the entire document as you create entries), choose References from the Insert menu, and click Index And Tables.

2 Click the Index tab. On this tab you see all the options you'll need to create your document index (as shown in Figure 6-6 on the following page).

3 Begin by clicking Mark Entry. The Mark Index Entry dialog box opens. Here you will enter the entries and subentries for the index.

4 Move the cursor to the point you want to insert the first entry. (Word will insert an index code at the cursor position.) Type your first entry in the Main Entry box (for example, Services). Add a Subentry if desired (for example, Layout). Click Mark to add the code.

5 Continue moving the cursor and adding entries in the Mark Index Entry dialog box.

6 When you've finished, choose Cancel to close the dialog box.

7 Position the cursor at the end of the document (or wherever you want to generate the index). Choose Insert, Reference, and Index And Tables.

8 With the Index tab displayed, click OK. Word then compiles the index and places it at the cursor position.

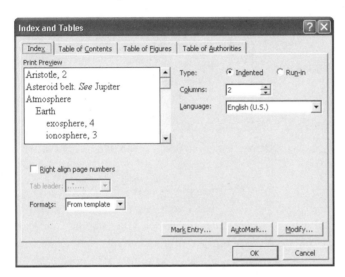

Figure 6-6   Word's indexing feature is a bit more complex than ordinary tasks, but worth the effort to learn.

If you find that you've misspelled an entry in the index, or want to modify some of the page numbers listed, you can simply click in the index and edit it as you normally would.

Recording and Running Macros

And finally, we get to *macros*. Macros help you save time and effort by recording your repetitive tasks and playing them back on command. For example, you might create a macro for applying a certain format, adding a header you always use, searching and replacing an outdated style, or creating a table of contents.

> **Lingo** A *macro* is simply a sequence of tasks that you record so that Word can automatically execute the steps next time.

A macro records the individual steps you take and then runs through them automatically when you play the macro later. This means that, in order to work with macros, you have to go through two stages: creating the macro, and then running it.

To create a macro, position the cursor at the point you want to begin, and choose Macro from the Tools menu. When the submenu appears, select Record New Macro. The Record Macro dialog box appears, as shown in Figure 6-7.

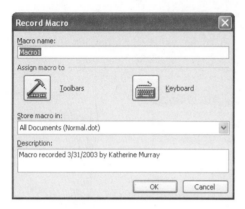

Figure 6-7   You can record a macro to automate tasks you find yourself performing over and over and over.

First, enter a name for the macro. Then choose whether you want to assign the macro to a tool, a shortcut key combination, or an unused function key (for example, F12). You also need to tell Word whether you want to save the macro in the Normal template (the default) or save it in the current document only. Click OK to begin recording. A small palette containing two tools—Stop Recording and Pause Recording—appears over your Word work area.

> **Caution**   When you're assigning a macro to a key, be sure to choose a key combination that isn't being used. Otherwise, you will overwrite the function of the existing key combination with the new macro you create.

The macro now records your every on-screen action. For example, suppose that you move the mouse to open the Insert menu, choose References, and click Index And Tables. You then click the Table Of Contents tab and click OK to generate a quick TOC. Now click Stop Recording. The macro is saved under the name you entered.

To play the macro, choose Macros from the Tools menu (you can also press Alt+F8). The Macros dialog box appears. Simply click the macro you want to play, and click Run. The macro is executed, automatically repeating the steps you saved.

Fast Wrap-Up

- Creating sections in longer documents enables you to vary the format from section to section.

- You can add many different items to headers and footers in your Word documents.

- The Clip Organizer stores your picture, sound, and video files. The new Picture Library enables you to edit, compress, and share your images with others. Word includes a built-in diagramming feature that offers you six types of diagrams, from mapping processes to relationships to flowcharts.

- Creating hyperlinks in Word for documents, Web pages, e-mail, buttons, and more is simple with Ctrl+K.

- The full XML support in Word that is available in Office System Professional enables you to create and tag XML data, attach your own schemas, and use transforms. In Standard and Basic editions, you can save documents in XML format.

- You can use Word for high-end tasks such as generating a table of contents or index for your long document. Additionally, you can record macros to automatically step through tasks that used to be repetitive chores.

Part 3
Effective Microsoft Office Excel 2003: Analyze and Organize Data

If working with numbers is a regular part of your daily routine, you may find that Excel's new look, added functions, and Extensible Markup Language (XML) support enable you to work faster and smarter than ever. This section shows off the new features and takes you through all the important Excel tasks you're likely to need—from creating a basic spreadsheet to adding functions to producing charts and printing worksheets. In the chapters that follow, you'll find everything you need to know to master Excel tasks quickly.

Creating and Saving a Spreadsheet

7

10-Second Summary
■ Create a basic spreadsheet

■ Enter data

■ Name ranges and navigate the worksheet

■ Work with functions and formulas

■ Share worksheets

■ Use XML in Excel 2003

Microsoft Office Excel 2003 makes it easy—even for those of us who weren't math majors—to do sophisticated things with numbers. Want to create an amortization table for that new home you're thinking about? Need to create a professional-looking balance sheet to give potential investors a good sense of what they're putting their money into? Want to download data lists from the Web and include them in your reports to stockholders?

Whatever your intent, if your project has something to do with numbers, Excel can help you create it. This chapter explains how to create a worksheet, and shows you how to enter data, work with formulas, share data via the Web, and create and map XML files.

New Features in Excel 2003

In addition to Excel's new look, which follows the Windows XP theme, Excel 2003 includes a number of features that extend the capabilities of the program and the data you prepare with it:

■ **Ink support**   Full support for the Tablet PC enables you to add data, annotate worksheets, draw diagrams, and hand-draw charts, even when you're away from your desk.

■ **Internet faxing**   A new offering in the Send To submenu of the File menu enables you to send faxes without leaving your Excel worksheet.

■ **Windows Rights Management**   Now Excel users working with Windows Rights Management (WRM) can protect sensitive data by assigning various roles to file recipients. Someone assigned as Viewer can view files as read-only but cannot make any modifications; Reviewer enables a user to make comments in a file and add information; Editor grants editing privileges so the file can be modified.

- **Research while you work**   The Research task pane enables you to search specific resources to find information you need as you work. The Translation feature converts foreign phrases and words using multi-language capabilities.

See Also For more about working with Excel's new XML features, see the section, "Using XML in Excel 2003," later in this chapter.

- **XML support**   The Office System Professional editions provide full support for industry-standard XML, which enables businesses to prepare, save, and share information in the common XML format. In Standard and Home editions of the Office System, users can save Excel files in XML format but cannot perform high-end XML tasks.

- **Links to SharePoint Team Services**   Another significant enhancement in Excel is its seamless integration with Microsoft SharePoint Team Services. Now you can import SharePoint list data directly into your Excel spreadsheet, and export that data back to SharePoint just as easily.

What Can You Do with Excel?

Although Excel is a full-featured program that offers everything from simple math calculations to complex and sophisticated operations, you might find that you start using Excel to solve a simple problem or create a project. From there, as your familiarity with Excel grows, you'll be likely to try using it for other operations as well. Here are just a few ideas of tasks you can try in Excel:

- Track accounts receivable and payable for your small business.

- Create data lists to store your customer information.

- Create and track sales projections and results.

- Create and maintain a donor list for your small nonprofit organization.

- Handle all your standard business documents, including income statements, balance sheets, cash-flow reports, and more.

- Import XML data as the basis for comparison reports.

- Develop budgets for the various departments in your company.

- Produce cost-analysis reports.

- Publish financial information to the Web.

Excel Basics

When you first start Excel, the New Workbook task pane also appears on the right side of the workspace, enabling you to open an existing workbook, or start a new one from scratch, or from a template (see Figure 7-1). You can close the task pane to give yourself more room on the screen by clicking the Close box in the upper right corner of the task pane.

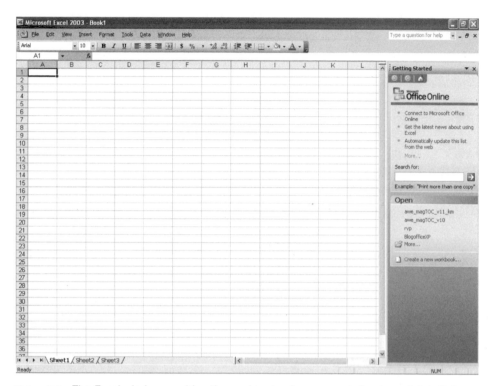

Figure 7-1 The Excel window provides the workspace for your worksheets and data lists.

The grid in the center of the workspace is the worksheet on which you'll do all your calculating tasks in Excel. Along the bottom and right sides of the worksheet area are two scroll bars—one vertical and one horizontal. You will use these to scroll to different areas of your worksheet when it gets too large to display on one screen.

At the bottom of the left side of the work area, you see the worksheet tabs, which enable you to move from sheet to sheet when you have created more than one worksheet in your Excel workbook. To move to a different worksheet, simply click the worksheet tab of the sheet you want to view. In addition, you can rename worksheets by right-clicking the tab to display a shorcut menu.

> **Lingo** A *workbook* in Excel is a collection of worksheets organized by a common topic or function.

Creating a New Spreadsheet

When you first start Excel, a blank worksheet opens automatically and the New Workbook task pane appears on the right side of the window. (If the task pane does not open automatically on your system, press Ctrl+N to display it.) If you want to open an existing worksheet instead of creating a new one, click the From Existing Workbook link and choose the worksheet you want to use from the dialog box that appears.

Aha!   Creating a Workbook from a Template

Excel 2003 also includes professionally designed templates you can use as the basis for your worksheets. This is a great help, especially if you are unfamiliar with the traditional forms of common financial documents such as balance sheets or a sales invoice. To start a worksheet from an Excel template on your computer, click the On My Computer link in the Templates area of the task pane. If you want to view the huge gallery of templates available at Microsoft Online, click Templates on Office Online.

Adding Column and Row Labels

The column and row labels you use in your spreadsheet tell others (and remind you) what the data in the cells means. There's no hard and fast rule for what types of labels you use—your own projects will determine that. Generally, however, many people create row labels that refer to the data being tracked (for example, Region 1, Region 2, Region 3), and the column labels refer to the period of time used to track the data for each of the regions (Quarter 1, Quarter 2, Quarter 3, and so on).

> **Lingo**   The intersection of each column and row is called a *cell*, and each cell has a unique address, which is a combination of the column letter and row number.

To enter column and row labels for your worksheet, click the cell where you want to enter the first label. Type the label and press the Tab key if you're entering column labels (this moves the highlight to the next cell) or Enter to move to the next row.

Aha!   Entering Labels Automatically

If you are entering a common series of labels, such as *January, February, March* or *Quarter 1, Quarter 2, Quarter 3*, you can have Excel enter the labels for you. Type the first label and then click the small box in the bottom right corner of the selected cell. Drag the cell to encompass the entire area for which you want to add labels. A ScreenTip appears to show you the entered labels as you drag. Release the mouse button and the labels are entered automatically.

Entering Data

To enter the data in your worksheet, click the cell and type the value. When you first begin entering information, the default format of the cell is General, which applies no particular format to the information you type. Table 7-1 explains the different types of data you can enter in Excel.

Table 7-1 Data Types in Excel

Type	Description
Numbers	This is the most common type of data, and you can format numbers in several different ways, including General (303), Number (303.00), and Currency ($303.00). In addition, you can use the Accounting format to align the numbers by their decimal points and currency symbols.
Date	You also can store date values in your worksheet, which is important for tracking information over time, dating reports, sorting according to date, and more. Once you enter date information, you can apply a wide range of date formats.
Time	Time also is an important value for many items you'll be tracking in your worksheets. You can format time values in a number of different ways in Excel.
Text	Not only can you enter text as row and column labels in your worksheet, but you can also track names, addresses, and product IDs, enter serial numbers or product codes, and add comments to your entries. Text data is formatted as text, and can be sorted alphabetically in ascending or descending order.

Aha! Having Excel Read Back Worksheet Values

Want to have your computer read back that last column of numbers so you can make sure you got it right? Excel can read the data to you by using Speech playback. To play back your data, highlight the column or row of data you want to hear, choose Speech from the Tools menu, and select Show Text To Speech Toolbar. Click Speak Cells on the Text To Speech toolbar. A computer-generated voice reads the values beginning at the top of the column or the left end of the row. If you want to have Excel read you each entry after you enter it, select Speak On Enter at the right end of the Text To Speech toolbar.

AutoFilling Cells

In addition to simply clicking and typing, you can use the Fill feature of Excel to fill spreadsheet cells with data. You might use this, for example, when you are entering sequential check numbers in a row. To autofill the cells, follow these steps:

1 Click the cell and enter the starting value.

2 Click the small rectangle in the lower right corner of the cell and drag across the row or down the column.

3 At the end of the area you want to fill, release the mouse button. The area fills with a copy of the value you entered in the initial cell.

4 Click AutoFill and a list of choices appears (see Figure 7-2). To create a sequential series, click Fill Series.

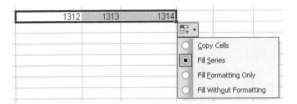

Figure 7-2 You can use the AutoFill button to fill data in a sequential series.

Note   The choices on your AutoFill button list will vary depending on the type of data you are using. The choices here allow you to simply copy the cells in the selected range, apply only the formatting of the cell to the other cells, or add only the data without copying the formatting.

Importing Data

You have another option for entering data in your worksheet: You can use data you have stored in other programs. To import data from another program (or from another Excel workbook), follow these steps:

1 Select the sheet onto which you want to import the data by clicking the worksheet tab.

2 Click the cell you want to serve as the upper left corner for the imported data.

3 Choose Import External Data from the Data menu and choose Import Data.

4 In the Select Data Source dialog box, navigate to the folder storing the data file you want to import.

5 Click the Files Of Type down arrow and select the program type from the list.

6 Locate the file in the list, click it, and then click Import.

7 Depending on the type of program from which you're importing, options will appear, asking you to select the table you want to use. Click the table choice, and then click OK.

8 The Import Data dialog box appears, asking where you want to add the data. (You've already positioned the cell pointer in a new worksheet, which takes care of this step.) Click OK.

You might need to do a little formatting to display the data the way you like it, but by importing an existing file, you've saved yourself the time and trouble of re-entering information, and you've reduced your margin for error at the same time.

Entering Data on the Tablet PC

Tablet PC support is a feature Excel shares with the other Office System applications. Now you can edit a worksheet, create a chart, e-mail a report, or add figures wherever you go. Ink support enables you to do the following things in Excel 2003:

- Add handwritten notes to a worksheet you're reviewing

- Enter data and convert the handwriting to typed text

- Sketch out a chart by hand

- Select a range of cells to be copied and e-mailed to a coworker for double-checking

See Also For a great guide on using the Tablet PC, see Jeff Van West's *Tablet PC Quick Reference* (Microsoft Press, 2003).

Moving Around and Selecting Cells

Once you enter information in your worksheet, you need to be able to navigate the worksheet and select the cells you want to use for various operations. Table 7-2 gives you a quick overview of the important keys for moving around on the worksheet.

Table 7-2 Keys for Navigating the Excel Worksheet

Press This Key	To Move Here
Enter	Next cell down
Tab	Next cell to the right
Shift+Tab	Next cell to the left
Any arrow key	One cell in the direction of the arrow
Home	Column A
Ctrl+Home	Cell A1
Ctrl+End	The last cell in your worksheet
Page Down	Down one screen
Page Up	Up one screen
Alt+Page Down	Right one screen
Alt+Page Up	Left one screen

Aha!   Moving to Cells Quickly

Two quick ways to move to the cell you want: Click in the Name box, type the cell address or range name, and click Enter; or press F5 to display the Go To dialog box, type the destination cell or range, and then click OK.

Selecting Cells

After you get to where you're going on the worksheet, you need to know how to select cells. Here are some of the different ways in which you'll select the cells you want to work with:

- To select a single cell, either click the cell or type the cell address (for example, B7) in the Name box in the left side of the Formula bar and press Enter. The highlight moves to that cell.

- To select a range of cells, click the first cell and drag to the last cell in the block. The area highlights as you drag the mouse. When the range is the size you want, release the mouse button.

  Lingo A *range* is a group of selected cells. You use ranges when you work with multiple cells in formulas, copy and move operations, chart creation, and so on.

- To select noncontiguous (that is, not touching) ranges or cells, select the first cell or range as just described. Then press and hold Ctrl while selecting subsequent cells or ranges. When you've selected all the cells you want, release Ctrl and perform your task as needed.

- To select the entire worksheet, press Ctrl+A. The entire area is highlighted.

Naming and Moving to Ranges

In some cases you may want to save the selected cells as a range that you use in common operations. For example, suppose that you often use the yearly sales figures for each salesperson (cells F5 to F20) in worksheets and reports that you create. You can name that range so that you can refer to it by name in other operations, and Excel will automatically know which cells you're referring to. To create a named range, follow these steps:

1 Highlight the area you want to name as a range.

2 Click the Name box on the Formula bar on the right side of the worksheet.

3 Type the name you want to assign to the range, and then press Enter.

> **Caution**   Be sure to start range names with letters, and don't use spaces (use underscores to separate words instead). Otherwise, Excel won't know what to do with the name and will display an error box asking you to enter a valid name.

Now you can move right to that range by typing the range name in the Name box, or by clicking the Name box down arrow and selecting it from the displayed list.

> **Aha!**   Fast Range Names
> If you prefer, you can press Ctrl+F3 to display the Define Names dialog box. Then simply type the name for the range, and click OK to save it.

Working with Functions and Formulas

Functions in Excel do most of the heavy work when it comes to complicated operations. Luckily, you can put away your trigonometric calculator and relax, because Excel has the know-how you need and the support to help you use it.

Checking Out the Formula Bar

You'll use the Formula Bar as you enter and edit Excel formulas and functions. The following graphic shows you the different parts of the bar:

The Name box displays the location of the cell that's currently selected. You can use the Name box to move to other cells or select named ranges. The Cancel and Enter buttons abandon or accept the function you've entered, and the Insert Function button displays the Insert Function dialog box so that you can insert it in the function box.

Deconstructing Formulas

A *formula* is an equation that carries out a particular operation on specified values. You'll use formulas to calculate sales projections, estimate taxes, average your expenses, total your income, and tally your inventory, among other things. A *function* is a preset formula that carries out a specific kind of operation. For example, you use the =SUM function to add a column of numbers; you use =AVERAGE to display the average of a group of cell values. Excel functions always appear in this form:

=FUNCTION (argument, argument)

Here's a step-by-step explanation:

- The *equals sign* (=) tells Excel that what follows is a function. You always need to use the equals sign, or Excel won't know what to do with the data you enter and will display an error.

- The word *FUNCTION* above is where the actual name of the function appears. The function might be SUM, AVERAGE, IF, COUNT, MAX, or something else.

- The *(argument, argument)* text represents the part of the formula in which you tell Excel which values to use. Cell addresses are commonly used as arguments, but you can also use text, TRUE or FALSE, or numbers. For cases in which you'll need complex formulas (which is beyond our intention here), you can create *nested formulas* by including other formulas and functions as the arguments.

Entering a Formula

The process for creating a simple formula that uses a function is straightforward:

1 Click in the cell that will contain the function you want to use.

2 Click the Insert Function tool in the Formula bar. The Insert Function dialog box appears (as shown in Figure 7-3). Choose the function you want to use and click OK.

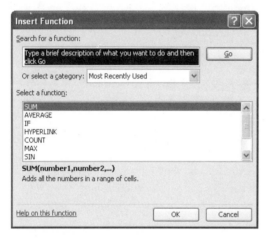

Figure 7-3 The Insert Function dialog box gives you three ways to find the function you need.

3 Choose the cells you want to include in the formula by entering them in the Function Arguments dialog box. Click OK to return to the worksheet.

Aha!   When You're Comfortable with Formulas

The fastest way to enter a formula, assuming you know what you're doing, is to type it in the Formula Bar. Begin with an equals sign (=); then enter the function name followed by an open parenthesis, the range of cells separated by a colon (:), and a closing parenthesis. Press Enter to perform the calculation. One even faster way to get formulas into your spreadsheet is to copy them; just select the cell containing the formula, press Ctrl+C, and paste the formula (Ctrl+V) at the new location. Excel will do the math and change the cell references relative to the new position—and the formula should function (no pun intended) just the way you want it to.

Special Formula Features

As your experience with Excel and with formulas begins to grow, there are a few features that will help you create accurate calculations. Remember to try the following features when you find yourself building more complex operations:

- The AutoSum tool (available on the Standard toolbar) allows you to enter common functions by selecting them from the AutoSum menu. You can choose Sum, Average, Count, Max, or Min, or click More Functions to display the Insert Function dialog box and use the Function Wizard to find the function you need.

- You can have Excel check your formulas for you to make sure there are no mistakes. To start the checker, choose Error Checking from the Tools menu. Excel will display any errors found in the formulas in your worksheet, and you can make corrections as needed in the formula bar.

- Whenever an error occurs in a formula in the spreadsheet, the Trace Error button appears beside the formula in the cell. You can click the Trace Error button to choose options that will help you run down and fix the error in the formula.

- You can watch a formula and keep an eye on its results by using the Watch Window feature. Start by selecting the cells with the formulas you want to watch, then point to Formula Auditing on the Tools menu and choose Show Watch Window. Next, click Add Watch, and then click Add to save the selected cells as the range you want to watch. You can then reposition and resize the Watch Window to keep it open in your workspace while you continue to work with the current worksheet. When any of the values or formulas in the watch range change, the value change is reflected in the Watch Window.

Sharing Worksheets

One of the major new features in Excel 2003 is the addition of the Shared Workspace feature, which enables you to share your worksheets, documents, and other projects easily in a shared space on the Web. The site is part of SharePoint Team Services, a Microsoft application that enables businesses and team members—within organizations and around the world—to organize projects and collaborate more effectively.

Start the process of sharing a worksheet by choosing Shared Workspace from the Tools menu. The Shared Workspace task pane appears, enabling you to name and choose a site where the document will be created. Click Create to create the workspace on the Web. Your current workbook is saved on the newly created shared workspace. You can click Open Site In Browser at the top of the task pane to see the created space (see Figure 7-4).

Figure 7-4   When you choose Shared Workspace from the Tools menu, you create a Web site team members can access to edit, discuss, and collaborate on your project.

Various areas on the shared site enable you to add team members, add tasks, create events, and more. The information related to your shared workbook is always available to you in the Shared Workspace task pane (see Figure 7-5).

Figure 7-5   The various tabs in the Shared Workspace task pane give you information about the project you're working on.

Aha!   Another Way to Share Workbooks

In addition to sharing a workspace online and working on collaborative projects, you can share an individual workbook by choosing Share Workbook from the Tools menu. Click the Allow Changes check box to enable multiple users to be able to work with and edit the current worksheet. The changes can then be merged into a master worksheet so that all edits are reflected in the final version.

Using XML in Excel 2003

In Chapter 6, "Special Tasks in Microsoft Office Word 2003," you learned about the new XML support in Word 2003. Excel 2003 also includes full support for XML in the Professional editions, allowing you to open, work with, and save data in a format that can be easily read and applied in any number of forms. The process of using XML in your Excel worksheets follows this basic path:

See Also For more about the basic workings and terminology of XML, see "Introduction to XML" in Chapter 6.

1   Open the document you want to prepare or work with as an XML document.

2   Attach a workbook map.

3   Use the visual mapping tool to tag the various data items in your worksheet in XML.

4   Save the file as an XML spreadsheet or XML data only.

> **Note**   Full XML support, which enables you to map XML data, attach your own schemas, and apply transforms, is available only in the Office System Professional editions. Standard and Basic editions of the Office System enable you to save files as XML data but do not allow for higher level XML tasks.

Attaching a Workbook Map

Your first step in preparing your file for XML is to attach the XML schema, also called the *workbook map*, in Excel 2003. Display the XML Source task pane and click the Workbook Maps button in the lower right corner. In the XML Maps dialog box, click the Add button and navigate to the folder in which the XML schema you want to use is stored. Select it, click Open, and Excel uses that file as your workbook map.

> **Aha!**   Creating a Schema from a Data File
>
> If you don't have an XML schema, but you have a similar data file that includes all the data elements you want to use, Excel can create a workbook map from that file. Click the XML file name, click Open, and Excel displays a message that it will create the schema based on the source data. Click OK to continue and attach the new document as the workbook map.

Using the Visual Mapping Tool

Once the workbook map is selected, the treelike structure of the data is displayed in the XML Source task pane to the right of your worksheet. You can map the XML data with the data tags you want to apply by dragging the item from the map in the XML Source task pane to the data in the worksheet. Figure 7-6 shows a data list that has been tagged as XML data. The List And XML toolbar provides additional tools for importing, exporting, updating, and working with XML data.

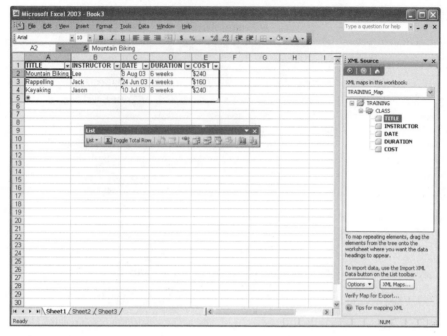

Figure 7-6   Preparing an XML file in Excel 2003 is literally as simple as drag-and-drop.

Aha!   Changing XML Properties

You can change XML properties by clicking the XML Map Properties tool in the List And XML toolbar. In the dialog box that appears, you can control issues around data validation and format, and import and export procedures.

Saving the Spreadsheet

When you're ready to save the spreadsheet, simply press Ctrl+S to display the Save As dialog box. To save the worksheet, simply navigate to the folder in which you want to save the file, enter a file name, and click Save. If you want to save the worksheet in a format other than traditional Excel workbook format (for example, you might want to save the file as an XML Spreadsheet or XML Data only), click the Save As Type down arrow and choose your format before you click Save.

Fast Wrap-Up

- Excel is a full-featured spreadsheet program that you can use to do simple or complex numeric operations.

- A workbook is a collection of worksheets in Excel. A worksheet is the page on which you perform mathematical operations. A cell is the intersection of a column and row, and stores one data value.

■ You add data to the worksheet—including number, text, date, and time values—by clicking a cell and typing the information.

■ You can use Excel's AutoFill feature to fill data cells quickly.

■ Tablet PC support in Excel 2003 enables you to edit, annotate, and sketch worksheet changes on the fly.

■ A range is a selected group of cells in a worksheet. You can name ranges that you work with regularly to find and reference them more easily.

■ Excel includes a number of preset functions you can include in formulas to execute common operations. Excel provides a number of features to help you find the right function and ensure that your formulas are correct.

■ Excel includes the Shared Workspace task pane to enable you to work collaboratively on projects with team members near and far. The feature uses SharePoint Team Services to create a shared Web site that houses important collaborative documents.

■ XML support in Excel enables you to create, import, work with, and export XML data files and spreadsheets. You use a visual mapping tool to simply drag-and-drop XML tags to data items on the worksheet.

■ Excel allows you to save your worksheets in a number of different file formats, including Web pages, XML Spreadsheets, text files, and files supported by other popular spreadsheet and database programs.

Editing, Formatting, and Printing Spreadsheets

8

10-Second Summary

- Learn editing techniques for data, text, and formulas
- Copy, move, and paste cells and ranges
- Change data formats
- Choose text font, style, and size
- Add borders and shading

Entering and saving worksheet data is only a fraction of what you can do with Microsoft Office Excel 2003. Next steps involve making sure your worksheet is as accurate as it can be and making it look professional by choosing fonts, colors, pictures, and more. When you've got the worksheet the way you want it, you can preview it to make sure the page breaks occur in the right places, and choose your favorite options before you print.

Aha!   The Fastest Ways to Format

Microsoft Online includes a gallery of common worksheet templates you can use to build worksheets you are creating. If you want to apply formats to an existing worksheet section, you can use AutoFormat, available in the Format menu. See the section, "Fast Formatting," later in this chapter for details.

Editing Spreadsheet Data

What does editing look like in your business? In one department, editing might involve passing the sales projection worksheet among team members for their changes and suggestions. In another department, editing might involve double-checking formulas, switching ranges, and correcting misspellings. This section shows you quickly how to edit your worksheets to ensure their accuracy.

> **Aha!**   Commenting on Worksheets
>
> If you're the lucky person who is reviewing another's work, you will find that the Comment feature comes in handy. On your desktop system or Tablet PC, you can add your thoughts and suggestions in little pop-up boxes without adding information in the worksheet itself. To add a comment, click the cell to which you want to add the comment and choose Comment from the Insert menu. Type your message in the little message box that appears; then click outside the cell.

Editing Techniques

Depending on what you need to correct in your worksheet, you might use any or all of the following editing techniques to check and correct things:

- **Correct typos and incorrect data**   The easiest way to make an editing change in an Excel worksheet is to click the cell you need to change, type the correct information, and press Enter.

> **Note**   If you want to edit quickly in the cell without typing in the Formula bar, double-click the cell (or press F2 to turn on Edit mode), delete the errant data, and type the correct information; then click outside the cell or press Enter.

- **Check spelling by pressing F7**   This starts the spelling checker, which displays any unrecognized words so that you can correct them or add them to the spelling dictionary.

- **Check your formulas with the Error Checker**   Excel includes a feature you can use to double-check your math on the worksheet. Choose Error Checker from the Tools menu to start the process.

> **Aha!**   Setting Error Checking Options
>
> To display the settings the Error Checker uses by default, choose Options from the Tools menu and click the Error Checking tab. Here you can specify whether you want Excel to check errors in the background while you work, or wait for you to choose the command from the Tools menu. You can also control which errors Excel looks for by default.

Copying and Pasting Cells and Ranges

At times you may need to make bigger edits—the kind that require highlighting a range of cells and then copying, cutting, pasting, or dragging them to another location, perhaps on a new worksheet. You'll use block copy and paste operations to do that. Here are the steps:

1 Select the area you want to move to the new sheet. If you have previously named the range, choose the range name in the Name box to select it. If you have not saved the area as a range, drag to select the area.

2 Copy the cells by pressing Ctrl+C. This places a copy of the selected range on the Office Clipboard. A dotted outline (often called *marching ants*) appears around the perimeter of the range.

3 Click the Sheet2 worksheet tab. Click in the cell where you want the data to be placed, press Ctrl+V to paste the cells, then press Enter.

Notice that the copied data brings with it any formats you previously applied, except the cell widths on the new sheet, which appear at their default setting. If you want to retain the column width and row height settings when you paste cells in your worksheet, click the Paste Options button that appears beneath and to the right of the pasted cells (see Figure 8-1). Click the Keep Source Column Widths option; Excel then preserves the column widths with the pasted information.

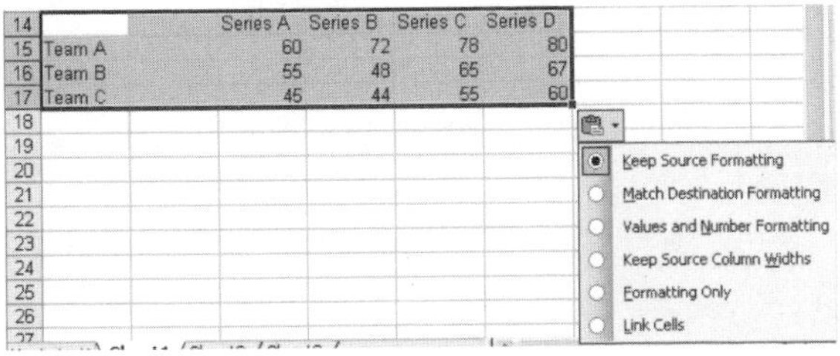

Figure 8-1 Paste Options enable you to preserve the format of the cells you paste.

Lingo The *source column* is the column from which you've copied data; the *destination* is the new area where the copied cells will be placed.

Caution Be sure that you are pasting data into a clear area, because the incoming information will overwrite the data in existing cells without any warning from Excel.

Clearing Data

Once you've placed the copied data into the second worksheet, you can clear the information from the first worksheet. To do that, follow these steps:

1 Click the Sheet1 worksheet tab. The information you previously highlighted is still selected.

2 Choose Clear from the Edit menu and then select All. The cell contents are cleared.

There's another way to handle this copy-paste-and-clear operation: You can select the information on the first worksheet, choose Cut from the Edit menu (or press Ctrl+X), move to the new worksheet, click the area where you want the data to go, and press Ctrl+V (or Enter) to paste. This removes the data and places it in the new worksheet in one process; you don't need to go back and clear the data later. Note that when you use Cut to remove data, the format and cell contents are cleared, and the blank cells are preserved in the worksheet.

Clearing vs. Deleting Data

At first glance, it may not be obvious why we need two commands that seem to remove data from a worksheet. However, there's a subtle difference between clearing and deleting data.

When you clear data by using the Clear command in the Edit menu, you are telling Excel to wipe the cell clean of all contents, formats, and comments. The cells remain intact, but now they are simply empty.

When you use the Delete command from the Edit menu, you are actually removing the selected cells from the worksheet. The other cells in the worksheet are moved to close that void, which means that the cell references in your formulas are automatically updated.

When you highlight a range and then press your Delete key, or use the Backspace key to delete data, you are removing the data only; the format of the cell remains in place. For that reason, when you want to remove all data and formats within a given range, and intend to plug other data into the blank space you've created, use the Clear command. When you want to condense the amount of space on your worksheet and remove the unnecessary rows or columns, use Delete.

Working with Rows and Columns

Some of the rearranging you need to do might involve changing the width or height of columns and rows. By default, Excel's columns are set wide enough to display 8.43 characters (yes, it's an odd number), and the rows are set to 12.75 points, or slightly more than 1/6 of an inch in height, since 72 points equals 1 inch.

When you want to make a change to a column or row, you need to begin by selecting the one you want to work with. To select an entire column, click the column label. To select an entire row, click the row label. Then use the following steps to make the changes you want to make:

- To change the width of a column, choose Column from the Format menu and select Width. In the Column Width dialog box, type a new width for the column and click OK.

- To set the width of a column or the height of a row to automatically accommodate the largest data entry, use AutoFit. Choose Column from the Format menu and then select AutoFit Selection to resize a column automatically. Choose Row from the Format menu and click AutoFit to resize a row.

■ To change the height of a row, select Row from the Format menu and choose Height. In the Row Height dialog box, type a new value in the text box and click OK.

> **Aha!** Resize Columns and Rows Quickly
>
> You also can resize columns and rows by selecting the divider line in the column or row label area and dragging the divider in the direction you want. Dragging a divider line down in the row labels increases the row height; dragging a divider line to the right in the column labels widens the column. All other rows and columns are moved accordingly to allow for the size change.

■ To insert columns and rows, select the column or row beside which you want to add another column or row. Then, depending on what you've selected, choose Rows (or Columns) from the Insert menu. If you add a row, the new row is added above the selected row; if you add a column, the new column is added to the left of the selected column.

> **Aha!** Inserting Multiple Columns and Rows
>
> If you want to insert multiple rows or columns, highlight the number of columns or rows you want to add before you choose Rows or Columns from the Insert menu. Excel will add as many rows or columns as you have highlighted.

■ To hide columns and rows, you can again choose Row or Column from the Format menu and choose Hide (or, alternatively, Unhide). But there's also another way: right-click the column or row you want to hide. A context menu of row or column options appears, and you can choose Hide to hide the selected column or row.

> **Note** Unhiding Columns
>
> How do you select a hidden column to "Unhide" it? If you have hidden column C, for example, select columns B and D, and then right-click the column label area. Choose Unhide from the context menu, and column C reappears.

Formatting Spreadsheets

Now you're ready to focus on making your worksheet look good. Adding special formats, cool fonts, attention-getting graphics, and lines and borders may not be the most important thing about your worksheet—but it lends a professional touch that may help others give your work a closer look.

> **Aha!**   Color-Coding Worksheet Tabs
>
> Color-coding your worksheet tabs can help people viewing the workbook understand what the different tabs mean. To set the color of a tab, right-click the tab, choose Tab Color, and select the color you want from the Format Tab Color palette. You may want to create a "key" on the opening workbook page so others know what the colors represent.

Fast Formatting

If you want a quick-and-easy spreadsheet that looks professional and will get at least a few appreciative blinks from the crowd, try AutoFormat. Excel's AutoFormat is a set of worksheet formats you can apply to your data. To use AutoFormat, follow these steps:

1 Begin by selecting the area of the worksheet to which you want to apply the format. If you want to apply the format to the entire worksheet, click Ctrl+A.

2 Choose AutoFormat from the Tools menu.

3 Scroll through the list of formats in the AutoFormat dialog box (see Figure 8-2). Click the format you want and click OK.

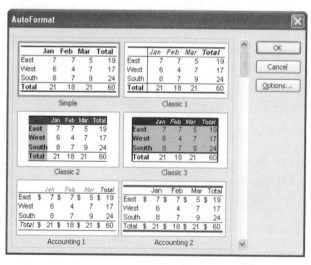

Figure 8-2 AutoFormat gives you a number of fast formats to apply to selected data.

By default, AutoFormat applies its own format for number, border, font, pattern, alignment, and width/height settings. If you want to turn off the automatic formatting for any of those items, click the Options button in the AutoFormat dialog box and click the check box of the item you want to clear. Then click OK to apply the format to your worksheet.

> **Aha!** Formatting Conditionally
>
> Excel also includes a feature called Conditional Formatting, which enables you to apply formats to data based on certain conditions. For example, you could specify that a cell highlight in red if its value falls below a certain level—this would be good for an inventory tracking worksheet or spreadsheet that monitors your cash flow. To use this feature, choose Conditional Formatting from the Format menu.

Choosing Data Formats

The most common formatting task you'll do in Excel is formatting the data you enter. When you first type numbers, text, dates, and times, they are placed in a generic format based on the data type Excel recognizes. (For more about this, see Chapter 7, "Creating and Saving a Spreadsheet.") As you work with your worksheets, you will need to know how to display data in the necessary format. To set the format of cell data, follow these steps:

1 Select the cell you want to format. (You can also choose a range, column, or row if you want to apply the same format to multiple cells.)

2 Right-click the selected cell(s). Choose Format Cells from the context menu.

3 The Number tab is displayed by default. Click the format you want in the Category list on the left. Each time you choose a different format, options related to that format, as well as a general description of the format, appear on the tab (as shown in Figure 8-3).

Figure 8-3 You can control all kinds of formatting tasks in the Format Cells dialog box.

4 Select the format you want, specify any options you need, and then click OK.

> **Aha!**   Using Formatting Tools
>
> This section shows you how to use the Format Cells dialog box to apply different formats to the data in your worksheet—but remember that you can apply many format changes quickly by selecting the cells and clicking the appropriate format-ting tool on the Formatting toolbar. You can change font, style, alignment, and color by using tools on the toolbar. Additionally, you can change common number formats, add borders and lines, and fill worksheet areas with a color of your choosing. If you're not sure which formatting tool is which, position your pointer over the tool and a ScreenTip will display the tool's name.

Changing Alignment, Font, Style, and Size

As you can see, the Format Cells dialog box is a one-stop shop for all your Excel formatting needs. The various tabs in the dialog box contain options related to a specific task. You'll use the options in the Alignment tab to control how the data appears in the cells of the selected area. And the Font tab—well, that's obvious, isn't it?—allows you to choose a dif-ferent font, style, size, and color for the data in your worksheet.

To set the alignment for your data, display the Format Cells dialog box by right-clicking in the selected cell and choosing Format Cells. Then click the Alignment tab and change any necessary settings. You may not use Alignment much for ordinary worksheets, but it does come in handy when you want to create special effects, such as vertical or skewed text labels or worksheet titles.

To change the font, style, size, and color of your data, follow these steps:

1 Display the Format Cells dialog box and click the Font tab.

2 Scroll through the Font list to find a typeface you like, then choose the Font Style and Size you want by clicking them (see Figure 8-4).

3 If you want to change the color of your data, click the Color down arrow and click the color you want from the displayed palette.

4 Set other options and effects as needed; then click OK.

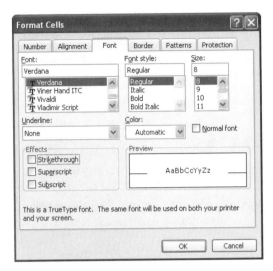

Figure 8-4 Make your changes for text font, style, size, and color on the Font tab of the Format Cells dialog box.

Limiting Changes with Rights Management

Office System now includes a feature that enables you to control how, when, and by whom your worksheets are modified. You can block users from changing formatting styles; you can disable the printing feature; you can keep worksheets from being distributed and restrict distribution to only those people who need access to the information. To use Rights Management in Excel, choose Permission from the File menu. Then choose Do Not Distribute and in the Permission dialog box, click the Restrict Permission to the Workbook checkbox.

Next, add the email addresses of users who can read (but not change, print, or copy) worksheet information. Additionally, you can specify those users who will be able to view, modify, and save changes. If you want to see further options for restricting what users can do with your worksheet file, click More Options. After you set up the permissions the way you want them, click OK to return to the worksheet.

Adding Borders and Shading

Once you've mastered the formatting of cells and labels, you'll start thinking about sprucing up your worksheet in new ways. Borders can add a professional look and give you more flexibility than simply drawing boxes around worksheet areas or charts. You can use Excel's Border feature to add horizontal or vertical lines, grid lines, surrounding borders, or specialty lines. You can work with borders three ways:

■ Select the area to which you want to apply the border, and then click the Borders tool, shown below, to display the Borders palette and select the tool you want.

■ Display the Borders toolbar, shown below, by clicking the Borders tool and choosing Draw Borders. You can then select the cells you want to border, select the Draw Border tool, choose your line style and color, and draw the border by dragging the pencil tool in the areas you want to draw. Press Esc to turn off border drawing.

■ Select the cells you want to border, right-click the selection, and choose Format Cells. Click the Borders tab in the Format Cells dialog box and choose one of the Presets, or click one of the Border lines to create a custom border. Choose the line style and color you want and click OK. The border is applied to the selected cells.

Shading Worksheet Areas

Another feature that goes hand-in-hand with bordering your worksheet cells is colorizing them. You can change the background color and pattern of cell areas using the Patterns tab in the Format Cells dialog box. You might want to change the background color of column labels or row labels, for example, or perhaps highlight an area of your worksheet that you want to stand out in a unique way. To change the color of your worksheet cells, follow these steps:

1 Select the cells you want to change, right-click, and choose Format Cells from the shortcut menu.

2 Click the Patterns tab in the Format Cells dialog box. Click the color you want in the Cell Shading area.

3 Click the Pattern drop-down arrow, producing a palette that offers you additional patterns you can apply in the color you selected, as shown below.

4 Click the pattern you want, and then click OK to apply the colored pattern to the selected cells.

> **Aha!**   Filling Quickly with Color
>
> If you want to apply color to cells without opening the Format Cells dialog box, you can simply select the cells you want to color, and then click Fill Color on the Formatting toolbar. This applies the currently selected color to the highlighted cells. If you want to use a different color, click the Fill Color down arrow and choose the color you want from the displayed palette.

Printing Spreadsheets

Once you get your worksheet looking just the way you want it, you will probably want to print a copy. Even if your goal is to send the file over the Internet or post it on the Web, having a printout to stick in a file somewhere is a good idea for very important documents. The process of printing a spreadsheet in Excel is basically this: choose what you want to print, and print it. Here's a quick run-down:

- **To get a fast print**   Click the Print tool on the Standard toolbar. A quick status box appears, telling you that the file is being sent to the printer and then—voilà!—there it is. Fast and easy.

- **To print a selected area**   Save the area as a print area. Begin by selecting the cells you want to include, and then choose Print Area from the File menu and select Set Print Area. A dotted outline surrounds the range, indicating that it is now marked as a print area.

> **Note**   Clear the print area you've selected by choosing Print Area from the File menu and choosing Clear Print Area.

- **To preview the worksheet area before you print**   Click the Print Preview tool on the Standard toolbar. The print area you selected appears in the preview window, showing the orientation, margins, and the header and footer of your worksheet.

> **Aha!**   Adding Headers and Footers
>
> If you want to add a header and footer, or change the margins for your worksheet before you print it, display the worksheet in Print Preview mode (click the Print Preview tool on the Standard toolbar), and click the Setup button at the top of the Preview window. In the Page Setup dialog box, click the Margins tab to set margins and the Header/Footer tab to enter a header and footer for the worksheet. After you make your changes, click OK to return to Preview mode.

- **To set print options**   Press Ctrl+P to display the Print dialog box. Choose the page range you want to print, number of copies, and so on. Click OK to print.

Faxing from Excel

Excel 2003 gives you the option of faxing your worksheet—or a portion of it—while you're still working on the file. Begin with a connection to the Internet and your worksheet open on the screen. Choose Send To from the File menu, and click Recipient Using Internet Fax Service. The first time you do this, a message box appears telling you to click OK to choose an Internet fax service; you are then taken to a Web site where you can make your choice and enter your information.

Fast Wrap-Up

- Editing in Excel is as simple as clicking the cell you want to correct and typing the new data. Use F7 to check spelling, and the Error Checker to make sure your formulas work.

- You can copy, cut, and paste cells by first marking them as a block or a range, and then using the commands on the Edit menu, or the appropriate tools on the Standard toolbar.

- When you clear cells, all data and formats are removed and the blank cells remain. When you delete cells, the data *and* the cells are removed from the worksheet.

- You can use Excel's AutoFormat feature to quickly apply professional designs to the worksheet.

- The Format Cells dialog box (available when you right-click selected cells) contains all the options you need for controlling the format of cells on your worksheet.

- You can add borders by clicking the Borders tool, or by working with the Draw Borders toolbar.

- Print your worksheet or selected worksheet area quickly by clicking Print on the Standard toolbar, or by selecting Print from the File menu and choosing your print options. To make sure that the pages will break correctly in your printed worksheet, choose Page Break Preview from the View menu.

Charting Spreadsheet Data

9

10-Second Summary
- ■ Recognize chart elements
- ■ Create a chart
- ■ Learn chart editing techniques
- ■ Use ink to annotate a chart

People get tired of looking at numbers. They want to see color, diagrams, and pictures that illustrate what you're trying to say. Charts enable you to show at a glance what your numbers are leading up to. Readers will know instantly which region sold the most, which subsidiary is most profitable, or who has the highest turnover. And depending on the type of chart you choose, you can show complex relationships among various data items or a simple, easy-to-read bar chart.

> **Lingo** A *chart* is a graphical representation of your data that's designed to show readers at a glance the trends that your data suggests.

Microsoft Office Excel 2003 enables you to create a number of different charts, and gives you a Chart Wizard to lead you quickly through the process. Along the way, you have the option of creating associated details as you want them—adding chart titles and labels, displaying a legend, coloring the chart, and more. This chapter shows you how to make the most of Excel's charting feature in the shortest time. You're just a few clicks away from a few good-looking charts.

A Charting Toolkit

At its most basic level, a chart is a picture of the data in your worksheet. You choose the data that you want Excel to illustrate, select your chart type, and Excel does the rest. You'll see the following elements commonly used in charts (see Figure 9-1):

- ■ **Data series**   The data series is the data you are tracking. The column or row labels are used as the labels in the chart legend.

- **Data marker**   The data marker is the item used to represent your data graphically. In Figure 9-1, the data marker is a bar. In a pie chart, the data marker is a pie slice; in a line chart, the data marker is a point on the line for an individual data series.

- **Axes**   The horizontal and vertical lines along the left and bottom sides of some charts (including bar, line, and area charts) are known as *axes*. The x-axis is the horizontal bar, and the y-axis is the vertical bar. The data values in the chart are plotted in relation to the categories shown on the x-axis and y-axis.

- **Gridlines**   The gridlines extend by default off the y-axis in some charts, giving you a visual clue about the value of individual data items. You can add gridlines, and customize the ones already there, by changing the increment between them or hiding them completely.

- **Chart title and axis titles**   The title of the chart typically appears at the top of the chart. Subtitles appear along the x-axis and y-axis as applicable.

- **Legend**   The legend advises how to read the data markers that readers see in your charts. The legend labels are taken from the data series row or column labels you select.

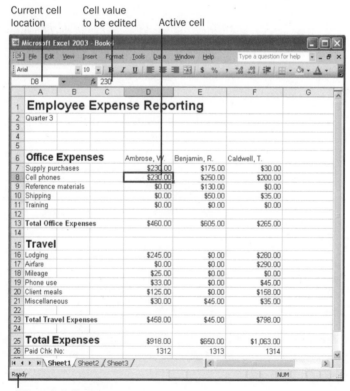

Current cell location   Cell value to be edited   Active cell

Edit mode indicator

Figure 9-1 The most common chart types share these traditional chart elements.

> **Note**   Not all Excel charts use all these elements. A radar chart, for example, is created using only a y-axis, and pie and doughnut charts do not use either an x-axis or a y-axis. You will add titles and axis titles, and change the gridlines and legend as necessary as you create the chart using the Chart Wizard.

Creating Effective Charts

The best charts are clear, colorful, and easy to understand, giving readers the information they need and helping them grasp it quickly. Charts also add visual interest to pages of mind-numbing numbers, and give readers' eyes a break. Here are some suggestions for ensuring that your charts accomplish what you intend:

- **Choose a chart type that will be easy for your readers to understand**   The most common chart types—the ones everybody is used to seeing—are bar, line, pie, and area charts.

- **Make sure your chart shows something worthwhile**   Don't waste your audience's time depicting data that won't mean much to them. Use charts to highlight the important comparisons you want to make, and use them sparingly to maximize their effectiveness.

- **Choose the right chart for the job**   Resist the temptation to use bar charts to show everything—from sales results to inventory to personnel hires to vacation time. Excel gives you a large collection of charts so that you can select one that shows your data in the best possible light.

- **Create clear titles and labels for your chart**   Don't leave your readers guessing about what the data items represent. Use an easy-to-read font and a comfortable font size so that people who might see the chart online, or in a slide presentation, can make out the items without straining.

- **Test new charts with others before you finalize them**   A quick review by friends or coworkers can reveal where your chart is hard to understand, or where you need to make an aesthetic change so that readers won't stumble on their way to your message.

Creating a Chart

Excel employs the Chart Wizard to help you build the chart that best portrays your data. First highlight the row or column labels and the data you want to include in the chart. Then click the Chart Wizard tool on the Standard toolbar (see Figure 9-2). The Chart Wizard appears, ready to lead you through the four steps of creating a chart in Excel. The following sections detail each of these steps.

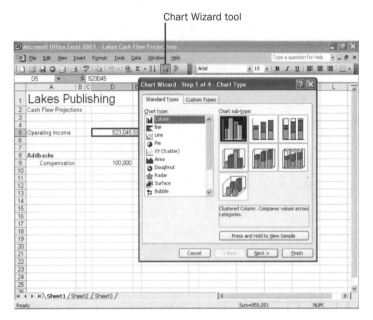

Figure 9-2   Click the Chart Wizard tool to start the process.

Choosing a Chart Type

The first page of the Chart Wizard shows you the library of chart types from which you can choose. Excel offers 14 chart types that portray data relationships. Table 9-1 introduces you to the various charts and explains when you might use each one.

Table 9-1   Excel Chart Types

Chart Type	Description
Column	The column chart enables you to compare data in different categories. For example, you might create a column chart that compares the number of proposals your consulting firm presented in June with the number of new accounts that resulted from those proposals.
Bar	This type of chart is great for showing comparisons among your data. If you want to compare the sales of apples, oranges, and mangoes during the first three months of the year, for example, the different colored bars tell the story at a glance.
Line	A line chart is another often-used type that is good for showing how data changes over time. You might track the number of hits on your Web site, the number of books signed, or the new donors added to your donor list during a specific period.

Table 9-1 Excel Chart Types

Chart Type	Description
Pie	The pie chart is commonly used to show how each individual data item (or slice) relates to the whole pie. You might use a pie chart to show how your department's expenses relate to company-wide expenses.
Scatter (XY)	A scatter chart enables you to compare pairs of data values. For example, you might depict a comparison of foreign and domestic sales of your product in relation to sales during a specific period.
Area	This type of chart shows how each of the data items relates to the whole (what percentage they represent) over time, or by category.
Doughnut	The doughnut chart shows how data items relate to the whole (similar to a pie chart), but it can also track multiple data series.
Radar	The radar chart plots data points along intersecting x- and y-axes.
Surface	A surface chart is similar to an area chart, showing relationships and trends in data over time.
Bubble	A bubble chart can compare three sets of data. The bubbles are sized according to the data values, giving readers a strong visual impression of which items in the chart have the highest value.
Stock	Stock charts are also known as high-low-close charts. These items track data series that include three distinct values. For example, if you are following a specific stock offering, you could use the stock chart to show the highest value, the lowest value, and the market closing value for a specific stock. You also could use this chart to show wholesale, retail, and discount prices on merchandise.
Cylinder, Cone, and Pyramid	These chart styles are simply different designs based on the Column chart type, which enables you to compare values in different series.

Note   For each chart type, Excel offers additional subtypes that allow you to choose different looks and designs for the primary chart. For example, when you choose a column chart, you can then select from the following subtypes: clustered column, stacked column, 100% stacked column, 3-D clustered column, 3-D stacked column, 3-D 100% stacked column, and 3-D column.

Lingo A *3-D* chart appears to "come off the page" because of the depth of the geometric shapes in the chart. 3-D charts are particularly popular for special effects charts or charts used in presentations.

To find the chart type that's right for you, follow these steps:

1 Click the chart type you want to see in the Chart Type list on the left side of the Chart Wizard dialog box.

2 Click a subtype (each time you click a different subtype, a description of it appears below the Subtypes window).

3 Click Press And Hold To View Sample. The wizard shows you how your data will appear in the kind of chart you selected.

4 If you don't like what you see, select a different chart type. If you're happy with the selected chart, click Next.

In addition to the standard chart types and subtypes, Excel gives you several custom chart types that are more difficult to categorize. Some of these charts have cool special designs, and are ready to place right into a presentation or on the Web. Click the Custom Types tab to see the additional charts. Click through the sample types and find one you like. (I'm partial to Columns With Depth, but that's just me.)

Specifying the Data Range and Series

The next step in the Chart Wizard enables you to specify whether you want the data series to be taken from the rows or columns in the worksheet. When you choose Columns, the data displayed in the columns is assigned to the data markers in the chart. For example, Figure 9-3 shows a simple column chart created from three months' worth of regional sales figures. This chart answers the question, "How did we do in the first three months of the year?" and groups the regions (rows) together to give a clear picture.

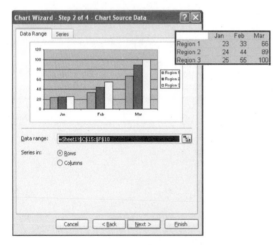

Figure 9-3   You can easily change the perspective of your chart by changing rows to columns in the Chart Source Data window.

If you wanted to answer a different question with this information, such as, "How did the sales regions do in the first three months of the year?," you can flip the data series so that Excel uses the columns instead of rows as the basis for the chart (as shown in Figure 9-4). To make that change, simply click Columns from the Series In area of the Data Range tab. You can see in a second how the different regions did in each of the three months. Same data, same chart, different perspective. When you're happy with the way the data is shown in the preview window, click Next.

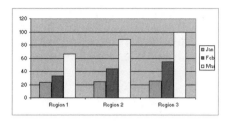

Figure 9-4 The chart displayed by Columns.

> **Aha!** Customizing Data Series
>
> To further customize how Excel uses data series, you can click the Series tab in Step 2 of the Chart Wizard. This tab offers you a number of different settings that allow you to add or remove new data series, move to the worksheet to choose a different name or value selection, or choose different axis labels. For simple charts, you probably won't need these items, but it's nice to know where to find them, just in case.

Setting Chart Options

The next step in the Chart Wizard lets you choose all the options you want for your chart. You set the various options by clicking the tab you want to change, and choosing the options you want to use. Table 9-2 explains the various choices available to you.

Table 9-2 Working with Chart Options

Tab	Description
Titles	Lets you add a chart title or titles to the x-axis or y-axis.
Axes	Helps you hide or display the x-axis or y-axis. You also can choose whether you want the x-axis to be selected automatically by Excel, or to be preset as a category or time-scale axis.
Gridlines	Enables you to choose whether you want to display or hide major and minor gridlines on both axes.
Legend	Lets you choose whether to display or hide a legend. If you want to show a legend, you also need to choose where the legend will be displayed in relation to the chart.
Data Labels	You can have Excel display the series names, category names, and values on the individual data markers to help your viewers understand your chart. (Note: Use this feature sparingly, because too many labels can make your chart difficult to read.)
Data Table	If you click Show Data Table on the Data Table tab, Excel will display a table of the data values used to create the chart beneath it.

Each time you make a change in the Chart Options dialog box, the preview window changes to show you the effect of your selection. When you're satisfied with the options you've added, click Next to move to the last page of the wizard.

> **Aha!**   Changing Charts After the Fact
>
> Once you've created a chart using the Chart Wizard, Excel changes the Data menu (which is normally in the menu bar at the top of the window) to the Chart menu whenever you click a chart to select it. The Chart menu contains all the commands you need to change settings you selected in the Chart Wizard. Depending on the type of chart you're working with, you may also see the 3-D View option, which enables you to change the current chart type into a 3-D display of the same chart type.

Choosing the Chart Location

The final step in the Chart Wizard involves specifying where you want the chart to reside. (You also can choose where to place a chart by selecting it and then choosing Location from the Chart menu.) You can place the charts you create directly in your worksheet, or you can create a chart sheet to store only the new chart. By default, after you select the worksheet data and create your chart, the chart is placed on the current worksheet. If you want the chart to be placed on a sheet of its own, click As New Sheet in the Chart Location dialog box. After you've made your selection, click Finish to create the chart.

Chart Editing Techniques

Once you click Finish, and the completed chart is placed on your worksheet, it is treated just like any other inserted graphic or picture. This means that when you click the chart, handles appear, and you can drag the mouse to resize, move, or rearrange the chart as you would any object. Here are additional chart editing techniques you may want to try:

■   Right-click any element in the chart to see a shortcut menu of editing options for that item. For example, when you right-click a data marker, options appear that enable you to change any of the settings you entered in the Chart Wizard. You can also add a trend line or clear the element you selected.

> **Aha!**   Working with the Chart Toolbar
>
> Excel gives you a handy Chart toolbar to use as you work on your charts. The toolbar is not displayed automatically, however; you'll need to look for it. To display the Chart toolbar, choose Toolbars from the View menu, and then select Chart. The Chart toolbar then pops up on your work area and you can dock it along with other toolbars or leave it floating over your workspace while you work.

■   If you really don't like the chart and want to start again, simply click the chart and press Delete. Be sure to click outside the main chart area and away from the legend; if you don't, instead of deleting the chart, you will simply select one of the chart elements for editing.

- Change the background color of your chart by double-clicking the chart background. In the Area section of the Format Walls dialog box, click the color you want to apply to the background, and then click OK.

- Remove the border of your chart by right-clicking the chart, choosing Format Chart Area, clicking None in the Border area of the Patterns tab, and clicking OK.

- Change the placement of the legend of your chart by right-clicking it and choosing Format Legend. Click the Placement tab, and choose the position you want; then click OK.

Aha!   Fixing Crowded Chart Labels

If your chart labels overlap, fix the problem this way: Double-click the scrunched text. In the Format Axis dialog box, click the Font tab. Choose a smaller size for the text (8 points often works well) or click the Alignment tab and, in the Orientation area, click the small red marker in the rotation diagram and drag the marker to angle the text labels. This places the labels at an angle in your chart so that the labels can be seen in their entirety.

Using Ink to Annotate Charts

Now because the Office System provides Ink support throughout all the core applications, you can use your Tablet PC to annotate charts in Excel. This means that when you're reviewing a spreadsheet chart with a coworker, you can add notes, draw Xs or arrows, and circle important elements on the chart.

> **Lingo** *Annotate* in this sense means to simply "make notes on." Ink support in the Office System enables you to write notes long hand and convert the handwriting to text, leave handwritten notes as they are, or draw on your charts as needed.

The Ink Annotations toolbar appears automatically when you create a chart on the Tablet PC, giving you the option of setting pen controls (choose Ballpoint Pen, Felt Tip, or Highlighter in a variety of colors). You can also erase, change color, and change line thickness as you go along. Simply click the tool and make your notes. It's like writing on a piece of paper—only better, because you can save, reuse, and share this information easily.

Fast Wrap-Up

- Excel includes 14 basic chart types—plus numerous subtypes and custom types—that you can use to help others understand your information.

- Use the Chart Wizard to go through the four-step process of creating charts.

- You can edit charts quickly by right-clicking the element you want to change and modifying the settings.

- Everything on a chart—titles, background, data items, labels, and more—can be customized by modifying the Chart Options.

- You can add notes to charts on a Tablet PC by using the Ink Annotations feature.

Part 4
Microsoft Office PowerPoint 2003: Present Ideas Powerfully

PowerPoint is one of those great programs that many people use only when they have to—which means that each time they return to it, there's a fresh learning curve involved. This part of the book focuses on the tasks you're most likely to want to accomplish with PowerPoint in the shortest possible timeframe. Whether you want a simple slide or an elaborate presentation that will wow your audience, the tasks in this section take you through the process quickly.

Creating a Presentation—From Start to Finish

10

10-Second Summary

- Start a presentation
- Add Slides
- Format Slides
- Arrange Slides
- Save and run the presentation

Some people are natural-born presenters. They just *love* getting in front of a crowd. They don't sweat it if they drop their note cards at the last minute; they're not stressed when the audiovisual equipment they need isn't there; and they don't swoon when they look out at the audience and see 350 people instead of the 30 they expected. I'm not one of those people. Are you?

Microsoft Office PowerPoint 2003 helps you prepare presentations that are easy, smooth, and professional, whether you're a seasoned veteran or a novice quaking in your boots. To those who would rather do just about anything than give a presentation, PowerPoint provides all kinds of help—professional designs, easy-to-use special effects, and even a wizard to help you with content. To experienced presenters, PowerPoint offers convenience, interesting effects, and the ability to take the presentation to people, to desktop, or to the Web. This chapter covers all the basics you need to know to put together a solid, professional presentation in PowerPoint. Maybe you'll be so excited about the result that you won't even notice those butterflies.

New Features in PowerPoint 2003

Some of PowerPoint 2003's most powerful features are shared throughout Office—the Instant Messaging capability, the Shared Workspace, Smart Tag capability (which is available in PowerPoint for the first time), and the Research task pane. Some new features are unique to PowerPoint, however:

- **Packaging presentations**   Say goodbye to the Pack And Go Wizard and hello to the Package To CD command. Now you can prepare your presentation and burn it to a CD that can be run on another user's system, even if that user doesn't have PowerPoint.

- **Slide show annotations**   New Ink support in PowerPoint 2003 enables presenters to add handwritten notes on slides as the presentation is going on, or save annotations to slides for later display.

- **Improved navigation tools**   The Slide Navigator has been replaced with an easier-to-use toolbar for moving to different slides in your presentation.

- **Larger movie display**   In PowerPoint 2003, you have the option of maximizing the movie so that it plays in full-screen view.

What Will You Do with PowerPoint?

Any situation—business or otherwise—that calls for acetate sheets, a flip chart, blackboard scribbling, or a slide projector, can be improved with PowerPoint. PowerPoint is a program that mixes all kinds of presentation tools to help you create effective, impressive, and professional-quality presentations. How can PowerPoint help you present your ideas? Here are a few examples:

- Present your next report to the editorial board as a 10-slide PowerPoint presentation, complete with printed handouts.

- Use a PowerPoint presentation instead of overheads in your next HR training class; print the slides as handouts for employees, so they can spend more time listening, and less time taking notes.

- Use PowerPoint (with embedded spreadsheets from Microsoft Office Excel 2003) to show the company why your department needs a bigger budget.

> **Note**   Feeling Creative?
>
> Presentations don't have to be "all business" in order to be effective. With PowerPoint's many media features, you can create a digital short film, mixing audio and video clips with still photos. Or you could produce a low-budget commercial for online broadcast or create a Web page that launches your annual report and gives visitors control over which elements they want to see, and when they want to see them.

PowerPoint's New Look

PowerPoint 2003 follows the new Office system's look and feel by providing a new effect for menus, toolbars, and more. The Getting Started task pane gives you instant links to Microsoft Online (a great source for image and media clips you can use in your presentations), and enables you to search for specific information (as shown in Figure 10-1).

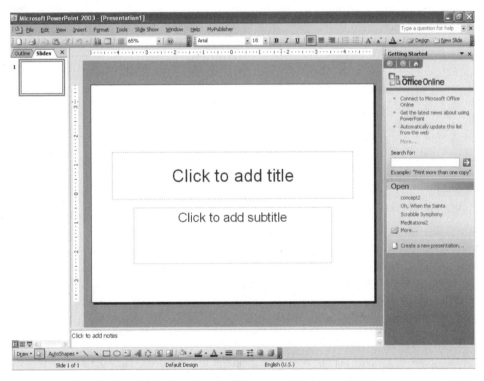

Figure 10-1   The Getting Started task pane gives you quick access to Microsoft Online when you launch PowerPoint.

Understanding the PowerPoint Views

When you first start PowerPoint, the application automatically displays Normal view in the center panel, with the Outline and Slide pane off to the left, and the Notes pane at the bottom of the display. PowerPoint includes three different views that you'll use for different tasks, depending on what you're trying to accomplish. The View controls, located in the bottom left side of the PowerPoint window (in the Outline And Slides pane) enable you to switch to these different views quickly. Table 10-1 introduces the different views you'll use in PowerPoint and tells you a little bit about each one.

Table 10-1 PowerPoint Views

Button	View Name	Use When ...
	Normal View	You want to work on individual slides or add notes to your slides.
	Slide Sorter View	You are organizing, reviewing, rearranging, or setting timing and transitions for your slides.
	Slide Show	You want to display a slide show based on the open presentation, starting with the currently selected slide.

Aha!   For Notetakers

You can also display the current slide in Notes Pages view, which presents a small version of the current slide atop a large notes area. This enables you to add notes (in the bottom panel in Normal view), and then review the notes while viewing the slide they're attached to.

To Master or Not to Master

If you're simply planning to create a quick and easy presentation, you might not want to worry about master pages. A *master page* is a page that works in the background of the slide, controlling such details as the format of headers and footers, the placement of slide numbers, the selection of a color scheme, background images or graphics used throughout the presentation, and so on. For longer presentations, or presentation styles you plan to use again, however, master pages can be great time-savers.

PowerPoint offers you three kinds of masters: A Slide Master, which controls format settings for individual slides; a Handout Master, which sets up the format of the handouts you create and print; and a Notes Master, which tracks the styles in effect for notes included with your presentation.

To create any of these masters, choose Master from the View menu, and then click the type of master you want to create. You are taken to the master page, where you can change the text style, insert a new master page, change the master layout, and modify the slide number, date, and footer information.

Starting with the End in Mind: Setting Up the Show

PowerPoint is so flexible that you can give your presentation in a variety of different ways. So the first question you should ask when you start a new presentation is: How will my presentation be delivered?

The answer to this question will affect the size of the presentation you create. You enter your choice in the Page Setup dialog box (which you display by choosing Page Setup from the File menu), shown in Figure 10-2.

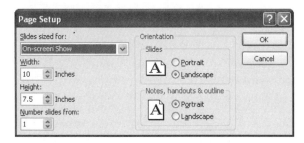

Figure 10-2 You use the Page Setup dialog box to tell PowerPoint how to gauge the size of the slides you want to create.

Choose your preferences for the way your presentation is set up by displaying the Page Setup dialog box (choose Page Setup from the File menu), and making the following choices:

1 Click the Slides Sized For down arrow to display the list of available options. On-Screen Show is the default setting, but you can also choose from a number of paper sizes, 35mm Slides, Overhead, Banner, and Custom.

2 If you want to change the width and height of the slides, click in the Width and Height boxes, respectively, and change those values, either by clicking the up and down arrows, or by typing a new value.

3 Enter the number you want PowerPoint to use as the first page number in the Number Slides From box.

4 By default, the Slides orientation is set to Landscape (horizontal, 11 × 8 1/2-inch mode). For most purposes, you should be able to leave this setting as is. The Notes, Handouts And Outline orientation setting is Portrait (vertical, 8 1/2 × 11-inch mode). This is a traditional orientation for the printed page, so this, too, should be fine as it appears.

5 Click OK to save your settings. You're now ready to begin creating your presentation.

> **Aha!** More Room, Please
>
> Before you start working on the presentation, close the task pane, if it's still visible, by clicking the close box in the upper right corner of the pane. This gives you more room to work with your slide on the screen.

Creating a Presentation

When you first start PowerPoint, a blank presentation opens on your screen. Next you need to choose how you want the presentation to look by selecting a design, and add the content for your presentation.

> **Aha!**   The New Presentation Task Pane
>
> If you want to start a new presentation when you've already been working with PowerPoint, click the task pane down arrow and choose New Presentation (or choose New from the File menu). In the New Presentation task pane, you can choose to start a new blank presentation, create one from a design template, use the AutoContent Wizard, or start a new presentation based on an existing presentation.

Choosing a Design

Click the Design tool in the Formatting toolbar to display the Slide Design task pane (see Figure 10-3). This task pane presents you with a wealth of design talent you can apply to your own presentations. Scroll through the list, and click the one that fits the look and feel you want to portray.

Figure 10-3   The Slide Design task pane displays all the professional designs you can use for your own presentation.

Adding Content

At any point in the process, you can begin to add content by clicking the Click To Add Here prompt and typing text. You can also add information by clicking the Slides tab in the Outline And Slides panel, and typing your slide text there. If you're relatively new to creating presentations, however, you may wonder what you should focus on. The AutoContent Wizard can help you create a general game plan for the details you'll fill in later yourself.

Getting Started with the AutoContent Wizard

But what if you're stumped about the type of information you want to include? The Auto-Content Wizard can help you with that.

To start the AutoContent Wizard, display the New Presentation task pane and click From AutoContent Wizard. The wizard begins (see Figure 10-4) and walks you through the following four steps:

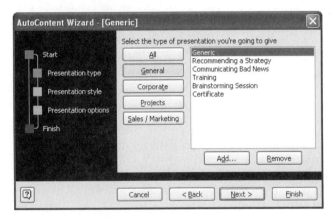

Figure 10-4 The AutoContent Wizard suggests topics, content, charts, and more for specific types of presentations.

1 Choose the category of presentation you want to create (General, Corporate, Projects, Sales/Marketing, or Carnegie Coach). Click Next.

> **Aha!** Seeing Them All
>
> If you want to see all the types of presentations the AutoContent Wizard has to offer, simply click the All button to display the entire list. Click the one you want, then click Next.

2 Select the kind of output you will use for your presentation. Click your choice (for most presentations, you will likely use either On-Screen Presentation or Web Presentation), then click Next.

3 Enter a title for your presentation and, if you want to include a footer (which might include your company or department name), type it in the Footer box. If you want the date and slide number to appear in the footer line, leave the options checked; otherwise, click the boxes to clear them and disable the options. Click Next.

4 Click Finish on the last page. The presentation is created and placed in the work area, ready for you to modify to your heart's content.

PowerPoint selects a design to fit the content of the presentation you've selected, but you can change it to suit your tastes (see "Choosing a Design," earlier in this chapter). Additionally, the wizard adds slide titles and suggested charts, bullet items, and more, to help spark your ideas about the specific content you'd like to include.

Adding and Editing Your Own Text

When you start with a blank presentation, or choose a design template, the text prompts within individual slides say such things as *Click To Add Title* or *Click To Add Text*. To add text, simply click in the box and type whatever you want to add. Click outside the box to accept the addition. If you've used the AutoContent Wizard to start the presentation, you've got all kinds of text in your presentation. You can change the text in the presentation two ways:

■ On the slide, you can click the text you want to change. The text box highlights and the cursor appears. You can then highlight the text you want to replace and type the new text. The AutoContent text is replaced as you type.

■ When all the text for that slide is highlighted in the Outline pane, begin typing. This replaces all the text in that slide.

> **Aha!**   Oops—I Wanted That
>
> If you accidentally erase more information than you intended to, press Ctrl+Z and PowerPoint will undo your last action.

Adding Slides

The AutoContent Wizard fills up your presentation with slides of its choosing, but if you have created a blank presentation, or started with a design template, it's up to you to add your own slides. Here's how to do it:

1 Display the slide before which you want to add a slide.

2 Click New Slide on the Formatting toolbar. The Slide Layout task pane appears, offering you a collection of different text and content layouts (as shown in Figure 10-5). Click the layout you want to use.

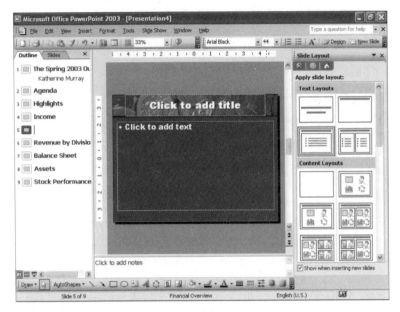

Figure 10-5 The Slide Layout task pane presents you with different slide choices for the one you add.

Changing Page Layout

You also can apply a new slide layout to slides you've already got in your presentation. This is helpful as you go through and edit your AutoContent-generated presentation to convey the information that is important to you. To change the page layout using the Slide Layout task pane, simply display the slide you want to change and choose Slide Layout from the Format menu. When the Slide Layout task pane appears, click the layout you want to apply.

Creating a Chart

Charts can be particularly helpful in presentations because they show data trends and concepts in easy-to-understand ways. When you want to add a chart to your presentation, follow these steps:

1 Begin by choosing a slide layout that has a chart placeholder in it.

2 Double-click the chart area to begin the chart-creation process. A bar chart is drawn by default, and a sample datasheet appears with dummy data already inserted.

3 Replace the data in the datasheet with your own information. Edit these cells the way you edit cells in Excel: click the cell and type the new information. Like an Excel spreadsheet, the column and row labels are used as the axis labels and the legend on the chart (see Figure 10-6).

4 Click the datasheet's close box to hide the datasheet and give yourself more room to work.

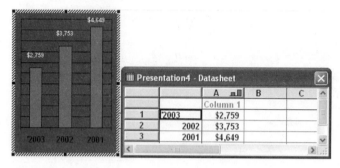

Figure 10-6 Enter chart data and labels in the datasheet.

Aha!   Changing Chart Type

If you want to change the type of chart used to portray your data, click the Chart Type tool on the Standard toolbar. A palette of chart styles appears, and you can simply click the chart type you want to use.

Importing Chart Data

PowerPoint allows you to import data into the datasheet if you want to use information you've created in another program. Just click Import File on the Standard toolbar, and PowerPoint displays the Import File dialog box. Navigate to the folder storing the file you want to import, click the file, and then click Open.

In the Import Data Options dialog box, select the sheet you want to import; then tell PowerPoint whether you want to import the entire sheet, or only a selected range. (If you want to specify a range, enter it in the Range box.) Finally, if you want the incoming data to replace the existing data in the datasheet, leave the Overwrite Existing Cells check box selected. Click OK to import the data and have PowerPoint redraw the chart.

Inserting Graphics

There are other types of visual aids you might want to add to your presentation. What about the architect's drawing of the new office? Or perhaps some clip art, or a few photos, would help liven things up a bit. Some people make the mistake of creating presentations that are simply pages and pages of text. But just as you need something now and then to break the monotony of reading page after page of this book, your audience will need a picture, a photo, or a splash of color every so often to give their eyes a rest, and help them pause a minute before they focus again on your words.

In other places in the book, you've learned how to add clip art, so I'll just give you a quick refresher here:

1 Select or add a slide with a Content layout area. (The small cartoon fellow represents clip art on the layout choices.)

2 Click the Insert Clip Art tool in the *Click Icon To Add Content* area of the slide.

3 In the Select Picture dialog box, click the picture you want to use, and PowerPoint adds it to the slide.

> **Aha!**   Searching for Art
>
> If you want to look for pictures that show something specific—such as people, animals, or trees—you can enter the topic in the Search text box and click Go. PowerPoint then displays all the clip art related to your subject. You can place the art by clicking it, and then clicking OK.

Formatting Techniques

Making formatting changes is a fairly simple task in PowerPoint. Usually, you can simply right-click the object you want to change to get a shortcut menu of choices related to that item. Here are some of the more common formatting changes you're likely to make:

- **Italicize or boldface a few words for emphasis**   Select the text you want to change and click Bold or Italic on the Formatting toolbar. You also can press Ctrl+B to boldface the selected work, or Ctrl+I to italicize it.

- **Change the color of a title**   Highlight the text and click the down arrow to the right of the Font Color tool on the Formatting toolbar. Click the color you want from the displayed palette.

- **Change the bullet characters on a bullet list**   Right-click in the list you want to change, and select Bullets And Numbering from the shortcut menu. In the Bullets And Numbering dialog box, click one of the alternate bullet styles, or click Customize to display the Symbol dialog box. Click the character you want to use as a bullet, then click OK.

> **Aha!**   Changing Fonts
>
> If you don't see a character you like, you might want to see what other fonts have to offer. Click the Font down arrow and choose a different font. The standard symbol fonts included in the Office System are Webdings, Wingdings, Wingdings 2, Wingdings 3, and Symbol, but your system may have others as well.

- **Change the alignment of text**   The easiest way to change the way text is aligned is to select it and then click Align Left, Center, or Align Right on the Formatting toolbar.

- **Modify indent levels**   If you want to increase or decrease the indent of text on the current slide, you can use the Increase Indent or Decrease Indent tools. You also can change indents by clicking the text you want to change and pressing Alt+Shift+Right arrow to increase the indent, or Alt+Shift+Left arrow to decrease it.

Change the Slide Background

Choose Background from the Format menu, and then click the down arrow in the color bar beneath the Background fill window in the Background dialog box to display the pull-down menu. Choose another color from the selected scheme, choose More Colors to select a different hue, or Fill Effects to choose a pattern, texture, gradient, or picture for the background. Click Apply to apply the change to the current slide; click Apply To All to change all slides in the presentation.

Aha!   Making Global Text Changes

When you want to make a font change that is applied throughout your presentation, you need to work on the master that applies to that slide type. Choose Slide Master from the View menu, and then make the changes—font, size, style, color, and alignment—that you want to make. When you're finished making changes, click Close Master View on the Slide Master View toolbar.

Changing Color Scheme

Perhaps you like the look of the presentation design, but you're not crazy about the colors. You can easily change that. Here are the steps:

1 Open the presentation you want to change.

2 Choose Slide Design from the Format menu.

3 In the Slide Design task pane, click Color Schemes. A selection of color schemes appears in the task pane.

4 Point to the one you like, and a down arrow appears. Click it and choose whether you want to apply the change to all slides, or just the selected slide. After you make your choice, the color change is made.

From Color to Grayscale

With a click of the mouse, you can see how your presentation would appear in black and white. This is helpful for projects in which you'll be printing handouts on a monochrome printer, and you want to see how your slides will look on the printed page. Click the Color/ Grayscale tool on the Standard toolbar, and a drop-down menu appears, giving you the choice of Color, Grayscale, or Pure Black And White. Click your choice and the change is applied to the current slide. The Grayscale View toolbar appears so that you can choose additional settings, or click Close Grayscale View when you're finished.

Arranging Slides

After you've created the slides you need (complete with text, charts, and pictures) and edited and formatted the slides the way you want them, you're ready to be a presentation producer. Now you need to take a look at the way your presentation flows from one slide to the next. Are your ideas arranged in a logical order? Should this slide come before that one? You use Slide Sorter view to make these kinds of changes in your presentation. Display the Slide Sorter view by clicking the tool in the lower left portion of the PowerPoint window.

Slide Sorter view displays all the slides in your presentation as thumbnails (as shown in Figure 10-7 on the following page). You can easily review the different slides in this view, and make choices about the order in which they are arranged. If you want to rearrange the slides, simply click the one you want to move and drag it to the new location. An insertion bar moves with the slide as you drag it to show you where the slide will be positioned when you release the mouse button. You can reverse a change you make by pressing Ctrl+Z.

See Also
Slide Sorter view is the place where you add slide transitions and set the timing of your presentation. You'll learn more about those tasks in Chapter 11, "Animating and Timing Your Presentation."

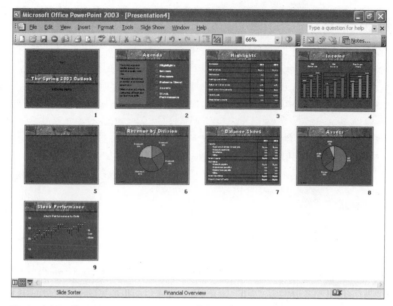

Figure 10-7   You can rearrange your slides easily in Slide Sorter view.

Take One: Running the Presentation

Are you ready to take a test drive with your new presentation? Press F5. The presentation starts, displaying the first slide in full-screen view. Advance to the next slide by clicking the left mouse button, or pressing Enter, the right arrow key, or the spacebar. If you want to return to a previous slide, press the left arrow key. When the presentation is finished, PowerPoint displays the message *End Of Slide Show, Click To Exit*. Click the prompt or press Esc, and you are returned to the view you were using before you pressed F5.

> **Aha!**   Annotating Slides
>
> The improved presentation toolbar in PowerPoint 2003 gives you a new way to display pen options. Now you can choose your tool by clicking the center button in the navigation toolbar, and clicking the Arrow, Ballpoint Pen, Felt Tip Pen, or Highlighter option. Select an ink color, and you can begin writing, circling, and sketching on your slides as needed.

Navigating the Slide Show

The navigation toolbar (a new easy-to-use feature in PowerPoint 2003) enables you to move easily from slide to slide in your presentation (see Figure 10-8). A new pen options menu enables you to choose the pen type and color you want to use for your annotations. You can display a specific slide by choosing it from the Go To Slide submenu; you can pause the presentation and go to a black or white screen while you have a discussion. You can also display the Speaker Notes dialog box to add specific comments, questions, or items you want to look up later by choosing Screen, and selecting the option you want.

Figure 10-8 The navigation controls are easy to use, and give you options while you are presenting.

Aha!   Switching Among Programs

The Switch Programs option on the Screen submenu displays the Windows Taskbar, so that you can easily display another program you have waiting in the wings. You might use this when you are giving a presentation introducing a new product to your regional sales managers. Before the presentation, you opened an Excel worksheet showing sales projections for the product, but you minimized it for use only if needed. When one of the regional managers asks a question about sales projections, you can choose Switch Programs, click the Excel icon in the Taskbar, and display and discuss the projections before returning to your presentation.

Saving Your Presentation

Congratulations! In one chapter, you've learned to create, edit, format, and run a simple presentation. The next two chapters build on these basics, so if you've started a presentation you may want to save it now. Press Ctrl+S to save the presentation, enter a name, and click Save.

Package to CD

PowerPoint 2003 includes a new Package For CD command on the File menu that enables you to create a CD of your presentation that can be run on other computers, even if they don't have PowerPoint installed. Choose the command from the menu, and insert a blank CD in your CD-RW drive. When you click the Copy To CD button, PowerPoint copies the files quickly to the CD, and then ejects it and asks whether you want to copy the same presentation files to another CD. You can click Options to specify how you want the CD to play the presentations, and to password-protect the presentation if needed.

Previewing for the Web

How quickly can you make a Web page? As fast as you can create a PowerPoint presentation. Once you've finished your presentation, choose Web Page Preview from the File menu. PowerPoint displays the presentation as it would appear on the Web (as shown in Figure 10-9).

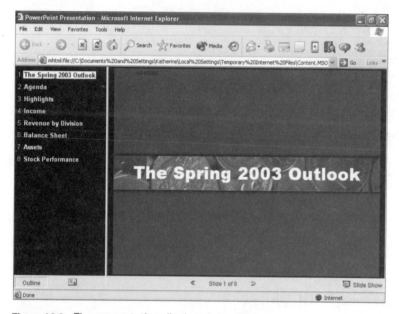

Figure 10-9   The presentation displayed as a Web page.

The presentation is created using frames to provide users with the links they need to get to other pages. The first page of the presentation appears in the right pane; on the left you see the titles of the other slides in your presentation. To go to another page, simply click the title.

Things to Watch for in Web Preview

As you're taking a look at your Web page in Web Preview, ask yourself the following questions:

- Is the text easy to read?
- Will visitors understand how to move from page to page?
- Have you used standard colors that can be displayed by most browsers?
- Are your charts large enough? Are they clearly labeled?

Click the browser's close box to close the Web Preview and return to the presentation. Make any changes that are needed, and then save the file in Web format.

Saving as a Web Page

To save your presentation as a Web page, simply click Save As Web Page from the File menu. The Save As dialog box appears with some special Web options. Beneath the file list in the Save As dialog box, click Publish to set further options, such as whether to save the entire presentation or a selected range, whether to include speaker notes, which browsers you want to support, and the title and folder for the saved Web page. Click the Open Published Web page in the browser check box if you want to see the page after it has been saved. Click Publish to complete the process.

Fast Wrap-Up

- Start a presentation by selecting a blank presentation, working with a design template, or using the AutoContent Wizard to suggest content based on the topic you select.

- Changing the layout of a slide is a simple matter: choose Slide Layout from the Format menu, and choose the layout you want from the thumbnails displayed in the task pane.

- PowerPoint includes layout templates that make it easy for you to add charts, clip art, tables, pictures, diagrams, and media clips.

- You use the tools on the Formatting toolbar to make simple changes; additional options are available on the Format menu, and on individual objects' short-cut menus.

- Click Design on the Formatting toolbar to display the Slide Design task pane, then choose Color Schemes to choose a different color set for your presentation. You can also see how the presentation will look in black and white by clicking the Color/Grayscale tool on the Standard toolbar.

- You will use Slide Sorter view to rearrange the slides in your presentation.

- Run your presentation by pressing F5, and advance the slides by clicking the left mouse button, or by pressing the right arrow key, Enter, or spacebar. Return to a previous slide by pressing the left arrow key.

- You can save your PowerPoint presentation as a Web page. Choose Save As Web Page from the File menu to save a browser-ready version of your presentation.

Animating and Timing Your Presentation

11

> **10-Second Summary**
> - Set up the show
> - Use animation schemes
> - Add transitions to slides
> - Control slide display
> - Use speaker notes

Now that you know the tricks of creating, editing, and formatting your Microsoft Office PowerPoint 2003 presentations, you're ready to add the polish that turns it into a real show. In this chapter, you work in Slide Sorter view to add animation controls, apply transitions, set the timing of the presentation, and use speaker notes.

Working in Slide Sorter View

You got a brief look at Slide Sorter view in Chapter 10, "Creating a Presentation—From Start to Finish," when you learned to rearrange the slides in your presentation. But you need a closer look in order to add some of the finishing touches. Display Slide Sorter view by clicking the Slide Sorter view tool in the lower left portion of the PowerPoint window. Figure 11-1 on the following page shows you Slide Sorter view and highlights the important tools you'll be using here.

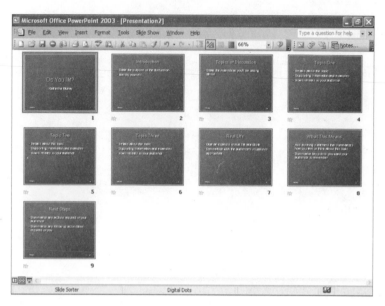

Figure 11-1   Slide Sorter view enables you to fine-tune your almost-done presentation.

> **Lingo** A *transition* is the effect applied to a slide as it is replaced by the next slide. Transitions can include animation, sound, and special effects such as fades, wipes, and dissolves.

Setting Up the Show

Start by taking a look at the basic setup for the slide show you're producing. Choose Set Up Show from the Slide Show menu. The Set Up Show dialog box, shown in Figure 11-2, appears.

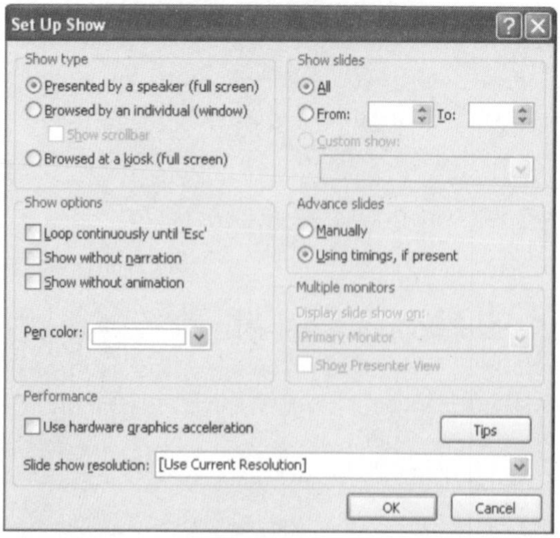

Figure 11-2   You make some basic choices for the way your presentation will operate in the Set Up Show dialog box.

> **Note** In Chapter 10, you made some initial choices in the Page Setup dialog box about the size of the slides you were creating. In the Set Up Show dialog box, you choose the type of presentation you will give, and choose settings (pen color, slide advance, and slide selection) that will be used in the actual presentation.

In the Show Type area, choose the form in which you'll be giving the presentation. Will you be presenting in front of an audience? Will someone be sitting at a computer, viewing the presentation on a monitor? Will the presentation be running on a terminal in a training room at your corporate office? Each of the options in the Show Type area adds unique features to the presentation, depending on what you're trying to do. The first option is the default selection—this is the normal, full-screen view. The second option, Browsed By An Individual, adds commands and navigational tools to help people move through the presentation in a way that's most comfortable for them. The third option, Browsed At A Kiosk, creates the presentation as a continuous loop that restarts automatically after five minutes of inactivity. Click the option that best fits how your presentation will be used.

The Show Options area enables you to control whether your presentation loops continuously, or goes from start to finish and then ends. If you want the presentation to loop, click the check box to enable the feature. Additionally, you can choose to run the presentation without narration or animation, if you're trying to keep the file sizes small and the special effects to a minimum. Finally, the Show Options area allows you to set the Pen color (click the down arrow and choose the on-screen color you want). You'll use the pen to draw on the screen while you present the slide show, circling or underlining important concepts.

In the Show Slides and Advance Slides areas, you specify which slides will be included in your presentation and how they will advance from one to the next. If you want the slides to change automatically, leave Using Timings, If Present selected (this is the default setting). If you want to give the user the ability to move on to the next slide by clicking a button or pressing a key, select the Manually option.

> **Note** Many of the discussions in this chapter—including setting slide transitions and rehearsing timings—are based on the idea that you have elected to advance the slides automatically. If you choose the manual method, the slide show's users will control when the pages advance.

The final options in the Set Up Show dialog box enable you to display the show on multiple monitors and improve system performance. If you have multiple monitors set up on your system, you can click the Show Presenter View check box to display a toolbar of Presenter tools, which enable you to display slide thumbnails, navigation tools, and speaker notes. If you have a graphics accelerator card in your system, clicking the Use Hardware Graphics Acceleration check box may accelerate the display of slides in your slide show. Once you're finished setting up the show, click OK to close the dialog box and return to Slide Sorter view.

Using Animation Schemes

Now that you've entered all the information on your slides, you can add special effects that really make them stand out. You can add *animation schemes* globally (which means the scheme is applied to all slides in your presentation), or you can apply different schemes to different slides. Here's how to add animation schemes to your slides:

1 Display the presentation in Slide Sorter view.

2 Click a slide to which you want to apply the animation.

3 Choose Animation Scheme from the Slide Show menu. The Slide Design task pane appears, displaying a list of animation schemes you can choose to apply to the current slide (as shown in Figure 11-3).

Figure 11-3 A list of animation schemes appears in the task pane. Click one to see its effect—the selected slide shows the result.

Lingo *Animation schemes* enable you to apply animation—that is, movement and special effects—to individual objects on your slides.

> **Note**   The animation schemes are organized by the kind of effect they produce. You can choose from Subtle, Moderate, or Exciting animation effects—or, of course, you can leave the slide set to the default of No Animation.

PowerPoint plays the animation effect on the current slide as soon as you click it, but if you want to see it again, click the Play button at the bottom of the task pane. If you want to see how the effect will look in the slide show, click Slide Show. And if you want to apply that animation scheme to all the slides in the presentation, click Apply To All Slides.

> **Aha!**   Adding Animation Effects to Multiple Slides
>
> To apply animation schemes to multiple slides, first select the group (press and hold Ctrl as you click additional slides), then click the scheme you want to use. If you want to use a fade effect for every section review in your presentation, for example, you can click all related slides, then choose one of the fade animation schemes.

Animating Individual Objects

Animation schemes apply an effect to all items on the slide—slide title, bullet points, and so on. But what if you want to have a chart slide in from the left while the bullet points are fading in? In this case, you need to animate objects independently, and you'll need to leave Slide Sorter view to do so. To control the order in which your objects appear, rotate, play, and fade, you need to work with Custom Animations on the Slide Show menu. First click the Normal View tool in the lower left corner of the PowerPoint window. Then choose Custom Animations. The task pane shown in Figure 11-4 appears.

Figure 11-4   When you want to control the appearance of individual objects on a slide, use the Custom Animation task pane.

Notice that the list in the task pane shows you the current (default) order of the items as they are sequenced. Numbers also appear beside the elements on the page, so you can easily see which item will be affected when you make a change. (This is a new feature with PowerPoint 2003, and it makes object animation *much* easier.)

To change the order in which the objects play, click the item you want to move, and click one of the Re-Order buttons to move it. You can also set additional options for individual objects by clicking the object's down arrow, and choosing what you want to change from the displayed list.

Adding Transitions to Slides

In addition to adding special effects to individual slides, you can control the way the slides appear and disappear on their way through the presentation. These appearances and disappearances are known as *transitions*, and they can add a solid sense of professionalism to even the simplest presentation.

When you want to add transitions to your slides, follow these steps:

1 Display the presentation you want to work with in Slide Sorter view.

2 Click the first slide to which you want to add a transition.

3 Click the Transition tool on the Slide Sorter toolbar.

> **Note**   If the Transition tool doesn't appear on your toolbar by default, you can display the Slide Transition task pane by clicking the task pane down arrow and choosing it from the displayed list.

4 In the Slide Transition task pane, click the transition effect you want to see (as shown in Figure 11-5).

Figure 11-5 Choose the slide transition you want from the displayed list and watch the selected slide to see the effect.

Changing Transition Speed

When you first select a transition for your slide, its Speed is set to Fast. This means that you might have trouble seeing the transition if you blink while it occurs. To slow the transition speed, click the Speed down arrow in the Modify Transition area of the task pane, and click either Slow or Medium. Test both to see which you like best for individual transitions.

Adding Sound Effects

You can also add sound effects to the transitions on your slides. By default, PowerPoint sets the transition to No Sound, but you can easily remedy that by clicking the Sound down arrow, and choosing the sound you want from the displayed list. Again, play around with the sounds to find the ones you like best, and remember to use them sparingly. If you want the same sound effect to be applied to the transition of each slide until you select a different sound (or choose Stop Previous Sound in the Sound list), click the Loop Until Next Sound check box.

See Also For more about adding sound effects, music, and narration, see Chapter 12, "Enhancing Your Presentations."

Controlling Slide Display

If you've set up your presentation to advance automatically from slide to slide, you must specify the amount of time you want each slide to be displayed. By default, PowerPoint sets up your presentation so that the slides will advance only when you click the mouse, press Enter, or the right or down arrow key. You can change this in the Slide Transition task pane by choosing to advance your slides automatically. Follow these steps to advance your slides automatically and specify the length of time each slide is displayed:

1 Set any transition and sound effects for the current slide.

2 In the Advance Slide area of the Slide Transition task pane, click the Automatically After check box. The timing 00:00 appears in the box beneath the option.

> **Aha!** Using Both Manual and Automatic Advance
>
> You can choose to leave both options selected in the Slide Transition task pane so that users have a choice of clicking to advance the slide, or waiting for the timing to play out. If you want viewers to just relax and watch, disable the On Mouse Click option so that the slide will not advance when someone clicks the mouse button.

3 Use the arrow to increase the time, or click in the box and type a new value. After you click outside the slide, the timing value will be displayed beneath the slide.

> **Aha!**   Using Apply To All Slides
>
> Because clicking the Apply To All Slides tool applies all the transition effects to all the slides in your presentation, you need to use this tool carefully. If you want to apply the same timing to all the slides, but you want to set individual transitions and sound effects, set the Advance Slide settings first, and then click Apply To All Slides. This will apply the same time to all slides (you'll see the small time indicator under the lower left corner of each slide in Slide Sorter view). Then you can go back and set transitions and sounds (and modify individual timings, if needed) without losing the unique effects of each slide.

Rehearsing Your Timings

Another way you can record the ideal timing for your slides is to use the Rehearse Timings feature. This feature enables you to go through your presentation as a slide show, manually advancing each slide after you've had enough time to read everything. Start the rehearsal by clicking the Rehearse Timings tool on the Slide Sorter toolbar. Your presentation begins, and a small Rehearsal toolbar appears in the upper left corner of your screen, as shown here:

The Slide Time value begins immediately, as it tracks the seconds you want the slide to display. When you click to advance to the next slide, PowerPoint records the time value, and sets the Slide Time value back to 00:00 for the next slide.

> **Caution**   Here's something tricky about the Rehearse Timings feature: If you have added Animation Schemes to an individual slide, each of the elements on that slide—such as the title, the bullet text, and any charts or graphics—might have individual animation effects applied. For those slides, you need to click Next on the Rehearsal toolbar to play the animated effect, and you might need to click Next several times before moving on to the next slide. Don't sit and wait an inordinately long time for an element to show up on an animated slide—PowerPoint is waiting for you to click Next, and those waiting periods will distort your timings.

At the end of the show, PowerPoint tells you how long the presentation is, and asks whether you'd like to keep the timings as you rehearsed them. If you click Yes, the timings you rehearsed will override any timings you entered in the Advance Slide area of the Slide Transition task pane. If you click No, the timings you entered manually will be retained.

Working with a Manual Show

If you decide that the Automatic-Advance method is not right for your audience, you can leave all the slides set to Manual Advance (or, if you've already changed a few of them, you can change them back to On Mouse Click, or click Apply To All Slides if you haven't applied transition effects). When you run the slide show, you can advance slides by clicking the mouse button, pressing Enter, or pressing the right and left arrow keys. You can also use the navigation bar to move around and add items (such as annotations) to your presentation. (For more information on navigating and adding annotations to your presentation, see Chapter 10, "Creating a Presentation—From Start to Finish.")

Notes for the Speaker

If you will be giving the presentation yourself, you'll probably remember that you need to leave extra time in slide 9 to accommodate the slower readers in your audience, or that you want to put in an optional question or two for particularly responsive audiences. But if someone else will be giving your presentation, you need some way of giving others the information about how to deliver individual slides. The answer to that problem is the Speaker Notes feature of PowerPoint.

You can add notes to individual slides that only the person who will be giving the presentation—or reading the handouts you've printed for their use—will see. To add speaker notes, click the Speaker Notes tool on the Slide Sorter toolbar. The Speaker Notes dialog box appears, as shown in Figure 11-6.

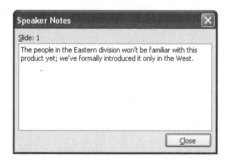

Figure 11-6 Speaker Notes enable you to add presentation suggestions and comments for others who might be giving your presentation.

To add your notes, simply type them in the available space. When you're finished adding notes, click Close. Or, if you want to add notes to another slide, click that slide and the Speaker Notes dialog box for that slide appears.

> **Aha!**   A Final Run-Through
>
> Once you make all your animation, transition, and timing changes, you'll want to go through the presentation from start to finish to see how everything looks. (And be prepared to modify the presentation a few times to get it running as smoothly as possible.)

Fast Wrap-Up

- Slide Sorter view enables you to organize your slides and add transition, animation, and timing effects.

- You use the Animation Schemes feature to apply animation features to the text and objects on individual slides.

- The Custom Animation task pane gives you what you need to animate individual objects on your slides.

- The Slide Transition task pane contains everything you need for controlling the way one slide disappears and the next appears.

- You can add sound effects to your slide transitions by choosing the sound you want from the Sounds list in the Slide Transition task pane.

- You can advance slides manually (by clicking the mouse button, or pressing Enter, or any arrow key), automatically, or a combination of the two.

- Click Rehearse Timings to go through the slide show and record the time used to display animated elements and advance to the next slide. You have the option of accepting these settings over any you entered on the Slide Transition task pane.

- Add Speaker Notes to help others who might be giving your presentation know how to present certain slides. (Of course, *you* may also find this helpful if you have a long presentation or tend to get nervous—Speaker Notes can prompt you if your mind goes blank.)

Enhancing Your Presentations

12

10-Second Summary

- ■ Add movie clips
- ■ Play music
- ■ Record narration
- ■ Broadcast your presentation

Your presentation should be looking good by now. You've learned to create and save a simple presentation in Microsoft Office PowerPoint 2003. You've learned to edit, format, and arrange the presentation, as well as coordinate its animation effects, slide transitions, and timing. You're probably eager to jump up in front of that group and get busy. Well, almost.

The features of PowerPoint go on and on—in fact, an entire book could be (and has been) written about using all the aspects of the program to create high-quality, imaginative presentations. But this section of the book wouldn't be complete without at least a quick look at some of the high-end effects you can achieve with PowerPoint. The tasks covered here may be reserved for special presentations—effects that include video, adding music, and broadcasting your presentation online.

See Also
For extensive details about working with PowerPoint, see *Microsoft Office PowerPoint 2003 Step by Step*, by Online Training Solutions, Inc., also from Microsoft Press.

What Kind of Enhancements Will You Use?

Now that you've had a chance to go through a presentation from start to finish and prepare it to run as you like, you may want to think about a "wish" list of additional features. Some great ideas might be a bit too much for your budget or schedule—a professionally produced, custom video showing interviews with all your top salespeople could be a great inspiration for your regional sales staff, but it would also cost a small truckload of money and take months to complete. But there are some enhancements you can easily add that will make your presentation more interesting, more enjoyable, and easier for viewers to navigate. Here are a few of the possibilities:

- ■ **Movie Clips**   Add two or three quick video segments to your presentation at strategic times—perhaps showing your animated company logo, walking up the steps of your new building, a few smiling faces, and so on.

- **Narration**   You can add voice-over narration to your PowerPoint presentation, welcoming your audience, giving directions on how to use the presentation, or inviting visitors to your Web site.

- **Music Clips**   The music you add to your presentation can be anything from a simple logo jingle to a full-score musical arrangement that plays while your presentation continues on the screen.

> **Aha!**   Using Your Resources
>
> You can get clips, templates, and more online by choosing Office on Microsoft.com from the Tools menu. This takes you to the Microsoft Office System site, where you can browse the latest utilities and download files that fit what you're looking for.

Adding Movies and Animations

Just a few years ago, it wasn't possible to add real moving pictures to your presentation without paying for an elaborate and expensive custom video produced by a production company. Adding video wasn't simply a matter of inserting a video file wherever you wanted it to play in your presentation. Today it is almost that easy. If you've got a digital video camera, or know where to find and download animations or video clips, you can add short *movies* to your presentation.

> **Lingo** A *movie* is a digital film of any length, complete with audio and video. An *animation*, on the other hand, is an illustration that moves.

PowerPoint makes it easy for you to work with video and sound files by giving you all the options you need in the Movies And Sounds command on the Insert menu. When you choose this command (you need to display the presentation in Normal View first, by the way), a submenu appears, as shown below, giving you the following choices for adding movies:

> **Aha!** Adding Movies by Clicking
>
> As you learned in Chapter 10, "Creating a Presentation—From Start to Finish," you can also add objects to your slides by choosing a slide layout that includes a Content box. The Content box displays icons for adding six objects—tables, charts, clip art, pictures, diagrams, or media clips. To add a movie, click the Insert Media Clip icon.

Inserting a Movie Clip

To add a movie clip to a slide in your presentation, begin by displaying the slide you want to use. Then choose Movies And Sounds from the Insert menu and select Movie From Clip Organizer. The Insert Clip Art task pane appears so that you can choose the movie clip you want from the displayed list (as shown in Figure 12-1).

Figure 12-1 You can choose the clip you want to add by clicking it in the Insert Clip Art task pane.

When you click the movie, it is added as an object in the center of your slide. PowerPoint asks whether you'd like the movie to play automatically when the slide is displayed in a slide show, or wait until the mouse is clicked. Click Yes to have the movie play automatically; otherwise, click No.

> **Aha!** Adding a Custom Clip
>
> If you want to use a digital file you've captured, or you have a video clip you've downloaded from the Web, use the Movie From File option to add the file. Choose the option from the Insert menu; the Insert Movie dialog box appears. Navigate to the folder storing the movie you want to add, click it, and then click OK.

Capturing Your Own Movies

If the digital film producer in you is just dying to work some original video into your presentation, go ahead and use that QuickCam or Sony digital camcorder. You can use your camera's software to download the video file, then clean it up in a digital editing program, such as Adobe Premiere, and place it as a media object in PowerPoint. Once your original file is ready for your presentation, just add it to a slide by choosing Movies And Sounds from the Insert menu and selecting Movie from the File menu. Then choose your file in the Insert Movie dialog box and click OK.

Alternatively, you can add the movie to the Clip Organizer and then place it in your presentation. Start with a slide that includes the content prompt (the small palette containing the object icons), and click the Insert Media Clip icon to display the Media Clip palette. Click Import and navigate to the folder in which your file is saved, then select your file and click OK. The clip is added to the Clip Organizer, and you can now select it as usual and click OK.

Sequencing Your Movie

Once you get the movie file placed where you want it to be played, choose Custom Animation from the Slide Show menu to display the Custom Animation task pane. Then verify that the objects on the slide appear in the order in which you want them. For example, suppose that you want the slide title to appear, then you want the movie to begin, and finally you want the text box to rotate in at the bottom of the slide. Make sure that each item appears when it should in the Animations list in the center of the task pane. If you need to change the order of the items, click the Re-Order button to do so. (For a refresher on sequencing the objects on your slides, see the section "Animating Individual Objects" in Chapter 11.)

Display Movies Full-Screen

A movie clip is considered an "object" in PowerPoint, and you add it to your slides in much the same way you add a picture: by clicking a slide with a content layout, then clicking the Insert Media Clip icon.

In previous versions of PowerPoint, movie objects played in a small rectangular area on the presentation slide. In PowerPoint 2003, you have the option of maximizing the movie so that it plays full-screen. This allows you to launch a short video of a new product or an interview with the product designer, run it full-screen, and then return seamlessly to the presentation.

To tell PowerPoint to play the movie full-screen, right-click the movie clip after you place it on the slide. Choose Edit Movie Options from the shortcut menu and, in the Display Options area of the Movie Options dialog box, click Zoom to Full Screen; then click OK.

Adding Sounds and Music

Do you want your presentations to sing? Were you hoping to have a cricket chirping through your new presentation about the nature center? Did the board think it would be nice to have the board members say their names at the introduction to the new staffing video? Did you want to have Frank Sinatra singing "Fly Me to the Moon" behind your new junior high school presentation about the effects of gravity? Whatever your intentions for sound and music, you can add the objects easily—and have them play automatically—in PowerPoint.

When you're ready to insert a sound object on your slide, follow these steps:

1 Display the slide on which you want to add the sound.

2 Choose Movies And Sounds from the Insert menu, then choose Sound From Clip Organizer. The Insert Clip Art task pane reappears along the right side of your PowerPoint window, this time showing all the sound files stored in the Clip Organizer.

3 Click the sound you want to add to the slide. PowerPoint will ask you whether you want the sound to play automatically during your slide show, or play only when clicked.

Aha! Checking Out Sound Properties

If you're unsure whether you've got the right sound clip, you can play it by clicking the button on the right side of the file icon and choosing Preview/Properties. The Preview/Properties dialog box appears and the sound plays automatically. You can also review, edit, and add keywords related to the sound (which can be helpful if you use certain sound clips for certain items in your presentation).

Recording and Playing Sound Effects

You might not have the vocal quality to do voice-overs for movie trailers, or the creative wherewithal to generate funny or interesting noises for special sound effects, but including your voice—or the voices of your key managers or favorite clients—can be a fun and interesting addition to a more casual presentation.

If you want to record a sound for your presentation, display the slide on which you want to add the object, then choose Record Sound from the Movies And Sounds submenu. The Record Sound dialog box appears. Type the name you want to assign to the sound, and click the circle to begin recording (see Figure 12-2). Speak, sing, hiccup, bark, ring a bell, whatever—and PowerPoint records it. After you've recorded your sound, click the square button to stop recording.

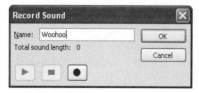

Figure 12-2 Use the Record Sound dialog box to capture customized sound elements for your presentation.

PowerPoint adds the sound object to your slide, and makes the sound available in the Sounds list in the Slide Transition and Custom Animation task panes, so that you can add the custom sound to other slides as well.

> **Note**   Use the Record Sound option when you want to add short sounds—bells and whistles, nature sounds, office sounds, and more. When you want to make a voice-over narration, use Record Narration in the Slide Show menu. For more about this option, see the section entitled "Recording Narration," later in this chapter.

Adding CD Audio

So what about Frank Sinatra singing "Fly Me to the Moon"? You can play a CD track (or an entire CD, for that matter) by using the Play CD Audio Track option in the Movies And Sounds submenu. Here's how:

1 Insert the CD with the recording you want to play.

2 Display the slide on which you want to add the object. If you want the CD track to play for the duration of your presentation, display slide 1.

3 Choose Movies And Sounds from the Insert menu, then click Play CD Audio Track. The Insert CD Audio dialog box appears (as shown in Figure 12-3).

Figure 12-3 Choose the CD track you want to play, and then click OK.

4   In the Clip Selection area, choose the number of the track you want to start with (the Time value will be filled in automatically according to the track you select). Choose the number of the final track in the End area.

5   If the CD track is shorter than your presentation, you can make the track repeat by clicking the Loop Until Stopped check box.

6   Click OK to add the CD track to the slide.

7   Play your presentation by pressing F5.

Recording Narration

Here's another opportunity to do a little vocal work. Suppose that your CEO is a very gregarious guy. People like him. He inspires trust. The board decides he's the one to deliver the news to shareholders that earnings were up 15 percent in the last quarter.

Adding narration, at least in theory, isn't any more difficult than speaking into the microphone attached to your computer. But similar to the speech-recognition features discussed in Part 1 of this book, narration still has a long way to go before it is fully, no-fuss functional. To start narrating your presentation, follow these steps:

1   Display the slide on which you want to add the narration. (You can add narration to more than one slide.)

2   Choose Record Narration from the Slide Show menu. The Record Narration dialog box lists the amount of room you've got on your hard drive for recorded voice (as shown in Figure 12-4). Remember, sound files take up massive amounts of space.

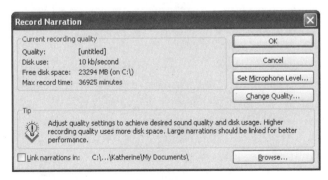

Figure 12-4 The Record Narration box provides everything you need for setting up and recording narrations.

3   Click OK to start recording. As your presentation begins running in a slide show, begin your narration.

4   When the slide show finishes (or you press Esc), PowerPoint displays a message box asking whether you want to save the slide timings and the narrations on each slide. Click Save if you do; otherwise, click Don't Save.

5   Press F5 to display your presentation and listen to the narration.

Managing Recordings

You can keep your presentation file relatively small by linking—rather than embedding—the narration file. Linking causes the narration to be stored on your hard drive (which means you must have the source file available at presentation time); embedding saves the narration as part of the presentation file, which makes the file huge. To link the narration, click the Link Narrations In check box in the Record Narration dialog box, and click Browse to navigate to the folder in which you want to store the file.

High-quality sound files, which are enormous, are especially likely to cause a space problem. That's why PowerPoint automatically defaults to the lowest-quality sound available. If you feel you can afford the space and want to go with the higher-quality sound, click the Change Quality button and click the Name down arrow. You can choose from CD Quality (44.100 kHz, 16-Bit, Stereo sound—the highest quality), Radio Quality (22.050 kHz, 8-Bit, Mono sound), and Telephone Quality (11.025 kHz, 8-Bit, Mono sound—the default selection). You can click the Attributes down arrow to choose other configurations for the sound quality you select. Click OK to close the Sound Selection box and return to the Record Narration dialog box.

If, after hearing the narration, you decide you liked the presentation better without it, simply display the slides in Slide view and delete the sound icons in the lower right corner. This removes the narrations attached to the slides.

> **Note**   If you have other sounds on your slides, the narration overrides those sounds and they will not play. This does not affect any sounds applied as part of slide transitions, however.

Collaborating Online

Creating a presentation is often a group effort that requires input from a variety of people. You can use PowerPoint's Online Collaboration feature to share your presentation, gather notes, and discuss your progress whether your coworker is down the hall or around the world. To collaborate with others online, choose Online Collaboration from the Tools menu, and then select Meet Now, Schedule a Meeting, or Web Discussion. The feature works with Microsoft NetMeeting to access a shared server on which you and others can meet and discuss the project. PowerPoint displays an Online Collaboration toolbar for you to use while you're working with others.

And don't forget the Shared Workspace feature (available in the Tools menu) that enables you to use Microsoft SharePoint Team Services to create a Web site where you can share documents, resources, and links related to the presentation you are creating. (For a detailed explanation of the new Shared Workspace feature, see Chapter 3, "Creating and Viewing Documents."

Fast Wrap-Up

- For special presentations, you can easily add animations, movies, music, and more to your slides.

- You can add a movie clip in two ways: by choosing Movies And Sounds from the Insert menu and selecting Movie From Clip Organizer or Movie From File, or by clicking the Insert Movie Clip icon in the content palette on selected slides.

- Use the Clips Online link (found in the Clip Organizer and in the Insert Clip Art task pane) to find and download animations, movies, and sounds from the Web.

- You can record your own sound effects and save them in the Slide Transition task pane by choosing Record Sound from the Movies And Sounds submenu.

- You can use the Online Collaboration and Shared Workspace features to work with teammates as you prepare your presentation.

Part 5
Microsoft Outlook: Communicate, Collaborate, and Organize

This part of the book shows you how to take advantage of the many organizing and connecting features in Microsoft Office Outlook 2003, beginning by showing you how to let Outlook handle your online communications—creating, sending, receiving, and filtering e-mail. You also learn how to work with instant messaging to connect with others in real time. But the capabilities of Outlook go far beyond simple messaging; you can also use the Calendar, Journal, Address Book, Notes, and Task features to further organize your daily tasks.

The changes in Microsoft Office Outlook 2003 focus on fast communication and easy collaboration—and they are presented to you in a new, improved window that offers many different customizable views. Working with e-mail is easier than ever—you can contact peers, friends, and family instantly with a click of the mouse. Additionally, the Calendar and Tasks views each include new features that enable you to organize and share data more easily.

E-Mailing with Microsoft Office Outlook 2003

13

10-Second Summary
- Create and send instant messages
- E-mail with Outlook
- Send shared attachments
- Print messages
- Delete messages

You probably already know that Microsoft Outlook is far more than an e-mail application. Developed as a kind of personal data assistant to help you keep track of the myriad details of your daily life, Outlook includes a task scheduler, a calendar, a contact manager, a journal, and a notepad. But because e-mail has become so central to our personal and professional lives, it's nice to know that Outlook has at its core one of the best e-mail programs around. This chapter focuses on getting started with e-mail in Outlook.

Outlook 2003 with Business Contact Manager

A specialized version of Outlook that caters to the needs of small business owners and managers was made available with the Microsoft Office System. This version, Outlook 2003 with Business Contact Manager, enables you to add more detailed information about clients and leads, track meetings, record notes, and more. The emphasis is on contact management and easy integration with the other core Office applications. If you run or own a small business, it's worth a closer look.

A New Look for Outlook

Whether you're just beginning to use Outlook, or you're an experienced user from way back, you'll find the new look of the Outlook window easy to navigate and use (see Figure 13-1). By default, the window is divided into a three-column display, with these key elements:

- **The Inbox**   The Inbox is displayed by default in the center column of the Outlook window. Click the message you want to view in the Preview pane.

- **The Preview pane**   Now you can read the currently selected e-mail message without scrolling.

- **The Navigation pane**   This pane replaces the icon bar that stretched down the left side of Outlook XP and gives you more room on-screen. The default display shows the Folder List, but when you choose a different view (Calendar or Contacts, for example), other choices appear.

- **View controls**   Click one of the other views to change to that Outlook tool (Calendar, Contacts, or Tasks).

> **Note**   To display Notes, the Folder List, Shortcuts, or to customize the view options in the Outlook window, close one of the small icons in the bottom of the Navigation pane.

Navigation Pane   Inbox

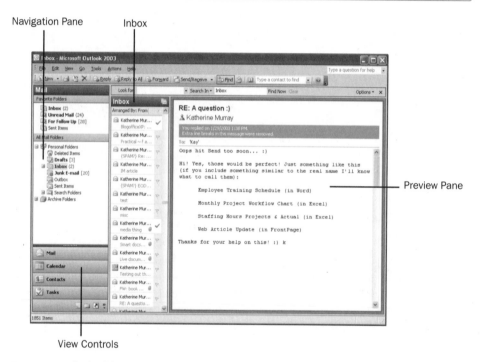

View Controls

Figure 13-1   Outlook's new design makes it easy to move among views and enter and organize information.

Instant Messaging in Outlook 2003

Instant messaging was available in the previous version of Office, but now it is available in all the core Office applications. Now you'll see the familiar Windows Messenger icon appear whenever you see one of your contacts' names in a document, a header line of an e-mail message, a spreadsheet, and so on. Instant messaging is a fairly recent addition to office communications, and enterprises are finding that it saves valuable time employees would otherwise spend waiting for returned phone calls, e-mail messages, and more.

When you have a quick question for a coworker, for example, you can send an instant message that pops up over her other applications. She answers you quickly and that's it—problem solved. Real-time communication that fits in seamlessly as you work—that's fast *and* smart.

Getting a .NET Passport

You need a Microsoft .NET Passport (or a Hotmail account) to begin using instant messaging in the Office System. (And only those contacts with a .NET Passport or a Hotmail account will be visible through Windows Messenger.) When you first begin using Outlook, the .NET Messenger Service dialog box appears so that you can enter your e-mail address and password (as shown in Figure 13-2). If you don't have a .NET account, click the Get A .NET Passport link at the bottom of the window—you are taken online to a Web page where you can sign up.

Figure 13-2 When you start Instant Messaging, you are asked for your .NET Passport user name and password.

> **Note** The .NET Passport is a free account that you are given automatically if you use Hotmail or MSN as your e-mail service; if you don't use either of these services, you'll have to click the link to get your Passport.

Once you have your .NET Passport user name and password, you can use the Log On command to start sending and receiving instant messages.

Receiving an Instant Message

When someone sends you an instant message, the message pops up over whatever you're working on. When you click the message to respond, it opens in a larger window (as shown in Figure 13-3). In the Instant Messaging window, you can do all kinds of things in addition to sending quick messages back and forth—including sending photos and files, making a phone call, sharing applications, and more.

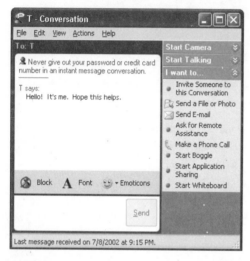

Figure 13-3   Trading text is only one part of what you can do with Instant Messaging.

Sending an Instant Message

Outlook uses the header of an e-mail message to let you know whether the user you are corresponding with is online. When you open an e-mail message from a person who is one of your contacts, for example, the Windows Messenger icon appears in the header, showing you that the person is online.You can send an instant message by clicking the icon and choosing Send Instant Message. A message window opens, and you can simply type your message and click Send.

Changing Online Status

The challenge of instant messaging lies in the fact that, once you're online, everyone who has your e-mail address listed as a contact can see you. And if you're popular, you might get lots of messages you didn't expect. There are two ways to handle this—the first is to log on only at the hours nobody else is online. A more practical answer is to learn how to change your online status so people know when you're busy or otherwise engaged.

You change your messaging status by displaying the Windows Messenger window (double-click the Windows Messenger icon in the status icon area on the far right side of the Taskbar). To change your status while you're online, choose My Status from the File menu and select the message you want to display (see Figure 13-4).

Figure 13-4   You control the status displayed to others within Windows Messenger.

Using Outlook as Your E-mail Program

To get started with e-mail in Outlook, connect to the Internet, start Outlook, and click Mail (if it doesn't come up as your default view). When you first begin working with Outlook, the program searches your computer for existing e-mail programs and accounts you've set up. Luckily, if you have existing e-mail accounts on your computer, Outlook imports the information so that it knows automatically how to send and receive mail using those accounts. Now you may want to add a new e-mail account, import an address book, or simply begin creating and sending e-mail. This section covers all those tasks.

Adding New E-mail Accounts

When you want to add an account to Outlook, choose Options from the Tools menu, click Mail Setup in the Options dialog box, then click E-mail Accounts. This displays a page on which you can change e-mail accounts or add new ones. Click Add A New E-mail Account, then click Next. On the Server Type page, choose the type of server your new e-mail account will use. (Most standard service providers use POP3 servers; Web-based servers use HTTP. If you're unsure which type your e-mail account requires, contact your Internet service provider for the necessary information.) Click Next to continue.

The Internet E-mail Settings page asks you for several kinds of information. You'll need your account user name, your e-mail address, and information about the server for incoming and outgoing messages. After you fill in the necessary data (again, contact your ISP if you're unsure), click Test Account Settings to see whether the settings you've entered will work as planned. Finally, click Finish, and your account is set up and ready to use.

Composing an E-mail Message

When you're ready to create an e-mail message, and the Mail view is displayed, click the New tool on the Standard toolbar. This opens the message window.

To create the message, follow these steps:

1 Choose your recipient by typing his or her e-mail address in the To line. If you are sending the message to more than one person, separate the e-mail addresses with a semicolon.

> **Aha!**   Changing the Look of Message Text
>
> You can change the font, size, color, style, and alignment of the text in your e-mail message by clicking the formatting tools you want on the message toolbar. You can further customize messages by adding a background picture or color, or by choosing special stationery.

2 If you want to send a copy of the message to someone else, enter the e-mail address in the Cc line.

3 Type a subject for the message that helps describe it briefly for the recipient.

4 Click in the message area and type your message.

> **Aha!**   Using Your Contacts
>
> If you don't know the e-mail address of the person to whom you're sending the message, but you know it's in your Contacts list, you can click the To button to display the Select Names dialog box. Click the name of the person to whom you want to forward the message; then click the To button to add the person's name to the Message Recipients list. Finally, click OK to add the name to the To line in the message window.

5 Click Send and Outlook sends the message immediately.

If you want to verify that your message was sent, click the Sent Items folder in the Favorite Folders panel of the Navigation pane. A list of sent items appears in the right pane.

> **Aha!**   Checking Your Spelling Quickly
>
> To do a quick spelling check of a single word, double-click the word to select it and press F7. The Spelling dialog box appears if the word is unrecognized, so that you can change it, ignore it, or add it to your dictionary.

Retrieving and Reading Your E-mail

When you first open the Inbox, you click the Send/Receive tool on the Standard toolbar (or press F5) to tell Outlook to go out to the server and retrieve any e-mail stored there in your account. An Outlook Send/Receive Progress status window appears while the message is retrieved and delivered. If you've previously created any e-mail to be sent, you can also see that transmission in this status window. When the new e-mail arrives, your computer plays a chime and the messages appear in the Inbox. Also, a note symbol appears at the far right end of the notification area on the Windows taskbar.

To read a new message, click it. The message opens in the Preview pane, showing the Subject line as the window title (as shown in Figure 13-5).

Figure 13-5   The received message appears in the Preview pane.

> **Note**   You can open the message in its own window by double-clicking it, which gives you the maximum viewing space available on-screen. You can reply to messages whether they are in Preview pane or full-screen view.

Replying to and Forwarding E-mail

Sending a response is simple. While the e-mail message is displayed on your screen, simply click Reply. The message is displayed in a new message window. The header information from the original message, which gives you information about the sender, the subject, and the date and time the message was sent, is copied into the body of the message.

When you receive an e-mail message that you think someone else needs to see, you can forward it to that person. To do that, click the e-mail message and click Forward on the Message toolbar. Again, the header information is copied into the message. Type the person's e-mail address into the To line, or choose it from the Select Names dialog box, add whatever text you need to introduce the forwarded message, and click Send. Outlook forwards the message immediately.

Responding to Meeting Invitations

One fast new feature in Outlook 2003 enables you to respond to meeting invitations without ever opening the message. When you receive a meeting request via e-mail, the header of the message includes the various response possibilities. Simply click the one you want (Accept, Tentative, Decline, Propose New Time, or Calendar) and Outlook communicates your intent, all without you ever having to type a word (see Figure 13-6).

Figure 13-6   Now you can respond to meeting invitations with a single click.

Attaching a File to an E-mail Message

But there's more to life than e-mail. There are files, too. You'll no doubt want to send files with your e-mail messages—files about the new product, report files, photo files, baby pictures, and more. To attach a file to a message, follow these steps:

1   Create the message as usual.

2   Choose File from the Insert menu.

3   In the Insert File dialog box, navigate to the folder storing the file you want to attach.

4   Click the file and then click Insert. The file name and an icon are added in a new Attach line beneath the Subject line.

> **Aha!**   Attaching a File Fast
>
> The fastest way to add a file to your e-mail message is to simply drag the file from the Windows Explorer window and drop it onto your open e-mail message.

Finish typing and formatting your message, then click Send. The message—and the attached file—are transmitted to your server to be delivered to the recipient you specified.

Sending Shared Attachments

Another new feature in Outlook 2003 enables you to send shared, or *live* attachments. You might do this, for example, when you are working with a team to produce a training manual, and several different people are involved in the creation of the document. By sending a shared attachment, you create a shared workspace for the document, and ensure that everyone has the latest available copy.

First attach the file as usual—by clicking the Insert File tool—and choose the file you want to attach. The Attachment Options task pane appears to the right of the message area (see Figure 13-7). Choose whether you want to send the attachment as a regular or shared attachment by clicking the option you want. Here's what each of those options do:

- Regular Attachments sends a static copy of the document on your drive to the recipient.

- Shared Attachments sends the recipient a copy of the document you sent but also creates a new document workspace and stores a copy of the document there.

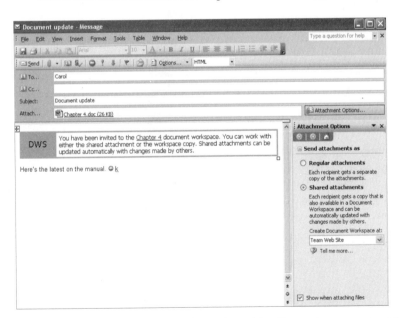

Figure 13-7   You can send a shared attachment to others when you are working on a collaborative document.

When you click Shared Attachments, a message appears above the text in the body of your e-mail message, giving a link to the new document workspace created for the attached document.

Printing Messages

When you receive a message you want to print, you can do so quickly by selecting it in the Inbox window and clicking the Print tool on the Standard toolbar. A Printing status box appears for a moment while the message is sent to the printer.

If you want to change the print options before you print, take the longer route by choosing Print from the File menu. This action displays the Print dialog box, where you can select additional options. You'll notice that your choices are fairly limited if you stick with the Memo Style (the default print format); the only choice you have is to print attached files. If you select Table Style, however, you can click Page Setup to control the format, font, margins, and more; specify the number of copies you want; and choose the range of rows you want to print. Click Preview after you've made your selections to see how the message will look when printed.

> **Aha!**   Printing Multiple Messages at the Same Time
>
> You can print a number of e-mail messages at once by selecting all the messages you want to print, right-clicking the selection, choosing Print, and clicking OK.

Deleting Messages

If you're like most of us, you're going to get many more messages you want to delete than messages you want to keep. *Spam*—unsolicited junk e-mail—is big business, and until you learn how to filter out unwanted messages (which is covered in Chapter 14, "Organizing with Microsoft Office Outlook 2003"), just expect to get lots of messages you don't want to read.

To delete the unwanted messages (or messages you've read and no longer need), select the messages and press Delete. The messages are sent to the Deleted Items folder and they will remain there (just in case you want to retrieve something) until you empty the folder by choosing Empty "Deleted Items" Folder from the Tools menu. When you choose this command, Outlook displays a message box asking you to confirm. Click Yes to complete the deletion.

Fast Wrap-Up

■ Outlook is a multi-featured program that enables you to organize your appointments, tasks, e-mail, journal entries, and more.

■ Instant messaging in Outlook enables you to trade short, fast messages with others who are currently online.

■ The Outlook window is organized into three columns to help make the most of on-screen space. The Navigation pane on the left in all views enables you to choose what you want to work with at any given time.

■ When you want to create a new message, click Inbox on the Outlook Shortcut bar; then click New. When the new message window appears, enter the recipient in the To line, type a Subject and the body text of the message; then click Send.

■ Attach a file to an e-mail message by choosing File from the Insert menu. Find the file you want to send, click it, and click Insert to attach the file. You can use the new Shared Attachment feature in Outlook to create a document workspace and make sure coworkers have the most current version of the shared document.

Organizing with Microsoft Office Outlook 2003

14

10-Second Summary
- ■ Manage your e-mail
- ■ Flag messages
- ■ Use search folders
- ■ Control junk mail
- ■ Work with contacts
- ■ Work with tasks and notes

Our biggest challenge today isn't finding the information we need; it's managing the information we find. If you're like most people, you get dozens—or hundreds—of e-mail messages each day. A major portion of your day can go to reading, sorting, filing, and deleting messages. Add in the time you spend creating appointments and scheduling meetings, and you've got a desktop full of details to track. This chapter shows you how to use Microsoft Outlook to sort and organize your mail. Additionally, you'll learn to keep track of your contacts, and create those important to-do lists, using tasks and notes.

Managing Your E-mail

Today, everybody uses e-mail. And we're not talking only about clients and coworkers—your son's coach, the car club president, your mother-in-law—*everybody* is online these days. Combine the proliferation of e-mail with the spam explosion, and you've got lots of mail to sort. This section shows you how to view, organize, and store the important messages you receive.

Viewing Your Mail

The new look in Outlook 2003 makes it easy to read a message quickly. The new Preview Pane displays the selected message without your opening it, which means no scrolling, and a fast read. You can also change the way messages are listed in your Inbox to get quicker access to specific messages. To change the way messages are listed, click the Arranged By line at the top of the Inbox, and select the view you want from the displayed list (see Figure 14-1).

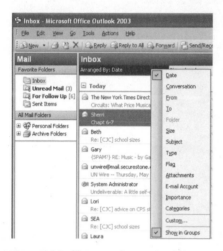

Figure 14-1   You can choose to view your messages in many different ways.

Aha!   Viewing Multiple Accounts

If you have more than one e-mail account depositing messages in your Inbox (for example, one for work and one for home), choose Arrange By E-mail Account to separate the messages. You can then easily scroll through only your work messages and find the one you need quickly.

Filing Your Messages

As you go through your messages, you'll find many you want to delete, and some you want to keep. Instead of leaving the keepers in your Inbox, you need to file them away where you can locate them easily later. Here are the steps for creating a new folder and storing your e-mail messages there:

1   Press Ctrl+Shift+E to display the Create New Folder dialog box (see Figure 14-2).

2   Make sure the Inbox is selected, type a name for the folder, then click OK. The new folder appears beneath the Inbox folder in the All Mail Folders pane.

3   Select and drag the messages you want to store to the new folder.

Figure 14-2 Enter a name and choose a location for the new folder.

> **Note** If you want to create a subfolder within another folder, click the expand button (+) to the left of the folder name.

Creating and Using E-mail Rules

E-mail rules offer you another way of cutting down the amount of time you spend reading and organizing your mail. When you create a rule, you tell Outlook to automatically perform a certain action when mail is received from a specific sender. For example, you can create a rule to file all e-mail from the district office in your Followup folder. To create a rule in Outlook 2003, follow these steps:

1 Select an e-mail message from the Sender for whom you want to create the rule.

2 Click the Rule tool in the Outlook toolbar.

3 In the Create Rule dialog box (see Figure 14-3), choose your settings. The options in the top half of the dialog box allow you to specify which messages are selected; the options in the bottom half enable you to tell Outlook what you want to do with the selected messages. For example, to move selected messages to a specific folder, click the Move E-mail To Folder check box, then click the Select Folder button to choose the folder in which the messages should be placed.

Figure 14-3 You can create e-mail rules to have Outlook take action whenever certain e-mail messages are received.

Aha!   Advanced Rules

You can further customize the messages that are selected and acted on by clicking the Advanced Options button in the Create Rule dialog box. These options allow you to fine-tune the selection procedure by selecting mail from specific accounts, with certain sensitivity levels, and so on.

4   Click OK to create the rule. A message box appears, asking whether you want to apply this rule to all the existing messages in your current folder. If you do, click the check box and click OK to continue.

Because I elected to create item alerts when messages with a certain subject were received, a listing of alerts based on the current folder appears for me to review (see Figure 14-4).

Figure 14-4   The New Item Alerts dialog box lists the new alerts related to the rule you created.

Aha!   More Alerts

If you are working with Microsoft SharePoint Team Services or a document workspace online, you can have Outlook let you know when the SharePoint site has been modified or added to by a team member. To enable alerts on your SharePoint site, display the shared document workspace, and click the Alert Me link in the left panel of your team site. Alerts will then be delivered to your Inbox, and you'll be able to click a link to move directly to the SharePoint site to see the change.

Flagging Your Messages

If you used the flagging feature in previous versions of Outlook, you'll be glad to know that there are more flags than ever in Outlook 2003. Now you can flag items in up to six different colors, which enables you to set one flag for business follow-ups, one for personal, another for a specific project, and so on. And now adding or modifying flags is easier than ever. Simply right-click in the flag bar to the right of the message you want to flag; a context menu appears listing all the different flagging options (see Figure 14-5). Click the one you want, and Outlook adds it to the message.

Figure 14-5   Choose the flag type you want to assign to the selected message.

> **Aha!**   Faster Flagging
>
> The fastest way to flag a message for follow-up is simply to click the flag bar. Outlook displays the default red flag to the right of the message. To indicate you've completed the follow-up, click the flag, and it changes to a check mark.

Using Search Folders

Outlook 2003 offers a new way of managing folders that can save you lots of time and message-scrolling effort. The new search folders enable you to create folders that contain links to messages related to a certain topic. For example, suppose that you're going to a conference on HR recruiting. You can create a search folder that enables you to find at a glance every message on your system that relates to that conference. To create a search folder, follow these steps:

1   Right-click the Search Folders icon in the All Mail Folders panel.

2   Choose New Search Folder.

3   In the New Search Folder dialog box (see Figure 14-6), choose the following items:

Figure 14-6 You indicate which messages you want to search for in the New Search Folder dialog box.

- In the Reading Mail area, specify which mail you want to search.

- In the Mail From People And Lists area, you can choose the names of specific people or distribution lists to search.

- In the Organizing Mail area, you tell Outlook to search for large messages, old messages, messages with attachments, or messages received within a specific timeframe or with certain words.

- In the Custom area, you can create a customized search folder by specifying your own criteria for the search.

4   Specify any necessary options (for example, if you selected Mail With Specific Words, you need to click the Choose button and enter the words in the field that appears); then click OK.

The new search folder appears in the search folder list as shown here:

Controlling Junk E-mail

What can we do to eliminate the massive amounts of time we waste dealing with junk mail? Happily, Outlook can help scuttle those unwanted e-mails. Outlook 2003 includes a number of features to help you reduce the amount of time you spend with unwanted mail:

- Outlook automatically files suspected junk mail in the Junk E-mail folder.

- Outlook blocks external HTML content to keep spammers from confirming your e-mail address.

- You can add junk mail senders to a Junk Senders list that blocks received e-mails.

- You can add approved senders to the Trusted Recipients List to indicate vendors, companies, and individuals from whom you want to receive e-mail.

Blocking HTML Content

When you receive some unsolicited e-mail messages, you often have a short wait while the image appears. What's actually happening during this time is that the e-mail message is notifying the sender that it "found" your address, and it's sending back to get the information to fill in the graphic. This data transfer capability is known as a *web beacon,* and it simply lets the junk mail provider know that your e-mail address is a live one. As a result, you can be sure you'll continue to receive plenty of spam, from this vendor and hundreds more just like him.

When Outlook blocks the external HTML content, the program keeps the data transfer from happening because the message doesn't go back to the external source to display the logo file. This keeps the site from ever knowing whether your address is live or not, which eventually lessens the amount of junk mail you receive. HTML content is blocked by default in Outlook 2003. If you want to remove the block, choose Options from the Tools menu, and click the Security tab. Click the Settings button, and click Block External Content In HTML E-mail to remove the check mark; then click OK to save the change.

Using the Junk E-mail Folder

When Outlook downloads a message it suspects is junk, it files the message automatically in the Junk E-mail folder, and displays a message box letting you know what's going on. You can click the Open button to display the Junk E-mail folder contents, or simply click OK. The messages are stored in the folder until you view them—and delete them by pressing Del, or dragging them to the Deleted Items folder.

Aha!   Clearing Deleted Items Automatically

You can have Outlook empty your Deleted Items folder automatically by choosing Tools, Options, and clicking the Other tab. In the General area, click the Empty The Deleted Items Folder Upon Exiting check box.

Marking Messages as "Not Junk"

One of the challenges of using the junk e-mail features effectively is making sure that important messages don't inadvertently get filed away as junk. To safeguard against this, Outlook includes a Not Junk tool you can use to identify approved senders. To specify a message as "not junk," click the message, and click the Not Junk tool in the Outlook toolbar. The Mark As Not Junk dialog box appears (see Figure 14-7).

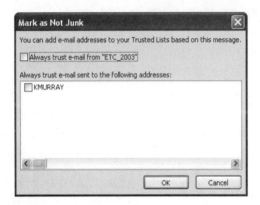

Figure 14-7   When you mark a message as "not junk," the sender is added to the Trusted Sender List.

Creating a Junk Senders List

One way to weed out those dastardly messages is to add the names to a junk e-mail senders list. To do this, right-click a junk message, and select Junk E-mail from the Context menu. Choose Add To Junk Senders List. Outlook records the entry, and checks against the list each time you receive new e-mail. If Outlook detects e-mail from that sender, the e-mail is treated according to the options you've chosen, either moving the e-mail to the Junk E-mail folder, or depositing it directly in your Deleted Items folder, depending on the options you've selected.

Archiving E-mail

If you're like me, and you're too busy to clean out your old e-mail messages regularly, you can use Outlook's AutoArchive feature to archive your old messages and move them to the location you specify. To use AutoArchive, follow these steps:

1 In Outlook, choose Options from the Tools menu.

2 Click the Other tab in the Options dialog box.

3 Click the AutoArchive button. The AutoArchive dialog box appears, offering a number of options for customizing how AutoArchive works (as shown in Figure 14-8 on the following page).

4 Change any items necessary. In particular, look at how often you want to run AutoArchive, what period of time you want to set for archiving (six months is the default setting), and whether you want to move the old items to a new location (click Browse if you want to change this setting to a different folder), or permanently delete old items.

5 Click the Apply These Settings To All Folders Now if you want the settings to go into effect immediately.

6 Click OK to return to the Outlook window.

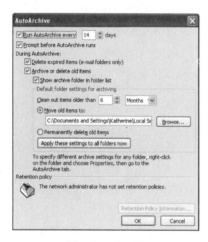

Figure 14-8 The AutoArchive feature files away or deletes old e-mail messages according to your instructions.

Aha!   Cleaning Up Your Mailbox

Outlook includes another feature, Mailbox Cleanup, to help you keep your Inbox orderly. This feature works hand-in-hand with AutoArchive, and relies on the Deleted Items folder as well. Choose Mailbox Cleanup from the Tools menu to display the dialog box. Choose the features you want to use (including AutoArchive and Deleted Items) and click OK to save your settings.

Working with Contacts

Have you ever heard that a business is only as healthy as its contacts list? Or how about this one: "It's not *what* you know, it's *who* you know." These sayings are probably a bit simplistic, but they do spotlight the importance of taking good care of your contacts. Outook's Contacts feature gives you a lot of room and some great features for collecting, organizing, viewing, and using your contact information.

Getting Started with Contacts

To display Contacts in Outlook, click the Contacts icon in the Outlook Shortcuts bar. Depending on the number of contacts you've entered (and if you imported your address book from another program, you may have quite a number of contacts), the names and e-mail addresses appear in the Contact window (see Figure 14-9).

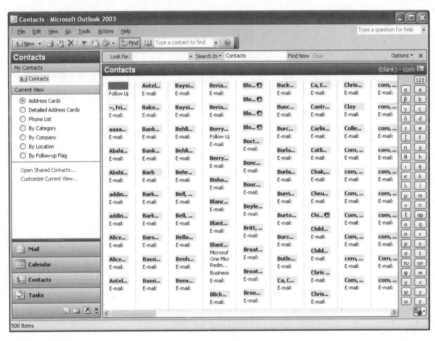

Figure 14-9   The Contacts window displays all contacts in the Preview Pane and shows the different view options in the Current View panel on the left.

To display the data on a specific person, double-click the entry in the Contacts window. The Contacts window for that person opens on your screen, filled with any information you've entered. Along the top of the Contact window, you'll notice a new toolbar to help as you work with contact data, as shown below:

Here's a quick list to give you an overview of what you'll do with the tools in the Contact window:

- Save And Close updates information you've changed, and closes the window.

- Save And New saves and closes the current contact, and opens a new Contact window.

- Print prints the selected entry (for more about printing, see the section entitled "Printing Contact Information," later in this chapter).

- Insert File lets you save a file along with the contact information (this might be helpful for adding an organization's annual report to the Development Director's data, for example).

- Follow Up enables you to flag an entry, and remind yourself that you need to make contact by a specific time on a specific day.

- Display Map Of Address does just that—it shows a map of how to get to the contact's office.

- New Message To Contact opens a new message window, so that you can send the contact an e-mail message.

- AutoDialer opens a New Call dialog box so that you can enter a phone number and call the person.

- Previous Item and Next Item allow you to scroll through the contacts preceding and following the current one in your Contacts list.

Where Does the Address Book Fit In?

If you've been working with Microsoft Office for any length of time, you're familiar with the Address Book. This feature allows you to store names, e-mail addresses, telephone numbers, and other contact information for the people with whom you work regularly. The Address Book is available within Contacts—it's a tool on the Outlook toolbar (to the left of the Contact Search box). If you click the Address Book, you'll see that it's pretty spare in the features department, compared to the huge Contacts utility.

If you're more comfortable working with Address Book to select, enter, and find data, feel free—when you go to edit contact information or add a new contact, Address Book moves seamlessly into Contacts, so you're working with the same Contacts window anyway. All data goes to the same place, which is the most important thing when you're trying to get organized and stay organized.

Creating a Contact

But let's assume for a moment that you don't have any contacts in your Contacts list. How do you add one? The process is simple:

1 Click the Contacts shortcut to display the Contacts window.

2 Click New. A blank Contact window appears (as shown in Figure 14-10).

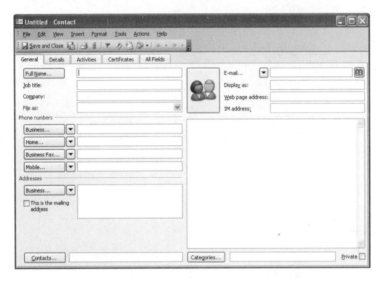

Figure 14-10 Simply fill in all the information you have for the contact, and click Save and Close.

3 Click the individual fields and enter the information you have to record.

4 When you're finished, click Save And Close to save the information you've added.

More Data! More Data!

Are you wondering what all these other tabs are for? As your experience with Outlook grows, you'll find that you can track *all kinds* of information—including free-form notes you've added about meetings, projects, interests, and more. The General tab, as you've seen, records all the important business contact information; the Details tab gives you room to add details about the person, and records NetMeeting settings. The Activities tab tracks the interaction you've had with the person by listing e-mail contacts, journal entries, notes, scheduled tasks, or appointments. The Certificates tab lists any digital signatures you use to correspond with the person, and the All Fields tab lets you create fields for recording additional information.

Finding a Contact

When you're trying to track down your information on a specific person, you can do it quickly by typing a name. Click the Contact Search box in the Outlook toolbar, type the person's name, and then press Enter. Outlook immediately finds the person's data and displays it in the Contact window, ready for your editing or review.

> **Aha!**   Find Names Fast
>
> To speed your search, you can enter only the person's first name (for example, *Larry*) in the Contact Search box. If your contact list includes more than one Larry, the Choose Contact dialog box will appear, asking you to select the Larry you want. Click the name you need, and then click OK.

Revising Contact Information

When you need to change contact information, simply display the contact's data by clicking Contacts in the Outlook Shortcuts bar, then double-clicking the contact's entry. The Contact window for that person then appears; you can click in the fields you want to change, and type the new information.

Printing Contact Information

When you want to print your contact information, you can choose to print individual contact information or print the whole list. Here are the steps for doing both:

- To create a printout of contact information for an individual, right-click the entry in the Contacts list, and choose Print from the Context menu. (You also can display the Contact window by double-clicking the entry and choosing Print from the toolbar.)

- To print the entire list, display the Contacts list, and choose Print from the File menu. In the Print dialog box, choose the Print style you want: Card Style, Small Booklet Style, Medium Booklet Style, Memo Style, or Phone Directory Style. Then select the number of copies you want, and click Preview to see how the document will look when printed.

> **Aha!**   Printing Selected Entries
>
> If you want to print only a few entries, select them in the Contacts list (click the first entry you want to print, then press and hold Ctrl while clicking the other entries). Right-click a highlighted entry, and click Print. In the Print dialog box, choose the Print style you want to use; then, in the Print range area, click Only selected items. Choose the number of copies you want, then click OK to print the selected entries.

As you can see, there's a lot more you can do with Contacts in Outlook. In fact, the way in which you can use the data in different Microsoft Office System applications is enough to fill a book. Experiment as you have time, and you'll soon discover favorite time-saving features in Outlook.

Outlook with Business Contact Manager

Outlook 2003 is available in yet another flavor: The Microsoft Office Outlook 2003 Business Contact Manager includes expanded contact management capabilities that enable you to track leads, calls, meetings, and more. For more about this expanded version of Outlook, go to *www.microsoft.com/office/preview/editions/contactmanager.asp.*

Journaling in Outlook

As an avid journal writer myself, I was thrilled to find the Journal feature in Outlook. "Oh, good!" I thought, "A place to record my deep thoughts while I'm working on other things!" Unfortunately (or fortunately, depending on your perspective), that's not what Outlook's Journal is about. Outlook's Journal feature enables you to record your involvement with a particular contact or task. By storing the information on a daily, weekly, or monthly time-line, the Journal can show you how you spent your time, and which of your clients gets the most of your time. This can be especially helpful when you work in a service-related area, and need to keep track of how much to bill different clients when you work on multiple projects during a day.

To start the Journal in Outlook, choose Journal from the View menu. The first time you choose Journal, Outlook will tell you that the Activities tab in the Contacts window does a good job of tracking information related to specific clients. If you want to use Journal only for those items you enter, click No when Outlook asks you whether you want to use it for automatic recording. If you want Journal to record items such as e-mail correspondence, scheduling, task entries and updates, and working with files, click Yes. The Journal Options dialog box appears, so that you can choose the items you want to track. If you choose this route, click the items you want Journal to record, then click OK to begin working with the Journal.

To record a new Journal entry, click New on the Outlook toolbar. The Journal Entry window appears (as shown in Figure 14-11 on the following page). Enter the subject for the entry, then click the Entry Type down arrow and choose the type of activity from the displayed list. Enter the name of the company the item relates to, then select the Start time by choosing the date and time you want to begin tracking the activity. You can then minimize the Journal entry, and go on about your work for that client company.

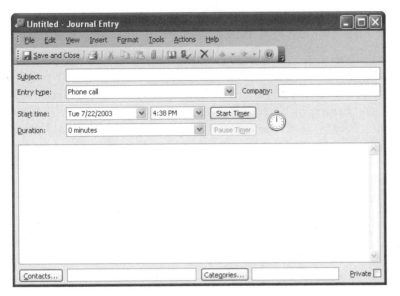

Figure 14-11　The Journal helps you track how much time you spend on individual pieces in a project.

When you're finished with the task at hand, redisplay the Journal entry by clicking the entry in the taskbar, then click Save And Close. The item is added to the timeline, and you can redisplay it, add to it, or edit the entry by double-clicking it.

> **Note**　There's much more you can do with the Journal in Outlook—and multiple views you can use to review the way your time information is tracked. Experiment with the various displays by choosing the different timeline views on the Outlook toolbar, or by choosing Current View from the View menu.

Working with Tasks and Notes

Does your to-do list grow during the day? Do things fall off the list accidentally, leaving unfinished details that are sure to catch up with you later? Do you have trouble reminding yourself about what you wanted to remember? Outlook includes two more features—Tasks and Notes—that can help you capture details that are in danger of falling through the cracks. Tasks enables you to reduce your larger projects into a series of manageable steps, while Notes helps you remember those great ideas that occur to you as you're doing a project.

First Tasks First

My mother had lists for everything. Her morning list began with "Make coffee," and ended with "Defrost chicken for dinner." I must admit that I'm not half the organizer my mother is—but, luckily, I know how to use Outlook's Task feature. I can track projects and people and personal events. If you're on the road to better organization, Tasks can help you get that sense of accomplishment at the end of the day.

To start Tasks, click the Tasks shortcut in the Outlook Shortcuts bar. The window shown in Figure 14-12 appears. To add a new task, click New on the Outlook toolbar. In the New Task dialog box, click in the Subject line, and type a name for the task. Click the Due Date down arrow to display a calendar, then click the due date you need. Fill in additional items, such as the Status, Priority, and Start Date if needed. You will automatically be reminded of the approaching deadline, until you click the Reminder check box to clear the check mark (as shown in Figure 14-13).

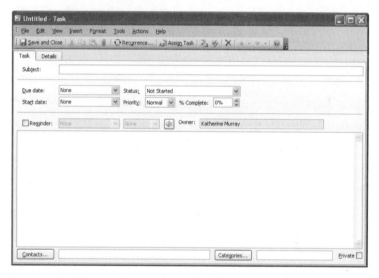

Figure 14-12   Create a new task by clicking New on the Outlook toolbar when the Tasks window is displayed.

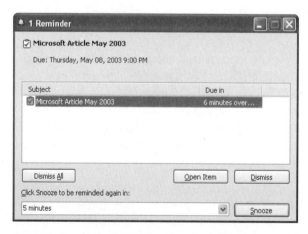

Figure 14-13   Outlook lets you know how many days you have before the task is due. Pressure, pressure.

> **Aha!** Fast Task Entry
>
> If you prefer to enter a task the fast way, click in the Click Here To Add A New Task box and type the task; then press Tab to move to the Due Date column. Click the down arrow to display a calendar, and click the date the task is due. Press Enter to save the task.

After you've entered the task information, click Save And Close to save the task. Outlook displays the task in the Task list. You can change the task data at any time by double-clicking the task in the list. When you complete an item, click the Complete check box (just to the left of the task). Outlook then marks out the task, like this:

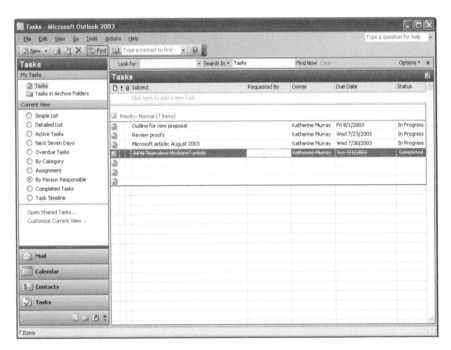

Closure. Nice. (Omigosh—did someone remember to defrost the chicken?)

Now the Notes

Notes is a rather small, but powerful, feature in Outlook. Start Notes by clicking the Notes shortcut icon in the bottom of the navigation panel on the left side of the Outlook window. If you've previously entered notes, they appear in the Notes area of your screen.

To create a note, click New. A notepad appears, showing the date and time along the bottom. Type your note, then either leave the note open on the screen, or click the close box to save the note in the Notes area. You can open a note later by displaying Notes view and double-clicking the note. The note appears over your work area, looking something like this:

As you can see, there are many features in Outlook that can help you get organized, whether you need to control e-mail messages, contact data, time, tasks, or thoughts. The only remaining problem is: which one will you tackle first?

Introducing Microsoft Office OneNote

If your work relies on good note-taking, the new OneNote application may make your professional life a lot easier. OneNote is a new utility that enables you to capture, store, organize, and use the notes you create. No more retyping text from wrinkled napkins or the backs of envelopes. If you've got OneNote on a Tablet PC, a Pocket PC, or installed on your regular work computer (with a writing pad peripheral), you can write, draw, or speak your notes as they're happening—and OneNote timestamps and saves the information for you automatically. Once you capture the notes, you can organize, use, and share them as needed— whether it's an audio clip of catch-phrases for your newest product, a diagram showing the potential restructuring of your business, a quick bit of conversation with a developer you just met, or a follow-up task list for the team. OneNote isn't part of the Office System per se, but it is available via download. Take it for a test drive, and discover how easy it is to capture, organize, and apply all those terrific moments of inspiration.

Fast Wrap-Up

- Create new folders to store your e-mail by pressing Ctrl+Shift+E. Drag the messages to the folder as needed.

- You can create rules to help you automatically organize e-mail as it is received.

- Outlook 2003 includes a number of junk mail features that cut down on the amount of spam you receive, and lessen the time you spend wading through unwanted messages.

- The Contacts feature in Outlook is an extensive data management tool that enables you to gather, update, sort, print, and use information about clients, companies, coworkers, and companions.

- Journaling in Outlook enables you to keep track of the time you spend on specific tasks during the day.

- Use Tasks to help you break down large projects into smaller, manageable chunks. You enter the task and due date, and check off the tasks when they're finished.

- Outlook Notes are pop-up boxes you can leave open on your screen as you work to remind you of important things you might forget.

- OneNote is a new note-taking application from Microsoft that enables you to take notes the way they occur to you—writing them by hand, speaking them into a microphone, or sketching them on a pad. OneNote is made available separately from the Office system, but it is compatible with all core Office applications.

Scheduling with Microsoft Office Outlook 2003

15

10-Second Summary

- Understand the Calendar
- Set appointments
- Use reminders
- Schedule meetings and invite attendees
- Create a meeting workspace

If you've ever felt like the frantic White Rabbit ("I'm late! I'm late!") from Alice in Wonderland, you know what a great thing it can be to discover a few extra minutes in the day. Microsoft Office Outlook 2003 includes a number of features that can help you make the most of your time. Using Outlook's Calendar, for example, you can bring your tasks and appointments together, and create schedules that make sense for everyone in your group. And now, scheduling and preparing for meetings is easier than ever. This chapter shows you how to organize yourself and your team using Outlook's scheduling features.

Understanding Outlook's Calendar

The Outlook Calendar provides you with numerous views, so that you can set, review, update, and compare appointments easily. You can use the Calendar as an electronic version of your appointment book or you can use Outlook's many features to do more. Specifically, you can categorize and color-code your appointments and tasks; add automatic reminders to have Outlook let you know when a deadline is looming set up and invite others to meetings; synchronize your appointments with your Pocket PC and Tablet PC; and share your calendar with others on your team.

Click the Calendar button in the navigation pane to display the Calendar window. The Calendar window displays several panels you can use to view appointments and complete tasks (see Figure 15-1). The main area of the screen shows the schedule for the current day, organized in 30-minute increments. In the top right corner of the window, you see a calendar displaying the current month. (You can display different months by clicking the arrows at either end of the calendar title bar.) The Tasks list appears in the lower right portion of the window, showing the tasks you've finished, as well as the tasks you need to do.

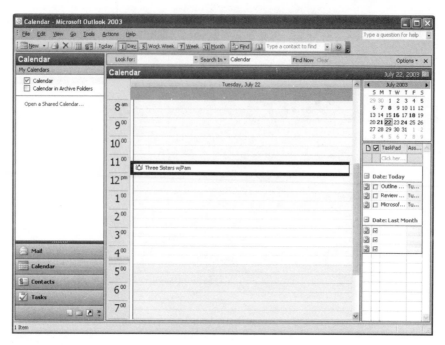

Figure 15-1   You view, organize, add, and modify appointments in the Calendar window.

> **Note**   If you don't see the calendar and task list on the right side of the Calendar window, open the View menu and choose TaskPad. You can also customize the appearance of the tasks by selecting the option you want from the TaskPad View submenu.

Creating Appointments

The fastest way to add an appointment is to display the Calendar in Day view, click the line corresponding to the time you want to add the appointment, type the text, and then click outside the entry.

When you want to create a more detailed appointment, however, with start and end times, reminders and more, you need to click the New Appointment tool in the Outlook toolbar (or double-click a line in the Calendar in Day view). This action brings up the Appointment window, in which you enter the information you need to set up the appointment (see Figure 15-2).

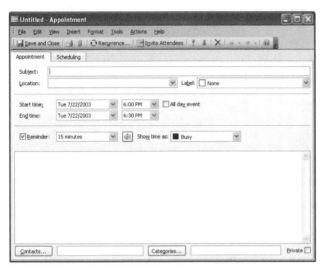

Figure 15-2   You fill in additional scheduling details in the Appointment window.

To create the appointment, follow these steps:

1 In the Subject line, type a phrase describing the appointment.

2 Enter a location or click the down arrow to choose a location you've entered previously.

3 Set the day and time you want the appointment to begin by clicking the appropriate down arrows and choosing the day and time from the displayed list.

See Also If you will be using Microsoft NetMeeting to meet online, see the section, "Holding an Online Meeting," later in this chapter.

> **Note**   If the meeting is an all-day event, select the All Day Event check box and the Calendar removes the time selections.

4 Choose the date and time your appointment will end.

5 Click Save And Close to save the appointment and add it to your daily calendar.

> **Note**   You also can create different types of appointments by choosing the one you want from the Actions menu. Choose from New Appointment, New All Day Event, New Meeting Request, New Recurring Appointment, or New Recurring Meeting to start with the appointment type you want.

Creating a Recurring Appointment

If you have regularly scheduled appointments (such as a Monday-morning staff meeting, or a Thursday-at-noon book club), you can create what Outlook likes to call a "recurrence." To do so, follow these steps:

1 Display the Appointment window. If you're starting a new appointment, click New on the Outlook toolbar; if you're transforming an existing appointment into a recurring appointment, display the appointment by double-clicking it in any Calendar view.

2 Click Recurrence on the Appointment toolbar.

3 In the Appointment Recurrence dialog box, enter a start and end time. (You don't need to enter the Duration value; Outlook will figure that out.)

4 In the Recurrence Pattern area, choose whether you want the appointment to repeat Daily, Weekly, Monthly, or Yearly. Depending on what you select (Weekly is selected in Figure 15-3, for example), the options in the right side of the dialog box change to allow you to specify when you want the recurrence to happen.

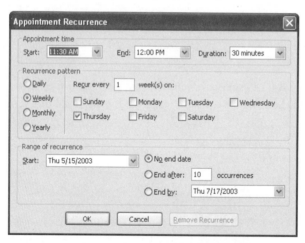

Figure 15-3 You can set up an appointment to repeat daily, weekly, monthly, or yearly.

5 Choose the date you want the recurring appointment to begin. (The current date is selected by default.)

6 Specify when you want the appointment to end. If you're setting an appointment to watch each of Bill Moyers's new PBS shows in a 13-week series, for example, you would click the End After box, and type **13**. If you know a specific date on which these appointments should end, you can enter it in the End By: box. And, of course, if you want the appointment to continue indefinitely, leave No End Date selected.

7 Click OK to create your recurring appointment. When Outlook displays your message in a Calendar view, a small Recurring symbol appears to the left of the appointment subject, as shown here:

> ↻ Meeting with Forbes on new blogging project (Virtual)

Aha! Quickly Changing an Appointment

When you want to revise details for an appointment you've already entered, you can do so easily by double-clicking the appointment in any Calendar view. This opens the Appointment window, showing all the appointment information you've entered. Click in the field you need to change, make your modifications, and then click Save And Close to update the appointment.

Canceling a Repeating Appointment

If you later decide to cancel the "recurring" aspect of an appointment, you can do so by double-clicking the recurring appointment. Outlook displays a small message box, asking whether you want to open only this appointment, or the entire series of recurring appointments. Click Open The Series, and then click OK.

In the Appointment window, click Recurrence, and then click the Remove Recurrence button at the bottom of the Appointment Recurrence dialog box. Click Save And Close to cancel the recurring appointment and return to the Calendar window.

Using Reminders

You've probably already noticed the Reminder check box in the lower portion of the Appointment window. By default, Outlook activates the Reminder feature when you create an appointment (until you turn the feature off in one appointment—then subsequent appointments appear without Reminder selected). A reminder in Outlook simply lets you know a few minutes (or however long you specify) in advance of the appointment that you've got something to do. A reminder works like this:

When Outlook sees that it's time to remind you about something, a chime plays (you can customize this feature, by the way—you'll learn how in the next section) and the Reminder dialog box appears (as shown in Figure 15-4 on the following page). You then have the following choices:

- Click Dismiss All to cancel all reminders on the current day.
- Click Open Item to display the appointment for editing or review.
- Click Dismiss to cancel the reminder on this item only.
- Click Snooze to reset the reminder to ring again in the period of time you specify.

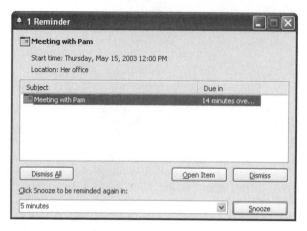

Figure 15-4   The Reminder window pops up when it's almost time for a task or appointment you've scheduled.

Modifying Reminders

You can customize when and how the Reminder lets you know what's coming. To change the amount of time, click the down arrow and choose a new time interval (from 0 minutes to two weeks) to let Outlook know how much forewarning you want.

If you want Outlook to play a different reminder sound, click the Reminder Sound tool (which is labeled with a megaphone symbol) to the right of the Show Time As option. The Reminder Sound dialog box appears, as shown below.

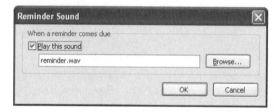

Click the Browse button to navigate to other sound files. If you want to disable the sound altogether, click the Play This Sound check box to clear it. After you select the new sound, click OK.

Aha!   Record Your Own

Any sound you've saved with a .wav extension (including ones you've recorded yourself) can be used as a Reminder Sound. You can use the Windows Sound Recorder to record your own custom sound.

Scheduling with Outlook

In addition to setting up appointments and events that affect your work and personal time, you can use Outlook to set up and schedule a meeting, invite participants, and reserve meeting rooms. While you're doing this, you can block out your time, so that you can easily see when you're busy, when you're out of the office, and when you have free time. Once you set up your schedule in this way, you can allow others to see the information as well, so they can make informed decisions about when to schedule their own meetings, if they want you to attend. Outlook 2003 also enables you to create Meeting Workspaces, Web sites that use Microsoft SharePoint Team Services (STS) to help you gather all the information you need as part of an upcoming meeting.

Planning a Meeting and Inviting Attendees

What if you held a meeting and nobody came? Hey, it happens to the best of us. (In my case, I scheduled an informal meeting at Starbucks, and then went to the wrong one. Big "Oops.") When you want to schedule a meeting that you'll be sure people will attend, you can use Outlook's scheduling features to help you. Here's how it works:

1 With the Calendar window displayed, open the Actions menu, and choose Plan A Meeting.

2 Click Add Others in the Plan A Meeting dialog box.

3 Choose Add From Address Book, then go through the names in the list that appears, clicking the ones you want. Then, click one of the following buttons:

   ● Required adds the name to the top group. These are the people who must attend in order for you to have the meeting.

   ● Optional puts the names in the middle group. You care about whether these people come, but if they can't make it, it's no big deal. You'll have the meeting anyway.

   ● Resources isn't a category for humans—it's for conference rooms and overheads. Okay, I admit that doesn't seem to make much sense. But before you can reserve resources using this category in Outlook, the item must have its own mailbox for reservations. If this is a bit too techie for you, check with your network administrator for the hows and whys of scheduling resources electronically.

4 Click OK. The names are added to the All Attendees list in the Plan A Meeting dialog box (as shown in Figure 15-5 on the following page).

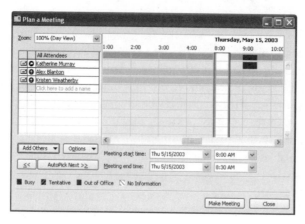

Figure 15-5 After you select attendees using the Add Others button, they appear in the All Attendees list.

> **Note** The first time you use this feature, the Microsoft Office Internet Free/Busy dialog box appears, asking whether you'd like to join the Microsoft Office Internet Free/Busy Service. This is a service that publishes your free times and busy times to the Internet, so that people who can't view your calendar can see when you are available. This is a protected service so that only those people who are members of the service, and who have your explicit permission, can view your calendar information. If you want to try the service, click Join; otherwise, click Cancel.

5 Enter the start and end times for the meeting.

6 Click the Make Meeting button. In the Meeting dialog box, type the Subject for the meeting, and enter the location (in my situation, that would be the address of the coffeeshop where we are meeting). In the message box, type a note to participants explaining the meeting, if you like. If you want to create a Meeting Workspace (more about this in the next section), click the Meeting Workspace button.

7 Click Send. Outlook sends the message as an invitation to the people you selected, enabling them to check their calendars, and respond to the invitation.

> **Note** Don't forget to invite yourself if you want to see what the invitations look like (and gauge when they arrive in your attendees' Inboxes).

Setting Your Schedule

Are you wondering how to tell Outlook to display time as free time, busy time, or out-of-office time? The Show Time As option in the Appointment or Message window is the key. In either dialog box, enter the other items as normal, then click the Show Time As down arrow, as shown below:

Click Free if you want the time you selected in the start and end times to be shown as available time. Choose Tentative if you've sent out invitations for another meeting during that time, or have an appointment pending. Select Busy if you're already scheduled for that time; or click Out Of Office if you plan to go swimming with the kids that afternoon.

Creating and Using Meeting Workspaces

Knowing that getting people together in the same time and space is important, Outlook provides the means for workgroups to gather in a meeting workspace on the Web. If your company uses SharePoint Team Services V2, or Microsoft SharePoint Portal Services (SPS), you can create shared workspaces with documents, photos, presentations, discussions, and more, all related to an upcoming meeting or critical event.

You can create a meeting workspace by clicking the Meeting Workspace button in the Appointment window. The Meeting Workspace task pane opens so that you can create a new workspace or select an existing one (see Figure 15-6).

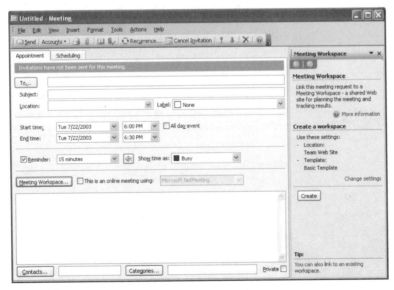

Figure 15-6 If your company uses SharePoint Team Services, you can create a shared meeting space on the Web where team members can gather, share information, and meet.

To create a Meeting Workspace, click the Create button. The Meeting Workspace task pane shows that the workspace is being created. When the process is finished, the following note appears in the task pane. Click the Go To Workspace link to display the newly created workspace.

Comparing Schedules

One of the challenges to successful collaboration is getting everyone on the same page—and in the same space—at the same time. Setting up meetings everyone can attend is tricky when you're trying to coordinate half a dozen busy professionals. The new side-by-side calendaring feature in Outlook 2003 gives you the ability to share your calendar with others and view others' calendars by placing them beside your own. That way, you can easily see which timeslots are open for everyone, and which are definitely a no-go.

You begin side-by-side calendaring by sharing your own calendar. In the Navigation Pane of the Calendar window, click the Share My Calendar link. Then, enter the information of those who have permission to view your Calendar, and click OK. This enables others to view your information.

To view others' calendars next to yours, click Open A Shared Calendar, and type the person's name, or choose it from your Contacts list. The other person must have previously selected Share My Calendar in their version of Outlook, and given you permission to view the calendar before you will be allowed access (see Figure 15-7).

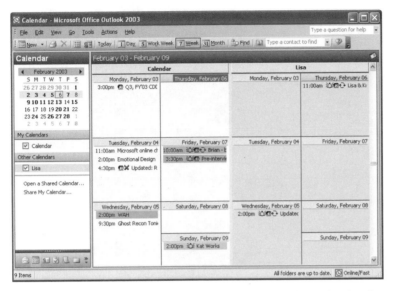

Figure 15-7 The side-by-side calendar view displays multiple calendars in a columnar format.

Holding an Online Meeting

In today's world, you may be as likely to have teleconferences or cyberspace meetings as you are to have real, face-to-face meetings. Outlook provides a feature that helps you schedule online meetings, using NetMeeting, or another conferencing utility, and an online meeting space. To schedule an online meeting using NetMeeting, follow these steps:

1 Click the time in your daily calendar when you'd like to schedule the meeting.

2 Click the New down arrow on the Outlook toolbar, and choose Meeting Request. (You also can press Ctrl+Shift+Q if you prefer.)

3 In the Meeting dialog box, enter the people you'd like to invite in the To line. (If necessary, click the To button to select the names, then click OK to return to the Message window.)

4 Enter a Subject for the meeting.

5 Click the check box to the left of This Is An Online Meeting. The dialog box changes to display additional options, as shown in Figure 15-8 on the following page.

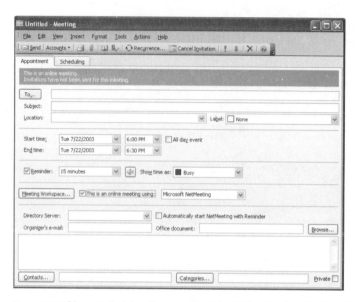

Figure 15-8 You can hold online meetings in Outlook using NetMeeting or another online conferencing service.

6 If you plan to use a conferencing service other than NetMeeting, click the drop down arrow to see what other services you have available, then click the one you plan to use.

7 Enter the Directory Server where you will "gather" with the other meeting participants. If you have a dedicated server used for this purpose in your organization, enter the address here.

8 Enter your e-mail address as the meeting's planner.

9 If you want NetMeeting to start automatically when Outlook reminds you of the meeting, click the Automatically Start NetMeeting With Reminder check box.

10 Set the other options as usual, entering the start and end times, and customizing the Reminder if you choose.

11 Click Send to send the meeting invitation to the people you want to attend.

> **Note**   If you are scheduling a meeting and inviting attendees who work in another time zone, their calendars are automatically adjusted for the time change, which means you won't have to recalculate their free times. Saves you trouble. Nice.

> **Aha!**   The Big Event
>
> When you set up an event (which is an appointment that lasts 24 hours or longer, such as a convention, a workshop, or a business trip), the appointment appears as a banner, rather than as a block of time on your schedule.

Printing Your Calendar

Having all your appointments, events, tasks, and meetings on your desktop is a great convenience, but there will be times when you're away from your desk and out of reach of a laptop, and you'll need a reminder to advise you of what's coming next. (Of course, don't overlook how easy it is to sychronize your Pocket PC or Tablet PC with your Outlook data, so you always have what you need on the go.) If you prefer to do things the old-fashioned, ink-and-paper way, you can print your Outlook Calendar in several different styles:

- Daily Style prints a listing of all scheduled appointments in a day's time.

- Weekly Style prints the entire week in a two-column format.

- Monthly Style prints the calendar in traditional monthly format.

- Tri-fold Style displays a three-column format with the daily calendar on the left, the Tasks list in the center, and the weekly calendar on the right.

- Calendar Detail prints only the items you have scheduled for the current day.

To print your calendar, click the Print tool on the Outlook toolbar. In the Print dialog box, select the printer you want to use, then click the Print Style that fits the look you want. Specify a Start date and an End date for the calendar entries you want to print, and enter the Number Of Copies you need. Finally, click Preview to see how the calendar will look before you print it. If everything looks good, click Print in the Preview window to display the Print dialog box a second time, and click OK to begin printing.

Fast Wrap-Up

- You use Outlook's Calendar to schedule your appointments, events, and meetings.

- Calendar gives you four views for your appointments: Day, Work Week, Week, and Month.

- Any tasks that you've added are displayed in the Day view.

- You can hide or show the Taskpad by choosing Taskpad from the View menu.

- You set new appointments by clicking New on the Outlook toolbar, entering a Subject and Location, and scheduling a start and end time.

- Outlook allows you to create recurring meetings of any frequency you choose—weekly, biweekly, monthly, or annually.

- You can use Reminders to let you know when a meeting or appointment is approaching. The Reminder plays a chime and displays a dialog box to alert you.

- Outlook uses a schedule to keep track of your time. You can create individual and group schedules to coordinate collaborative work.

- If you are using SharePoint Team Services V2, you can create a Meeting Workspace to organize and share important information related to an upcoming meeting.

- You can hold online meetings in Outlook, using NetMeeting or another online conferencing utility.

Part 6
Managing Data with Microsoft Office Access 2003

Microsoft Office Access 2003 isn't the intimidating, high-end database new users often think it is—it's actually a fairly friendly, powerful program that, in many cases, walks you through the data tasks you need to complete. Whether you are creating tables, designing reports, constructing queries, or working with Extensible Markup Language (XML) data, this part of the book shows you how to complete the most common data management tasks.

Getting Started with Databases

16

10-Second Summary

- ■ Understand database concepts
- ■ Start a new database
- ■ Create a new data table
- ■ Work with forms
- ■ Import and save XML data

Data, whether we call it that or not, is at the center of everything we do. Whether we are working with clients, shelving inventory, or preparing cupcakes for the class party, we are using information in many forms. Access 2003 is a program created to help you manage data—in large and small quantities, for simple or complicated tasks. This chapter gives you an overview of data management tasks and introduces you to the Access way of managing your information.

Note   Note that if you are using the Microsoft Office System Standard Edition, Access is not included as part of your system. Access is included only with the Professional edition of the Office System.

New Features in Access 2003

In the Professional editions of the Office System, Access 2003 shares the XML support available throughout other Office applications in the Enterprise and Professional packages. Now you can easily import and export data in XML. Other new features in Access 2003 include:

- ■ New smart tags point out potential errors in your databases.

- ■ Simplified linked table copying makes it easier to copy a relational table from one database to another.

- ■ New database backup feature enables you to create a regular backup of your entire database by choosing a menu selection.

- ■ A new feature makes it easy to identify dependencies in relational tables, helping you see how modifications will affect all aspects of your data.

Lingo *Linked tables* are tables that share a common field, creating a relationship that you can use to view and edit the data in either table.

What Can You Do with Access?

Let's start with the issue of function. What are *you* most likely to do with Access? There is an incredibly wide range of possibilities. Here are just a few ways someone might use Access at work:

- Develop a sales inventory database that interacts with point-of-sale software, updating inventory levels automatically at the close of each business day.

- Create a database for patient accounts in your optometrist's office that stores individual patient records, includes examination results, tracks office visits and prescription changes, and prints out a reminder card automatically one month before each patient's yearly checkup.

- Design a "back end" for a Web application, in which users take an online survey and answer questions about your company's product. The results are saved in an Access database, and can be used in further analyses and reports.

- Add a personnel database to your system that keeps track of each employee's start date, semiannual reviews, performance, payroll, bonuses, commendations, and vacation time.

> **Note**   As you begin to work with Access, you'll no doubt discover ways in which you can put the program to work for simple and not-so-simple data management uses. Once you discover how easy it is to create and work with data tables in Access, you won't have an excuse *not* to organize your data better.

The Access Window

When you first start Access, you'll see a pretty simple screen. There's not much going on—just the traditional menu bar, toolbar, and the Getting Started task pane (see Figure 16-1). You'll use the toolbar to create, modify, and link tables. The task pane includes all the selections you need to create new databases or work with existing ones.

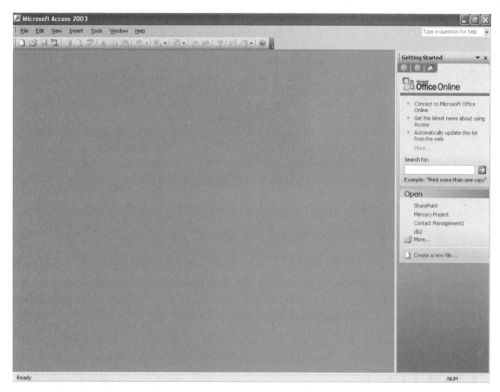

Figure 16-1   The Access window includes the tools and menus for creating, working with, and building relationships among data tables.

> **Note**   If you have previously opened a database table in Access, you might also see the Formatting toolbar, which appears beneath the Database toolbar. Access also features a Web toolbar that looks just like the Web toolbars in the other Office applications.

Database Overview

When you first begin creating a database, the task may seem daunting. This section explains a few database concepts that you'll use throughout this section of the book. Suppose you want to create a database that tracks information about the new litter of Newfoundland puppies you have.

There is an array of information items to capture about each pup, including birth weight, sex, dam, and sire. As time goes on, you will add weight data to track how quickly the pups are growing. You might add fields categorizing the individual characteristics—this pup has a white star on her chest; that pup is the leader of the group; another pup is the wallflower, and so on. You'll also record the amount of food the pups are eating, veterinary check-ups and shots, and any comments or additional bits of data you want to keep with each puppy's data. You'll enter the individual items you want to record—weight, sex, food, and so on—within *fields* in the data table. A collection of information about one pup is known as that pup's *record*. And the entire collection of data—all the pup records together—comprises the *database*.

> **Aha!**   More Than Words
>
> You can add pictures, video, and sound to your database tables, as well as text and numbers. This means you can put a photograph of each Newfoundland puppy on the record to help identify the pup later—and even add a sound clip of his bark if you choose. (Okay, okay, maybe I'm taking this example a bit far. Forget the bark.)

Once you have entered all the data, you might create a relationship between this database of puppies and your database of potential pup buyers. In the "potential buyer" database, you'd have the names, addresses, location, and desires of each prospective owner. This owner wants an all-black Newfie, so the pup with the white star is out. But this one wants a female with a laid-back temperament. By creating relationships and then querying the database (asking the database to display records with the characteristics you specify), you can match buyers with puppies and print a report.

> **Note**   Of course, a database doesn't have to be anything more complicated than a simple list of items, perhaps the names of your relatives and their birth dates, or the names of your East Coast sales reps and their Social Security numbers. This example just shows you how the different features of Access can be used together to get the most use from the data you've already got (which helps you work faster *and* smarter).

Starting a New Database

When you're ready to start a new database, you have two options. You can use the Access Database Wizard to walk you through the process and help you choose the fields you want in a specific type of database, or you can do it yourself by creating a new blank database.

Help Me, Mr. Wizard!

The first time you create a database, it's a good idea to use the wizard and see how Access does it. You begin by choosing a template of the style you want, then the automated wizard leads you through everything you need to know—all you do is answer the questions and select the options you want to use. Here's the process:

1 In the Getting Started task pane, click Create A New File.

2 In the Templates area of the New File task pane, click On My Computer.

3 In the Templates dialog box, click the Databases tab. Choose the type of database closest to the one you want to create; then click OK.

4 In the File New Data dialog box, enter a name for the new database and click
Create. The Database Wizard begins and leads you through a series of questions
that enable you to choose the types of tables you'll include, the way the data
labels will look, the kind of reports you want to create, and the title of the database. Make your choices on each screen, and click Next to advance the wizard.

> **Aha!**   Picture Data
>
> If you want to include a picture on the records (for example, if you have a business
> logo, a special symbol, or yes, a puppy picture you'd like to include), click the Yes,
> I'd Like To Include A Picture check box. Navigate to the folder containing the picture
> you want to use, select it, and click OK to return to the Database Wizard.

5 Click Finish to complete the wizard and create the new database.

Access displays a status window as it goes through and creates all the elements and tables
for the new database. After a moment, the Main Switchboard appears in your Access work
area (as shown in Figure 16-2). This is the menu you'll use to add, view, update, and print
the data in the new database.

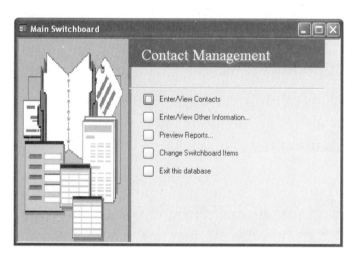

Figure 16-2   The Main Switchboard includes choices for the main Access tasks you're likely
to perform.

> **Aha!**   Using the Switchboard
>
> The Main Switchboard is available only if you have used the Database Wizard to create
> a database. It's a great way to put a friendly face on what can be complicated data-
> bases, especially if other people will be adding information to the database you've
> created. You can customize the Switchboard if you choose by selecting Change Switch-
> board Items.

Create a New Database from Scratch

If you're one of those people who'd rather *do* things, you can create a database with a few simple clicks of the mouse. The process isn't difficult, but what you miss is the create-it-all-at-once technique that the wizard offers.You also won't have the same look and feel for your data-entry form and your reports, but that's no big deal. You can learn those things as you go. (And besides, you'll learn how to create, format, and print reports in Chapter 18, "Preparing and Printing Reports in Microsoft Access.")

Here are the steps for creating a database from scratch:

1 In the Getting Started task pane, click Create a New File.

2 Click Blank Database in the New area of the task pane.

3 In the File New Database window, navigate to a folder in which you want to store the database file, enter a name for the file, and then click Create. The new database is created (in this case, the database for Newfie pups), and displayed in a database window with the file name you specified, as shown in Figure 16-3.

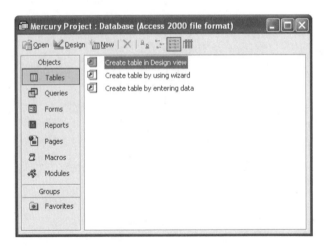

Figure 16-3 The new database file is created and displayed as a data table in your Access work area.

Creating Tables and Fields

When you create your database from scratch, you need to set up the tables and the fields you want to use in your database. (For the moment, all you have is a database file.) The tables collect the records related to a specific item (for example, you might have a "puppies" table and a "potential buyers" table). Fields store the individual data items that comprise each record—for example, name, address, city, state, product name, and so on. You'll use a different wizard to help automate the process of creating the tables and fields for your new database file. Here are the steps:

1 Open your database (if necessary) by choosing Open from the File menu, and clicking the new database name in the task pane. The database window opens in the Access work area.

2 Double-click Create Table By Using Wizard. The Table Wizard appears, as shown in Figure 16-4.

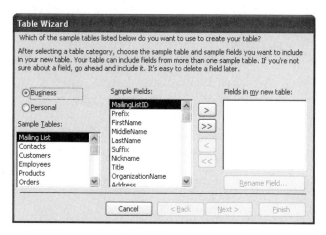

Figure 16-4 The Table Wizard prompts you to choose the fields you want to include in the new table.

3 In the Sample Tables list, click the table type you want to create. The Sample Fields list in the center of the dialog box changes to show the fields typically used in that table.

4 Click a field you want, and click the Add button to add it to your table. If you want to add all the fields in the Sample Fields list, click Add All.

> **Aha!** Adding Fields Quickly
>
> If you plan to use the majority of the fields, a quick way of adding the fields you want is to click Add All, and then, in the list showing your database fields, click the individual fields you *don't* want. Then click Remove to put them back in the Sample Fields list.

5 If you want to change the name of any field you add to your form, click the field you want to change, then click Rename Field. In the Rename Field dialog box, type the new name and click OK.

6 Enter a name for the table, leaving the primary key option set the way it is. (The primary key is the field by which Access first sorts your data. For example, Customer ID would be a good candidate for a primary key, because it uniquely identifies each customer record. For most purposes, you can let Access set this for you.) Then, click Next.

7 Choose whether you want to modify the table, enter data, or have the wizard create a form in which you can enter data. We'll create a form later in this chapter, so leave the middle option selected, and click Finish to create the table. The table appears, showing the fields you added, in Datasheet view, ready for you to add data (as shown in Figure 16-5).

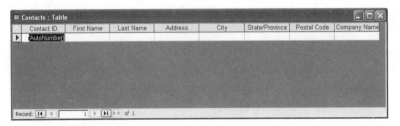

Figure 16-5 The Table Wizard creates the table and displays it in Datasheet view, with your field names as column headings and the first row selected, ready to receive the data you enter.

Aha!   Inserting a Field After the Fact

Did you forget a field you need? You can add it easily by clicking the column label to the right of the column you want to add. Choose Column from the Insert menu, and Access adds a new column with the label Field1. Double-click the field name to select it; then type a name for that field, and press Enter.

More Than One Way to Create a Table

The database window offers you two additional ways to create a table in your database. You can use Design view to create the table and add fields, or you can simply create the table by entering data. When you choose Create Table In Design View, Design view is displayed, and you add the field name, type, and a description for each field you create. Your field names can include as many as 64 characters, and you can choose a field type, which refers to the type of data that is to be stored in the field, by clicking in the Data Type column and clicking the down arrow that appears. Simply click the data type you want to assign to the field. (You can choose from Text, Memo, Number, Date/Time, Currency, AutoNumber, Yes/No, OLE Object, HyperLink, or Lookup Wizard.)

If you choose Create Table By Entering Data, Access creates the table, names it Table1, and displays a spreadsheet-like grid in which you can enter data. Change the field names by double-clicking the Field1, Field2 and similar labels, and type the name you want: **Name**, **Address**, and so on. You can then enter the information directly into the table, pressing Tab to move from field to field.

Adding Data

Now that you've created the database, you're ready to add information to it. In database parlance, this is known as "populating" the fields. Depending on how you created your database, you can use one of two methods to fill it with data:

- If you used the Access Database Wizard to create the database, you can use the Main Switchboard to enter data. This displays the data in a pre-designed form that makes it easy for you to add data.

- If you created the table from scratch, you can enter data in Datasheet view. You also can create your own form in place of the Datasheet (but I'll save that discussion for the section entitled "Creating a Form," later in this chapter).

Entering Data with the Switchboard

If the Main Switchboard is available (meaning that you used the wizard to create the database), click Enter/View Contacts and a data form appears on your screen (as shown in Figure 16-6).

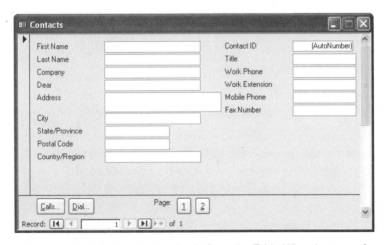

Figure 16-6 You add data in a simple form the Table Wizard creates for you.

Enter the information for each record by following these steps:

1 Click in the fields where you want to add information.

2 Type the data.

3 Press Tab to move to the next field (or click another field).

4 Click Page 2 to display additional fields.

5 When you're ready to move to the next record, click Next Record to display the next blank form.

Navigating Forms

There's a collection of buttons at the bottom of the Switchboard data entry form that you'll use to move among the records in your database and add records. This is what the different buttons do:

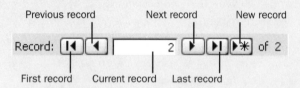

You can use the buttons to move to different records within the data table after you've entered your data, but you can also click in the Current Record box and type the number of the record if you know it.

Entering Data in the Datasheet

If you use the Tables Wizard to create the table in your database, or you choose the Create A Table By Entering Data option, the resulting table is automatically displayed in Datasheet view (as previously shown in Figure 16-6). There are two details about working in Datasheet view you need to remember:

- Each column is a unique field in the table. Column names might include Name, Address, Product ID, Customer Number, Social Security Number, or ZIP Code.

- Each row in the Datasheet is a unique record in the table. A record is a collection of fields related to one specific person, item, or product. In a Customer table, for example, each customer has his or her own record, and individual data fields (or columns) store the data for Name, Address, and so on.

Aha!   Entering Data in Datasheet View

Even if you are using the Main Switchboard, you can enter data in Datasheet view. To do that, close the Switchboard by clicking the Close box; then open the database window (which is minimized in the lower left corner of the Access window) by clicking the Restore button. In the database window, click Tables, then double-click the name of the table to which you want to add data. The table will open in Datasheet view, and you can type the data items and press Tab after each one.

To enter data in the datasheet, simply type the information and press Tab or Enter. The cursor moves to the next cell until you get to the last field in the record (row); then the cursor moves to the first field in the next record.

Importing XML Data

Access also allows you to import *XML* data directly into your data tables, which means you can easily share data with other programs that are capable of producing and using XML.

> **Lingo** *XML* (Extensible Markup Language) is an industry-standard data format that enables users to store data and formats separately, which allows the data to be used in many different forms and to be shared easily.

To import XML data into your Access database, follow these steps:

1 Open the database you want to use.

2 Choose Get External Data from the File menu, and click Import.

3 In the Import dialog box, navigate to the folder storing the XML file you want to import, then click the Files Of Type down arrow, and choose XML from the list.

4 Select the file and click Import. In the Import XML dialog box, click Options to make additional choices (see Figure 16-7 on the following page). Here's a quick explanation of each option:

- Structure Only imports only the schema of the data file

- Structure And Data imports the framework as well as the information in the file

- Append Data To Existing Table imports the data and places it in the appropriate fields in your data tables

> **Aha!** Transforming Your XML Data
>
> The Import XML dialog box also offers you the Transform button, which enables you to attach a *transform*, or a specific format, to the data you're importing. A transform is an XML file similar to a style sheet that tells the application how to display the contents of the data file.

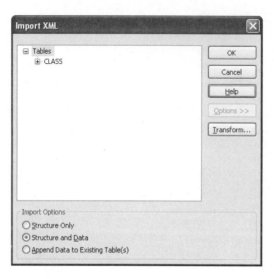

Figure 16-7 Click Options in the Import XML dialog box to make further choices about the XML data you import.

5 Click OK to import the data. Click OK a second time to close the message box that tells you the document has been imported successfully.

Importing Other Data

Of course, Access isn't limited to importing only XML data; you can use information previously stored in other Access databases, various dBASE versions, Microsoft Office Excel 2003, Lotus 1-2-3, Paradox, ODBC databases, and other applications and formats. The process for importing is the same: Begin with Get External Data in the File menu, and choose Import. Navigate to the folder you need. Then, in the Files Of Type list, choose the program format in which the data is currently saved. Depending on the format you select, different options will be displayed for you to choose specifically what you want to import. Figure 16-8 shows the Import Objects dialog box that appears when you import an Access database.

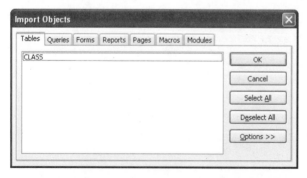

Figure 16-8 When you import data from another Access database, you have the option of importing the tools you created in that database as well.

> **Note** You also can use data from your Microsoft SharePoint Team Services data lists. To find out more about linking your Access database to SharePoint Team Services, see Chapter 17, "Working with Your Data."

Working with Forms

Many people find it easier (and friendlier) to work with forms instead of the datasheet. You can easily create forms that you or others can use with your Access data tables. And once you create the form, adding data is simply a matter of clicking and typing.

Creating a Form

To create a form, follow these steps:

1 Open the database you want to use.

2 In the database window, click Forms.

3 Double-click Create Form By Using Wizard. The Form Wizard steps in to help you create a data entry form for your database (as shown in Figure 16-9).

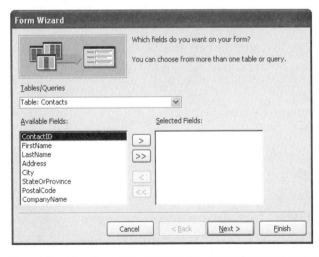

Figure 16-9 The Form Wizard walks you through the process of creating a data entry form for your data table.

Aha! Customized Forms

You also can choose Create Form In Design View, if you want to create a customized form on which you control where the fields and labels appear. This technique is a bit too involved for our purposes here (*fast* and *smart*, remember?), but feel free to experiment on your own.

4   Click the fields in the Available Fields list that you want to add to your form, then click Add after each one. The fields are added to your Selected Fields list.

5   When you're finished choosing fields, click Next. The Form Wizard asks you to choose a layout for the form you're creating. Select different options until you find the one you want, then click Next.

6   Choose the form style you like by scrolling through the list and selecting the one you want. Click Next.

7   Add a title for the form. You can choose to open the form after you create it or modify it. If you want to display a help window with information on working with forms, click the check box at the bottom of the Form Wizard window.

8   Click Finish to create the form.

> **Aha!**   Last Minute Changes
>
> If you choose to modify the form after you click Finish, the form is displayed in Design view. You can then change the look, color, alignment, and format of the labels and fields, using tools on the Formatting toolbar and the options available when you right-click the elements in the form.

Using a Form

When you are ready to add data by using the form you just created, display the database window and click Forms. Your new form appears in the right side of the database window. Add data to your data table using the form by following these steps:

1   Double-click the form name to open the form.

2   Click Last Record to move to the last record in the data table (if you've already entered data).

3   Click New Record to display a blank form.

4   Type the data in the fields, pressing Tab after each entry. At the end of the form, Access displays another blank form so that you can continue entering data.

5   When you're finished adding data, click the form's Close box. Access saves your data automatically and closes the form.

Saving a Database

Once you enter a database name, and save the database file in the File New Database window, Access takes care of saving your information for you automatically. Each time you add data to a form, Access saves the information and updates the data table. Whenever you close a datasheet view, Access asks whether you want to save what you've done. This is a nice feature, which saves you from entering an hour's worth of data, and then forgetting to save the file before you exit. All programs should be this thoughtful.

You can save Access data tables in other formats, however, so that you can use them with other things. Here are two options:

■   You can choose Save As on the File menu to save a database as a data access page (a Web page that also has a connection to a database).

■   You can select Export from the File menu to save the database in other popular formats, including XML documents, Microsoft Active Server Pages, HTML, Rich Text Format, and Excel.

For now, however, let's keep Access in Access and move on to the fun part—juggling all this interesting data you've collected.

Fast Wrap-Up

■   Access 2003 is a database program that enables you to collect, store, organize, use, and report on the data you collect.

■   Access gives you two methods for creating a database: You can use the Access Database Wizard or do it from scratch.

■   The database window contains the tables, forms, queries, reports, and other elements you'll work with in Access.

■   The Access Database Wizard suggests tables, fields, formats, and styles you can use for your data tables, forms, and reports.

■   When you create a database from scratch, you create only the database file; you'll need to add your own table, fields, forms, and reports.

■   When you create a database using the Access Database Wizard, the Main Switchboard enables you to enter, update, and report on data from a central menu.

■   Entering data in Datasheet view, or in a data-entry form, is a simple matter of typing the data and pressing Tab.

■   You can create a new table using the Table Wizard and a new form using the Form Wizard.

■   You customize a table or a form, arranging the layout and look of fields, by using Design view.

Working with Your Data   17

10-Second Summary
- ■ Sort data records
- ■ Search for data
- ■ Create and use queries
- ■ Work with relationships
- ■ Back up your data

Now that you've got the process of creating databases down, let's move on to what you'll actually do with the information you store. Although databases are good for storing information, their primary benefit is that they enable you to work with the data you've saved to see data trends, sales results, and future projects in new and enlightening ways. By sorting your data in a certain way, you'll be able to tell whether you sell more on the West coast or the East coast, for example, thereby helping you decide where to spend your advertising dollars. By searching for your top salespeople in the Northeast region, you can easily see who you need to take to dinner on your next trip north. And when you need to do damage control and orchestrate a recall (who purchased Model 2332 in Maine between July 15 and September 15 of last year?), you can use a query in Microsoft Office Access 2003 to find that information almost as quickly as you can type.

Sorting Data Records

One of the simplest operations you'll perform with your Access data involves sorting it. You can sort data by using either the datasheet or the data-entry form for a particular table. To sort records, follow these steps:

1 Open the database you want to use.

2 In the database window, double-click the data table or form you want to sort.

3 Click in the field that will be the organizing point for arranging your records. (For example, if you want to sort the records alphabetically by company name, click in the Company field. If you want the records sorted by customers' last names, click in the Lastname field.)

4 Click Sort Ascending or Sort Descending in the Standard toolbar. If you click Sort Ascending, the records are arranged from A to Z. If you click Sort Descending, the records appear arranged from Z to A.

> **Note**   If you prefer to use the menus, you can choose Sort from the Records menu and then choose Sort Ascending or Sort Descending from the submenu.

Searching for Data

See Also
Once you display the data you want to see, you can print the information in a report. See Chapter 18, "Preparing and Printing Reports in Microsoft Office Access 2003," to find out how to learn to print your displayed data.

Depending on what you want to do with the information you find, you can use a couple of techniques to search for data. The first technique helps you find a record you want. You might choose to search for a customer's address, for example, or to update a product code in your Products table. The second method involves searching for groups of records, by applying a filter that eliminates those records that are irrelevant. This section introduces you to both procedures.

Finding Specific Data

When you want to move to a specific record in your database, you first need to know what you're looking for. Are you looking for the record of a customer with the last name of Davis? That's enough to do a search. Here are the steps:

1 Display the data table or form you want to search.

2 Click in the field you want to search.

3 Choose Find from the Edit menu or press Ctrl+F. The Find And Replace dialog box appears (as shown in Figure 17-1). Notice that the selected field appears in the Look In box.

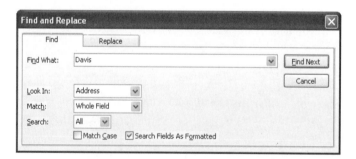

Figure 17-1 You can search for specific data items using the Find And Replace dialog box.

> **Aha!**   Search Everywhere
>
> If you're working with a large table and you're uncertain where the data you need to change is stored, you can have Access search the entire table by clicking the Look In down arrow, and choosing the name of the table.

4 In the Find What box, type the word, phrase, or characters you want to find.

5 Click the Match down arrow and choose whether you want Access to look for the information you typed in any part of the field, as the whole field (meaning that Access will display only records that show exactly what you typed in the field you selected), or as the beginning of the field entry.

6 In the Search list, choose whether you want Access to search Down through the database from the current selection, Up to the beginning of the database, or All the way through the entire database.

7 If you want Access to search for the capitalization you entered in the Find What box, click the Match Case check box.

> **Aha!**   If Appearances Are Deceiving ...
>
> The Search Fields As Formatted check box enables you to search for data as it is displayed, instead of how it is stored. This means, for example, that although a value might be stored as 2345, you can search for $2,345, if that's the way the information appears. This search feature can add extra time while you're waiting for results, however, so if you want your data fast, leave this box unchecked.

8 Click Find Next. If you are using a form, Access displays the next form with the information you're looking for. If you are using datasheet view, Access highlights the field entry that matches your criteria.

And Don't Forget Replace

The Replace feature comes in handy for times when you need to make a change throughout your database. For some reason, here in Indiana, they keep changing our area codes. Phone numbers in some areas that used to have a 317 prefix now have a 765 prefix. Talk about messing up someone's database! Now all your entries for Madison County are wrong. How will you fix it? Simply perform the following steps:

1 Open the data table with the entries you want to change.

2 Click in the field you want to change (in this case, Phone).

3 Press Ctrl+H (or choose Replace from the Edit menu).

4 In the Find What box, type the data you want to find (in this case, 317).

5 In the Replace With box, type the information you want to insert (in this case, 765).

6 Set the Match and Search options, then click Replace to replace the next occurrence of the data, or click Replace All to search the entire database and change all occurrences within the data table.

Applying Filters

A filter is a bit like a water purifier—it strains out all the elements you don't want. When you apply a filter to your data table, you tell Access to display only the data records that match what you're looking for. Here's the process:

1 Display the table or form to which you want to apply the filter.

2 Choose Filter from the Records menu, then choose one of the following:

- Filter By Form displays a form in which you can enter your filter conditions.

- Filter By Selection allows you to choose the filter by clicking existing data in the record.

- Filter Excluding Selection eliminates the selected data, and displays everything else.

- Advanced Filter/Sort displays a window in which you can construct a more detailed filter for your database.

3 For the simplest filtering tasks, you can select Filter By Form. A blank form appears (if you're viewing the datasheet, a blank table with one row appears).

4 Click in the field you want to use as a filter, then click the drop-down arrow that appears, and select your choice from the list. Figure 17-2 shows an Owner filter applied to the Contact Title field.

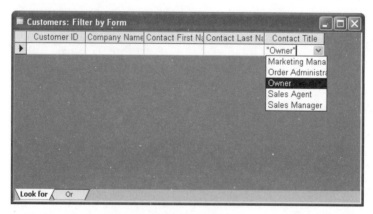

Figure 17-2 When you choose Filter By Form, you use a blank form or datasheet row to choose the data by which you want to filter your records.

5 Select any additional fields you'd like to use as part of the filter.

6 Click Apply Filter in the toolbar. Only the records that pass muster with your filter are displayed.

> **Aha!**   Getting Rid of Unwanted Filters
>
> Use Remove Filter/Sort from the Records menu (or click the Remove Filter tool on the toolbar) when you want to return the table or form to its full record display. If you want to use the filter again, you can choose Apply Filter/Sort from the Records menu (or click Apply Filter in the toolbar) to reapply the most recently used filter.

Working with SharePoint Data Lists

Access 2003 enables you to work with data stored on a Microsoft SharePoint Team Services Web site. SharePoint Team Services sites provide a gathering place for shared documents and meeting workspaces, giving you everything you need to organize projects, communicate with team members, assemble your resources, and share information. SharePoint sites include many different types of lists—for example, announcements, events, document libraries, links, tasks, contacts, and more—that you can import into your Access data tables.

To import SharePoint data, begin by opening the database you want to use. Choose Get External Data from the File menu, select Import, and in the Files Of Type field, choose SharePoint Team Services. When prompted, provide the URL of the SharePoint site you want to access, and click OK. The Import SharePoint Team Services Wizard begins (see Figure 17-3).

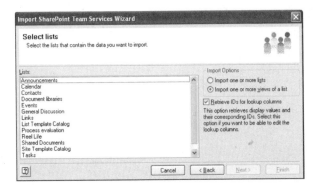

Figure 17-3   You can import data from all SharePoint lists by using the Import wizard.

Choose the list you want to import, and click Next. Choose the views that you want to import from the displayed list, and click Next again. Finally, click Finish. Access imports the information and places it in a table in the Database window.

Creating and Using Queries

The word "query" is one of those fancy-sounding words for something really simple. A query is a question. When you query an Access database, you ask it a question, such as:

- How many salespeople in Oregon sold more than 1,200 books last March?

- Which of our regional offices works the longest hours?

- How many students took advantage of our online courses last semester? And which classes were most popular?

You might think answering these kinds of questions would take hours of fact-digging. In fact, they can be answered in less than a minute in Access, if you've set up your fields correctly, and know how to use queries. This section introduces you to this time-saving feature.

Composing a Query

Your first task in creating a query that delivers the results you want is to tell Access what you need to find. Click Queries in the Database window to start the process. Then follow these steps:

1 Double-click Create Query By Using Wizard. The Simple Query Wizard appears (see Figure 17-4).

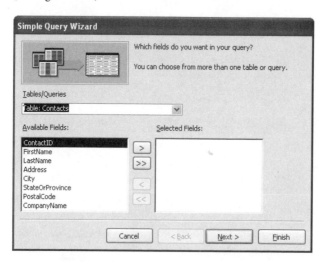

Figure 17-4 The Simple Query Wizard walks you through the process of creating your first query.

2 In the Tables/Queries box, choose the name of the table you want to use.

3 Click the field (or fields) from the Available Fields list that you want to add to the Selected Fields list (these are the fields you will use in the query). Click the Add button to add each field. Click Next.

4 Add a title for your query. Leave the other settings as they are. Click Finish. Click the Close box of the query window that appears.

Applying a Query

Now that you've created the query, you need to apply it to your database. Because you assigned the query a name, you can use that query on this or other tables at any time by selecting it from the Queries list in the database window. To apply a query to a table, follow these steps:

1 Display the database window for the database you want to query.

2 Click Queries in the left panel.

3 Double-click the query name from the list on the right. The information appears in the Query results window, showing you the latest query results based on the data in the data table as it currently stands.

> **Aha!**   Use Queries for Repeat Procedures
>
> Queries are very helpful when you need to know similar things periodically, such as who took the greatest number of vacation days last month, or which employees are due for rate increases. Once you create a query and name it, that query is available in the database window, and you can select it to apply it on your database monthly, weekly, and so on, to get the most up-to-date picture your data can present.

Modifying a Query

If you want to change a query you've created, you can simply edit the selections you've made. You do this using Design view. Here's how:

1 Display the database window for the database you want to use.

2 Click Queries in the left panel.

3 Double-click the query you want to use. The query opens in the query results window as usual.

4 Click Design View on the far left side of the Standard toolbar. The query appears in Design View (as shown in Figure 17-5 on the following page).

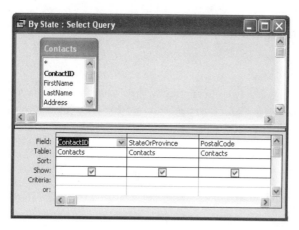

Figure 17-5 To modify a query, display it in Design View and change your selections.

5   To choose a different field, click in the Field entry and a down arrow appears. Click the arrow, and select the field you want from the displayed list.

6   If you want to choose a different table, click in the Table entry. Again, choose the table you want from the list that appears when you click the down arrow.

7   Make any other modifications as needed, then click Run on the toolbar. The modifications are applied to your data, and the query is saved in the new form.

Aha!   Delete Unnecessary Queries

If you want to do away with a query, simply click Queries in the database window, select the query you want to delete, and press Delete. Access will ask you to confirm that you want to delete the query. Click Yes to complete the operation.

More Fun with Queries

Queries are really wonderful, and can be quite complex, depending on what you want to do with them. Access includes five types of queries:

■   A *select query* allows you to select the data you're looking for.

■   A *crosstab* (short for cross-tabulation) *query* enables you to perform calculations based on the data values in query results.

■   A *make-table query* creates a table with the results of the query.

■   An *update query* goes through your database and updates records with new information.

■   An *append query* allows you to add information to the selected database.

For more information about working with these more specialized forms of queries, see *Microsoft Office Access 2003 Inside Out* by John Viescas, also from Microsoft Press.

Linking Tables

As you create tables and work with your data, you will begin to see ways that you can do even more with it. By linking tables, you can extend the functionality of your data by joining tables, and looking at the data in different ways. This section gives you a glimpse of relationships among tables, so that you can explore more thoroughly on your own.

Understanding Relationships

Access allows three kinds of relationships between tables:

- **One-to-one relationship**   This relationship is rarely used, because it typically can be handled within a single data table. However, an example of a one-to-one relationship might be when you want to link an employee's attendance record with a bonus schedule. The Employee ID field is the field unique to both tables, on which they would be linked.

- **One-to-many relationship**   This is the most common data relationship, in which one item in one table can be linked to many items in the second table. An example of a one-to-many relationship would be a link between a Sales Staff table and the Orders database. One salesperson can submit many different orders, but each order can have only one salesperson.

- **Many-to-many relationship**   This type of relationship is for complex data relationships, in which each item can be linked to multiple items. Access uses a third table, called a *junction table*, to store the primary and foreign keys (the fields on which the relationships are linked). An example of a many-to-many relationship is a book database, in which each book can be sold to multiple customers and be purchased from multiple vendors.

Creating Relationships

To create a link between tables, perform these steps:

1 Close any tables you have open, so that only the Database window is displayed.

2 Click Relationships on the Standard toolbar. If there are no relationships established in your database, the Show Table dialog box appears (as shown in Figure 17-6 on the following page).

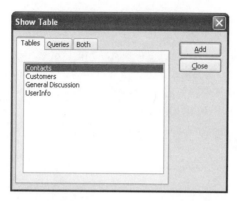

Figure 17-6 Use Show Table to choose the tables you want to use to set up relationships.

> **Note**   If you used the Access Database Wizard to create your database, links may already be established between your tables. In this case, the Show Table dialog box does not appear; instead, the Relationship window opens, showing the tables and the links established between them.

3   In the Show Table dialog box, click the Table, Queries, or Both tabs, depending on the items you want to include in your relationships. Select the tables you want to use, by clicking each one and clicking Add. When you're finished adding tables and queries, click Close, and the Relationships window is displayed (as shown in Figure 17-7).

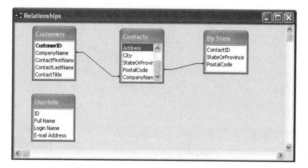

Figure 17-7 The Relationships window shows the tables among which you'll establish relationships.

4   To create a relationship between tables, drag the field from one table to the corresponding field in the second table. In the Edit Relationships dialog box, click Create. The link is made between the tables.

5   Close the Relationships window by clicking the close box. Access asks whether you want to save the layout of the tables. Click Yes.

Identifying Dependencies

When you begin to create relationships among tables, you create what's known as *dependencies*—that is, some tables, queries, forms, and reports rely on others to provide them with the necessary information. You can check the type and number of dependencies for an object you're thinking about changing by right-clicking the object in the Database window, and choosing the Object Dependencies option. The Object Dependencies task pane appears, listing the various items in your database, and showing you where dependencies exist (see Figure 17-8). You can show either those objects that depend on the selected item, or objects on which the selected item depends.

See Also
Chapter 18,
"Preparing and
Printing
Reports in
Microsoft Office
Access 2003,"
rounds out your
introduction to
Access by
showing you
how to generate
reports.

Figure 17-8   The Object Dependencies task pane shows you which other database objects depend on the selected one.

Backing Up Your Database

Access 2003 can easily create a backup copy of important database files by using the Back Up Database command directly from the File menu. When you choose the command, Access displays the Save Backup As dialog box, and names the database file with the current date, so that future backups do not overwrite previous versions (see Figure 17-9).

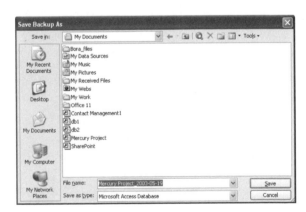

Figure 17-9   The new Back Up Database option enables you to easily create a backup copy of important files.

Fast Wrap-Up

■ Access enables you to sort your data easily—A to Z or Z to A—by clicking the tool you want on the Standard toolbar.

■ When you search for data in Access, you can use Ctrl+F to find a specific item, Ctrl+H to search and replace existing data, or a filter to display a group of records with the items you specify.

■ You can use queries to ask the database to show you something related to the data stored in the data tables. Access includes a wizard to help you create a query that will provide the best response to your question.

■ You can link tables to establish relationships among them. This enables you to perform operations—including sorts, searches, and queries—on a large table with many linked tables.

■ The new Object Dependencies command enables you to find out which objects depend on the selected object. This helps you make educated choices about what you want to change in the database.

■ Now you can back up your databases easily by using the Back Up Database command in the File menu.

Preparing and Printing Reports in Microsoft Office Access 2003

18

10-Second Summary

- Design a report
- Create the report
- Format and modify the report
- Save and print the report
- E-mail reports

They say we're all headed in the direction of the "paperless office," but I predict we're still at least a few years away from that scenario. As a general rule, we like to see things in black and white. We want to hand out reports at meetings; we want to give people printouts to take home and review; we need something to put in each other's mailboxes.

Once you've entered, sorted, modified, and organized your data, you're likely to want to produce some kind of cogent report. A report can show how well your business is growing—or where you need to cut back. A report can list your best-selling items, or shine a light on customer-service problems most likely to cause complaints. With Access, not only can you put your data in a logical, easy-to-understand form, but you can also make the results truly report-like, adding headers, footers—even charts and pictures that make your report visually appealing.

Note Once you create a report, Access makes it available in the database window, so that you can select it at any time. When you open the report, Access reads the data in the data table to which it is attached—which means that the report shows you the most current data you've entered each time you view it. An Access report is not like a static report you create in Microsoft Office Word 2003 or Microsoft Office Excel 2003; a report in Access retrieves any new data, so that you're always getting the most current picture of your database.

Creating a Report

Access once again comes to the rescue for the novice report writer, by providing a wizard to do the difficult part for you. The main steps for creating a report involve starting the wizard, answering the questions, and plugging in your own data. Here's the process:

1 Click Reports in the left side of the database window.

2 Double-click Create Report By Using Wizard. The Report Wizard starts (as shown in Figure 18-1).

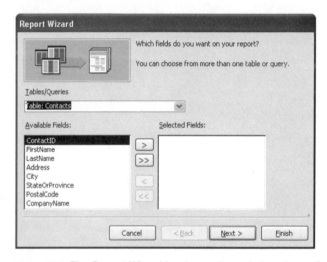

Figure 18-1 The Report Wizard leads you through the steps of generating a report based on the selected database.

3 In the Tables/Queries list, choose the name of the table or query that you want to use for the report.

4 In the Available Fields list, click the fields you want to add to the report; then click Add to display the field in the Selected Fields list. Click Next.

> **Aha!**   Everything, Please
>
> If you want to add all fields to the Selected Fields list at one time, click Add All in the center of the Report Wizard dialog box.

5 The next page of the wizard asks you to choose a grouping level for the report. If you want to add a *grouping level*, click the field you want to use, and click Add. Then click Next to move to the next page of the wizard.

Lingo A *grouping level* is a field by which the data is grouped. For example, when you group records by state, you display records with matching state values together.

6 Next, you must choose the sort order for your records. You can choose from one to four fields, each arranged in either ascending or descending order. If you first want to sort your records by state, and then alphabetically by last name, you would choose State, Ascending, for the first entry in this window, and Last Name, Ascending, for the second entry.

> **Note** Because Access tailors your choices depending on the type of table and fields you select, your options may be different from the ones I mention here. The process is the same, but the actual fields you select for reporting will be related to the data you are reporting on.

7 Choose a format for the report by selecting one of the following choices:

- Columnar format displays all data fields together in a list, with each entry representing one record.

- Tabular format shows data in datasheet array, with columns representing fields and rows representing records.

- Justified format displays the report in a form-like array, showing one record per page.

On this page of the wizard, you also choose whether you want the report to appear in Portrait or Landscape orientation. As you learned earlier in the book, Portrait orientation prints the page in standard 8.5 × 11-inch vertical format, while Landscape orientation prints the report in horizontal, 11 × 8.5-inch format. Make your selections and click Next.

8 Choose a style for your report. Click through the list to find the style you want. When you've found it, click Next.

9 Type a name for the report, and click Finish. The report appears in Print Preview so that you can view, customize, and then print it.

Sprucing Up Your Report

Once you generate a report in Access, you can make some changes to give it a different look. Start by displaying the database window, and clicking Reports. The report you generated appears in the list to the right. Double-click it to open it. The report appears automatically in Print Preview, which presents you with a new toolbar. Here are the tools you'll use to work with your Access reports:

On the Print Preview toolbar, you find the selections you need to display the report in Design view (which enables you to add details, such as headers, footers, and graphics), change the way the report is shown in Print Preview, use the report in Word or Excel, display the database window, add an object to the report, or print the report. The sections that follow show you how to use these tools to make a few changes to the report you have created.

> **Caution**   Once you step outside the familiar wizard territory in Access, you'll find that things can quickly get very complicated. Before you experiment with modifying the report in Design view, be sure that you've gotten the whole story on how those changes will affect the display of your data. To learn how to navigate like an expert in Design view, see *Microsoft Office Access 2003 Inside Out* by John Viescas, published by Microsoft Press.

Changing Margin, Page, and Column Settings

Use the Setup tool on the Print Preview toolbar to display the Page Setup dialog box (as shown in Figure 18-2). In this dialog box, you can use the Margins tab to change the margins for your report (you might need to do this, for example, if you're putting the report in a binder). To change the margins for your report, click the Margin setting you want to change, and type a new value. The Sample window changes to show you how the new setting will look.

Figure 18-2   You can change the print margins for your report using the Page Setup dialog box.

Click the Page tab if you want to change the orientation of the report. You might want to print the document in Landscape orientation, for example, if you are trying to fit as many columns on the page as possible. You can also use the choices on the Page tab to choose the paper size and source, and to select the printer on which you'll print the report.

The Columns tab enables you to control the columns in which your report is printed. One tricky point here: the word *columns*, in this context, does not refer to the fields in your report—instead, it refers to the column printout of the entire report. By default, this is set to one column, and unless you have a special use for columns in Access, leave the default as it is to avoid unwanted changes in your report.

> **Note** Are you wishing for an easier way to make your reports look good? The next section shows you how to publish your reports in Word so that you can fine-tune their layout and make them professional and polished.

Publishing Reports in Word

One of the great advantages about working with a system of programs such as the Microsoft Office System, is that you can share the talents of the different programs, no matter what kind of data you are working with. After you create a report in Access, you can use the OfficeLinks command to send it to Word, where you can fix it up with your favorite formats and frills. To publish a report in Word, follow these steps:

1   Click Reports, and select the report you want in the right panel.

2   Click Preview. The report appears in Print Preview.

3   Click the OfficeLinks down arrow on the toolbar; then select Publish It With Microsoft Word. A message box appears, telling you that the report is being printed to Word. The document is saved in a file with the same name as your Access report, but it is given the .rtf (rich text format) extension. The report appears in the Word window. You can now change the report in any way you choose, formatting or enhancing the report as a Word document.

> **Note** When you publish Access data in Word, the data does not remain linked to its original source in your Access database. This means that if you change the data in Access, the report published in Word will not reflect those changes. To make sure you have the most accurate, up-to-date information in your Access reports published in Word, be sure to use Publish It With Microsoft Word in OfficeLinks regularly.

Deleting Reports

When a report no longer serves your purpose, you can easily delete it from the database window to free up room for other new, improved, reports. Here are the steps:

1   Click Reports in the Database window.

2   Click the report you want to delete.

3 Click the Delete button, or press Delete. Access asks you whether you want to continue with the deletion of the report, and warns you that you cannot recover the file once it's deleted.

4 Click Yes to delete the report.

> **Aha!**   Data Remains Intact
>
> When you delete a report, you aren't doing anything to the data used to *create* the report. The data remains intact within the data table in which it is stored.

Printing Reports

When you're ready to print the report you've created in Access, you can do so in several ways:

- Right-click the report in the database window, and select Print from the context menu.

- Select the report in the database window and press Ctrl+P.

- Choose Print from the File menu.

- Click Print when the report is displayed in Print Preview.

The first three methods display the Print dialog box, so that you can choose your printer, specify the print range, and enter the number of copies you want. If you click Print while you're viewing the report in Print Preview, however, the report is sent directly to the printer with the default options.

E-mailing Reports

If you send a report to the home office regularly, you can e-mail it directly from Access. Here's how to do it:

1 Click Reports in the Database window.

2 Right-click the report you want to send in the right panel of the database window.

3 Select Send To in the shortcut menu; then choose Mail Recipient (as Attachment). The Send dialog box appears, as shown on the following page:

4 Select Text Files (which saves data in a tabular format), then click OK.

5 If the Choose Profile dialog box appears, click the Profile Name down arrow, and choose the name of the e-mail program you want to use to send the report. Click OK. A new e-mail message then appears, with your Access report included as an attachment.

Fast Wrap-Up

- The Report Wizard in Access helps you generate a quick report, and prompts you to choose the fields, sort order, style, and title you want.

- Once you create a report, use Print Preview to display it and review the data.

- You can add page and report headers and footers by working in Design view.

- If you want to add formatting enhancements to your report, you can use the OfficeLinks feature to publish the report in Word.

- You can print a report by pressing Ctrl+P, right-clicking the report name and clicking Print, or selecting Print while in Print Preview mode.

- To delete a report, simply select it in the database window and press Delete.

- You can e-mail a report by choosing Send To from the File menu, and choosing Mail Recipient (As Attachment).

Part 7
Microsoft Office FrontPage 2003: Design Effective Web Pages

Wherever you go in the Microsoft Office System, you'll find the ability to create Web pages—in Microsoft Office Word 2003, Excel 2003, and PowerPoint 2003. But when you want a real Web site—complete with multiple pages, numerous links, text, graphics, rollovers, and more—you want FrontPage 2003. This section shows you how to capitalize on the great new features in FrontPage 2003, and build professional-quality Web sites quickly.

FrontPage 2003 Basics 19

10-Second Summary
- ■ Create a Web site
- ■ Use a Web package
- ■ Add text to Web pages
- ■ Insert graphics
- ■ Create links
- ■ Preview and save Web pages

A Web page is really nothing more than a text file coded in a certain way that allows headings, text, and graphics to be displayed in a browser window. The codes themselves are quite simple, and the rules are pretty easy to remember. You create a *link* in your document that enables visitors to move to another page by clicking the link. The page links to another page, which links to another page, and so on. Before long, you have the World Wide Web.

FrontPage is a powerful, yet surprisingly easy, Web creation program that gives you a friendly way to create sites without having to work with Hypertext Markup Language (HTML) code. You can use the menus, tools, options, and palettes to add the items you want in the way you want them to appear. FrontPage also helps you work with what could be very complicated elements—forms, rollovers, animations, and more— in an easy-to-use, no-coding interface. For those of us who slept through most of computer science, that's good news.

Note For the first time in the Office System, Frontpage 2003 is offered as a stand-alone product. To find out more about FrontPage go to *www.microsoft.com*.

New Features in FrontPage 2003

FrontPage 2003 includes many new features that expand what you can do with the Web pages you create and make the creation process easier than ever. Here are some of the new features you'll see in this version of FrontPage:

- ■ The new window layout gives you more room on-screen to work.
- ■ New Web packages help you create data-driven sites quickly.

- Improved views enable you to design, code, and preview your pages more easily (you can also use Split view to see both Code and Design views at the same time).

- Layout tables take the hassle out of table formatting, and give you a library of tools for your own customized effects.

- Extensible Markup Language (XML) support throughout FrontPage lets you add XML functionality to your Web sites.

- Dynamic Web templates allow you to create and share an HTML template that updates all pages based on that design template.

- Now you can create Web modules for use with SharePoint Team Services sites that enable you to package a specific Web part and distribute it to other sites.

> **Note** These are simply the most prominent of the new features in FrontPage 2003, but there's a lot more to see. To learn more about new and improved features for creating, editing, publishing, and maintaining your site, display the Microsoft FrontPage Help task pane, and click What's New in the See Also section.

What Can You Do with FrontPage?

The most obvious answer to this question is, of course, *create a Web site*. But perhaps the bigger question—and the one you'll need to spend some time considering before you start work—is, What do you want to *do* with your Web site?

In its relatively short life span, the World Wide Web has grown from a fairly ugly, primarily text-based medium to a high-energy, moving, colorful communications channel that offers text, graphics, video, and sound. Once the domain of engineers and data architects, the Web now belongs to everybody—from governments to companies, from grandparents to schoolteachers. And today we're finding more uses for the Web as well. Instead of simply using Web pages as a way to provide information to those who are looking for it, we can buy and sell almost anything, and store, share, and work with our information on the Web in new and exciting ways.

So, what will you do with a Web site you create in FrontPage? Here are just a few possibilities:

- Create a professional Web site for your company, complete with an About Us page, a corporate directory, a customer-service page, and a page describing your products and services.

- Publish your college coursework to the Web, so that your distant students can follow along with the presentations you give in class.

■ Make the annual reports of your nonprofit organization available online, so that potential donors can find out more about you and what you do.

■ Create an e-commerce site for your small business that enables you to sell items from an online catalog (see the section on Microsoft bCentral later in this chapter).

■ Design a team site your employees can create and use collaboratively, using Microsoft SharePoint Team Services.

See Also
Chapter 21, "Publishing Your Pages," walks you through the steps involved in actually getting your pages on the Web.

The FrontPage Workspace

Start Microsoft FrontPage by clicking Start, choosing All Programs, Microsoft Office, and selecting Microsoft FrontPage 2003. The FrontPage window opens (see Figure 19-1). You'll recognize the familiar Office menu bar and toolbars, as well as the Getting Started task pane.

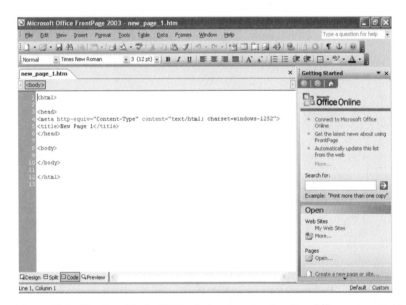

Figure 19-1 The FrontPage 2003 window has the familiar Office menu and toolbars, but includes special features related to Web work.

FrontPage Views

FrontPage 2003 has made viewing and working with your site—and individual pages—easier than ever. When you're working in the Web Site tab, six different site views are available:

📁Folders 🖳Remote Web site 📄Reports 🔀Navigation 🔗Hyperlinks ⏱Tasks

- **Folders view**   Shows the folders and files of the open Web page.

- **Remote Web site**   Enables you to compare local and remote sites, and publish and synchronize files.

- **Reports view**   Allows you to check the status of various elements in your site.

- **Navigation view**   Shows you the navigation structure users will follow as they use your site.

- **Hyperlinks view**   Displays all the links among pages in your site.

- **Tasks view**   Lists the various tasks that still need to be completed, and shows their current status.

When you are working on an individual page, a different set of view controls appears that enables you to choose the way you want to see a specific page:

📃Design 🗗Split 🖻Code 🔍Preview

- **Design view**   Displays the page, showing text boundaries and placeholder items.

- **Split view**   Shows a two-panel window with both Code and Design views.

- **Code view**   Displays the HTML and XML code for your Web page.

- **Preview view**   A read-only view that shows you how the page will look on the Web.

Although you may do most of your work in Design view, the new Split view makes it easy to switch back and forth between Design view and Code view. That means you can make a change in the HTML code for your page, and immediately see it reflected in the Design portion of the Split window.

Where Will Your Web Site Go?

Before you create a Web page, think about where it will appear. You'll need to have a hosting location for the site—an account with an Internet service provider, or ISP. There are many national and local ISPs who can set you up with a Web account and give you a Universal Resource Locator, or URL (often known as a Web address). The URL is the piece of information you need to tell FrontPage where your finished Web site will appear.

Creating a Web Site

The process for creating a Web site is easier than you might think. If you don't need to add anything fancy—perhaps just a couple of headings, some body text, and a picture or two—you
can create a Web page in just minutes. We'll take this simple path to illustrate Web page basics.

1 Start Microsoft FrontPage. If the task pane doesn't appear, choose New from the
File menu.

2 In the New Web Site area, click One Page Web Site.

3 In the Web Site Templates dialog box, shown in Figure 19-2, click the different
template icons to find the one you want. The Description area changes to show
you what each of the Web sites are meant to do. Select the template you want to
use, then click OK.

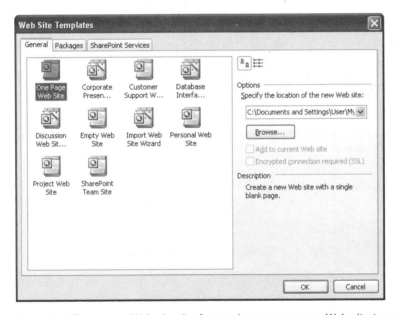

Figure 19-2 To create a Web site the fast and easy way, use a Web site template.

Some Web site templates include wizards that walk you through the process of creating the
Web site; others do not. The Corporate Presence Wizard, used in this example, illustrates
the various steps in putting together a Web site. For example, the Corporate Presence Wizard asks about the following:

■ The main pages you want on your site (for example, What's New, Products/
Services, and so on).

■ The topics you want to be displayed on your home page.

■ The topics you want to address on your What's New page (assuming that you
selected it as a main page you want to include).

- The number of products and services pages you want to create.

- Specific details about what you want to include for information about your products and services.

- The information you want to request from visitors filling in the feedback form on your site.

- Whether the information in the feedback form should be saved in tab-delimited format so that you can easily use it in a database.

- Items about your table of contents page, such as whether you want to update it automatically and use bullets to identify main pages.

- What you want to appear at the top (header) and bottom (footer) of each Web page in your site.

- Whether you want to display an "under construction" icon on those pages that you're working on.

- The title of your company, the short name (if you have one), and the company address.

- Your company's contact info, including telephone, fax, and e-mail addresses.

As you can see, the FrontPage Web Wizard doesn't leave much to chance. Once you answer all these different questions, you can click Finish, and FrontPage builds the site, displaying all the created pages and folders in Folders view in the Web Site window (see Figure 19-3).

> **Note** If you use the Corporate Presence Wizard, one last question asks whether you'd like to see what needs to be done next in Tasks view. When you click Finish, Tasks view appears, with the various Web-creation tasks listed in order of priority.

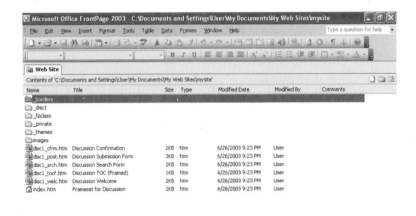

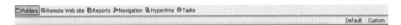

Figure 19-3 After FrontPage creates the site, the pages and folders appear in Folder view in the Web Site window.

Aha!   A Quick Look at Pages

To open any one of the pages you've just created, double-click it in Folders view. To return to Folders view, simply click the Web Site tab to display all pages and folders for the current site.

Using a Web Package

FrontPage includes so many features that it's a bit of a challenge to find all the things that could make your use of the Web smarter and more efficient. For that reason, FrontPage 2003 includes Web packages that help you easily create data-driven Web sites for several different functions. You can choose from an Issue Tracker for recording, organizing, and resolving issues in your project; a News and Reviews Site, and a Web Log, which enables you to post log entries, have discussions, add links, and more.

Begin using a Web package by choosing New from the File menu, and clicking Web Package Solutions in the New task pane. Then, in the Web Site Templates dialog box, choose the package you want to create (see Figure 19-4 on the following page), and click OK.

Note   FrontPage will display a message that the package must be created on a system running SharePoint Team Services. If you do not have SharePoint running on your local system, you can enter the URL of your SharePoint Team Services site, and create the package at that remote location.

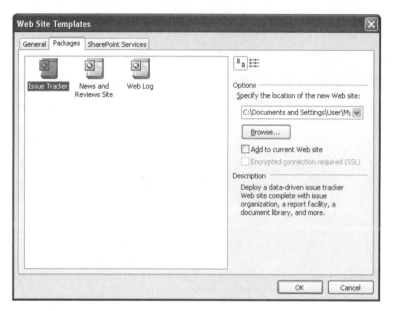

Figure 19-4   You can use one of FrontPage's new Web packages to create a specialized data-driven site.

In the Import Web Package dialog box, click the items you want to import into your new Web site, and click Import. The Web site is built, and you can add text, graphics, and create links as usual.

FrontPage and SharePoint Team Services

Throughout this book, you've learned about SharePoint Team Services, the Microsoft Web application that enables you to easily gather, store, organize, and share data, and work collaboratively in a central location online. SharePoint Team Services enables you to create custom team Web sites with announcements, events, links, discussions, document libraries, and more.

Within FrontPage, you have the capability of creating your own SharePoint sites and publishing them on the Web. You create a new SharePoint team site by choosing SharePoint Based Team Web Site in the New Web Site area of the New task pane. In the Web Site Templates dialog box, choose SharePoint Team Site, enter the URL for the site in the location box, and click OK. FrontPage builds the site on the server you specified, and displays the pages and folders in Folders view. Click default.aspx to display the default Team Services page and begin adding your own content.

Working in Tasks View

Tasks view (shown in Figure 19-5) isn't the prettiest display in the world, especially if you are eager to see what your newly created Web site will look like. But Tasks view serves a useful purpose, and that's why we're exploring it here. Especially when you are new to creating Web sites, remembering what you need to do—in what order—can be difficult. Tasks view takes that guesswork out of Web creation, by giving you a list of tasks to complete. Once you finish them, you're done. It's that simple.

Figure 19-5   Tasks view gives you a list of items to accomplish on your way to a finished Web site.

Double-click the first task in the list. The Task Details dialog box appears (see Figure 19-6), showing you the status of the task, and information about it. Click Start Task to begin working on your new Web site. FrontPage changes to Page view, and displays the new site in the work area.

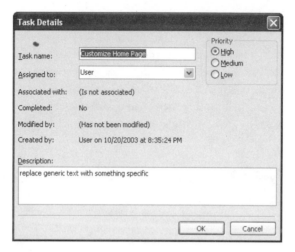

Figure 19-6   Double-click a task to change its status and assignment.

Web Lingo

The Web has brought with it a new language. The following list gives you a quick overview of what each of these terms means:

- **Hand-coding**   Using HTML codes to prepare a document for the Web. You can use any text editor (such as WordPad in Microsoft Windows XP) to hand-code Web pages. FrontPage allows you to use menus and tools to bypass coding (although you can still work with code if you like, by clicking the HTML tab at the bottom of the work area).

- **Home page**   The page of a Web site that appears when a visitor first logs on to the site.

- **HTML**   An acronym for Hypertext Markup Language, HTML is the simple coding system used to prepare documents for display on the Web.

- **Hyperlink**   Also called a *link*, this is a connection established between pages that enables a visitor to move from one page to another.

- **URL**   An acronym for Universal Resource Locator, the URL is the Web address of the site, often appearing in the form *http://www.webaddress.com*.

- **Web site**   A collection of Web pages organized around a particular topic, company, school, or group.

- **Web page**   An individual page within a Web site.

Adding Text to a Web Page

The next step in making your Web site truly your own is adding text to the home page. When you open that first task, the page you'll see is the home page created by the Web wizard. Prompts are entered in the various areas on the page to give you ideas about what you might enter there.

To replace a comment with your text, click in the comment to select it, highlighting the entire paragraph. Type the text you want to add. Depending on the template you used to create the site, the text you enter might appear in a different color than the prompt text (this is a helpful feature that keeps you from accidentally leaving prompt text on the page); the font and style of the text you enter is the same as the prompt text. Continue replacing the prompt text with your text until you've added everything you need to add.

> **Aha!**   Copy and Paste into FrontPage
>
> You also can copy text from another Office System program into FrontPage. If you select and copy a bulleted list in Word, for example, the list appears in FrontPage with the same formatting applied in the original document. This gives you a quick way to use text you've already entered once (and can help you make sure your Web site is consistent with other documents you've created for your company).

Modifying Text

You can change the font, style, and color used on your Web site, in much the same way you change text in a Word document: Highlight the text you want to change, then click the tool you want to use on the Formatting toolbar. Here are a few ideas of the kinds of text changes you might want to make while you're working on your Web site:

- Click Font Color to change the color of selected text.
- Click the Font down arrow to choose a different font.
- Click Align Center or Align Right to change the text alignment.
- Click Increase Font Size or Decrease Font Size to make the selected text a size larger or smaller.
- Click the Border tool to add a border around selected text.

Applying a Web Theme

Whether you use a wizard or a template to create your Web page, you may want to change the design scheme—colors, fonts, and more—to get a different look. You can experiment with overall design by changing your site's Web theme. Here's how:

1 Choose Theme from the Format menu.

2 In the Theme task pane, scroll through the list of themes, and click the down arrow on the right edge of the one you want.

3 Choose whether you want to apply the theme as the default for the entire site or for the selected page only (see Figure 19-7). FrontPage applies the new theme as you select.

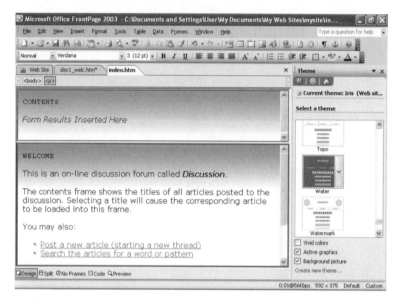

Figure 19-7 You can choose a theme to give your Web site a coordinated look and feel.

Aha!   Limiting Graphics

If you want to limit the graphical effects in the theme you choose, click the Active Graphics and Background Picture check boxes to remove those special effects. The samples shown in the task pane change to show you the difference; you can select the theme you want, and know that it is as lean in the graphics department as possible (which means it will appear on your visitors' monitors faster).

Aha!   Test in Different Browsers

Not all browsers display Web pages the same way. What looks great in Internet Explorer might be less attractive in Netscape. So even though you enable these options to make your site look the best it can, be sure to test the display in more than one browser.

Inserting Graphics for the Web

One of the great advantages of the Web wizards in FrontPage is that they take care of a lot of the design for you. But when you have your own images to import, how do you do it? Simple. Start in Design view, then choose Picture from the Insert menu. A drop-down list of choices appears. Here's what each of those choices does:

- **Clip Art**   Displays the Clip Organizer, so that you can choose a piece of clip art to include on the page or download clips from the Web.

- **From File**   Displays the Picture dialog box, so that you can navigate to the folder you want, and select the file you want to insert.

- **From Scanner Or Camera**   Displays the Insert Picture From Scanner Or Camera dialog box, so that you can begin scanning or downloading images from your scanner or camera.

- **New Photo Gallery**   Opens the Photo Gallery Properties dialog box, so that you can create and insert a collection of photos on your page.

- **New Drawing**   Displays the drawing tools, so that you can add your own art to the Web page.

- **AutoShapes**   Displays the AutoShapes palette, enabling you to add pre-drawn shapes on your site. AutoShapes are great for adding buttons quickly, or creating special design elements for your site.

- **WordArt**   A feature that allows you to do special things with text. To use WordArt, choose the option from the menu, and then select the style you want from the WordArt Gallery. In the Edit WordArt Text dialog box, type the text you want to add to the Web page, then click OK. The text item is placed as an object on your page, so that you can move it, resize it, or rotate it as needed.

- **Video**   Displays the Video dialog box, so that you can choose a video file you've prepared for the Web.

Aha!   Add a Photo Gallery

If you have a collection of photos you'd like to display on a favorite Web site, you can use the FrontPage Photo Gallery feature to gather and display them in the format you want. In Design view, choose Picture from the Insert menu, then click New Photo Gallery. In the Photo Gallery Properties dialog box, click Add; then choose Pictures From Files, or Pictures From Scanner Or Camera, depending on whether you're using files you've saved, or scanning or importing digital images. Select the image(s) you want, and click Open. Finally, click the Layout tab, and choose the layout you want for your images; then click OK.

Viewing Navigation Paths and Links

Once you create the Web site, add the text, and insert the pictures, you're ready to see how your site fits together. When you use a wizard to create the site, the navigation system (the way in which you move from page to page) and the linking is already done. The navigation buttons appear along the left, top, and bottom of the page (depending on the choices you selected in the wizard), and the links are already made, so that when you click the Preview tab and click one of the buttons, you are taken to that page.

When you want to view the navigation system the wizard established for you, display the site in Navigation view by clicking the Navigation icon on the Views bar at the bottom of the Web Site tab. The Navigation window shows icons of each page, with lines connecting the pages to which they are linked. You can collapse and expand the navigation diagram by clicking the minus (-) and plus (+) buttons in the bottom center of linked pages (as shown in Figure 19-8).

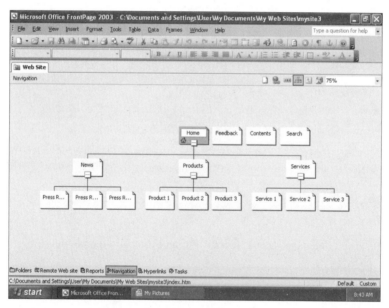

Figure 19-8   The Navigation window shows you how the pages in your Web site are linked.

While you're working in Navigation view, you can add new pages, move linked pages to a different page, include selected pages on navigation bars, rename pages, and delete pages. To work with an individual page, right-click the page, and choose the option you want from the shortcut menu that appears.

You also can use Hyperlinks view to see which pages are linked. This is a pretty amazing view—worth at least a quick look. When you have displayed some of the links by clicking the + buttons beside each page icon, the display looks something like Figure 19-9. Staggering, isn't it? By viewing the links on this simple wizard-generated site, you get an idea of why this medium is known as the "Web."

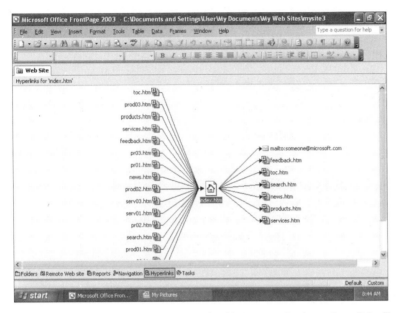

Figure 19-9   The links between pages (and between sites) are the sticky fibers that make this online world a Web.

Selling on the Web

Selling on the Web is becoming big business, although most retail outlets are still having trouble maintaining their equilibrium in a rapidly changing online marketplace. Not to be daunted by folding dot-coms, however, new Internet businesses spring to life hourly around the globe. And everybody is thinking about e-commerce. How will your business make money on the Web? And how much do you have to shell out to create a professional—and profitable—e-commerce-capable Web site?

Microsoft has at least one answer for small businesses who want to dip a toe into the Internet marketplace without mortgaging the farm to do it. Microsoft bCentral is a FrontPage add-in and service that helps you build e-commerce capability into your Web site. When you download the bCentral add-in, you are given templates that help you design your own catalog and e-commerce pages, add a shopping cart, create an online store, manage your sales, and process the orders you receive. Then, once your site is in place, you can subscribe to the bCentral.com service, and pay a monthly fee to have bCentral manage all these different e-commerce components for you. For more information about these and other bCentral.com services, visit *http://www.bcentral.com.*

Aha!   Showcase Your Services

Microsoft Office Online also includes the Office Marketplace, which enables you to list your services in business-to-business categories such as Creating Documents, Reference, Calendars and Printing, Content Management, Communication and Collaboration, Analysis Tools, and Training and Assistance. To visit Office Marketplace, make sure you're online, display the Help task pane, and click Connect To Office on Microsoft.com.

Previewing the Page

Previewing the Web site is simple—just click Preview in the page view tabs along the bottom-left side of the work area. The text and graphic frames are hidden, so that you see what the visitors to your Web page will see. FrontPage 2003 gives you additional controls over Preview, so that you can view your site in a variety of different screen resolutions and browsers. To see your range of choices, click the down arrow to the right of the Preview in Microsoft Internet Explorer 6.0 tool. The following list of preview choices appears so that you can click your choice:

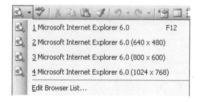

Aha!   Adding Browsers

If you want to add browsers to the preview list, click Preview in Microsoft Internet Explorer 6.0, and choose Edit Browser List. In the Edit Browsers List dialog box, click Add, and enter the name of the browser you want to use, as well as its startup command. Click OK to add the browser, and click OK a second time to return to your Web page.

Preview is a read-only mode, which means that you can only view—and not edit—the page in Preview mode. If you see changes you want to make, click Normal to make your changes in that view.

> **Aha!**   From Web to Print
>
> To get a quick printout of the current page as it will appear on the Web, click the Print button on your browser's toolbar. This prints the page without frame lines, so that you can review how the page shows up on the Web.

Saving the Page

When you're ready to save your Web site, choose Save from the File menu. If you had opened the page from Tasks view, a shortcut box appears, asking whether you want to mark the task as completed. If you do, click Yes. If you plan to work more on the task later, click No.

> **Note**   Because the wizard generates the pages, and names them so that each link refers to the correct page file, you do not specify a new name during the Save procedure, as you would when saving other application files. It's important that the home page is named index.htm and the additional main pages keep their original names.

Okay, now you've been through the process of creating a Web site with FrontPage. Hopefully it was easier than you thought. This chapter has touched on the basic instructions for creating a site. You continue the process in Chapter 20, "FrontPage Special Tasks," where you learn how to add some bells and whistles, and then you'll publish the site to the Web in Chapter 21, "Publishing Your Pages."

Fast Wrap-Up

- FrontPage 2003 is a stand-alone Web site creation and management program that works seamlessly with your other Office applications.

- You can use FrontPage to create sites quickly from scratch, using the program's Web templates. New Web packages make it easy to create data-driven Web sites.

- The four basic page views available when you're working on a page—Design, Split, Code, and Preview—enable you to see your Web site from different perspectives.

- The six different site views—Folders, Remote Web Site, Reports, Navigation, Hyperlinks, and Tasks—let you work with the overall site in specific ways.

- Tasks view lists the items you need to accomplish during the creation of your site.

- Add your own text to a Web page by clicking the prompt text to highlight it and then typing. You can change the font, style, color, and alignment of text, as you would in a word-processing document. You also can copy text from other programs into FrontPage.

- FrontPage includes a number of options for the kinds of graphics you can add to your pages. You can use clip art, scanned images, WordArt, AutoShapes, and more. You also can create your own Photo Gallery, complete with captions, for display on a specific page.

- FrontPage 2003 allows you to preview your page in multiple browsers and screen resolutions. This shows you the way your site will appear on the Web, complete with working links, and enables you to see how other users will be viewing your site.

Microsoft Office FrontPage 2003 Special Tasks

20

10-Second Summary
- Add a table to your Web page
- Work with frames
- Add lines and boxes
- Create rollovers
- Work with HTML code

In the last chapter, you learned to use a Web Wizard to create a Web site, and then add text and graphics to your pages. With the templates and packages in Microsoft Office FrontPage 2003, you might wonder why Web development companies charge an arm and a leg to do this kind of thing. But rest assured that, although you are now a Web designer in your own right, there are still *many* things to learn. We've only scratched the surface of the capabilities of Microsoft Office FrontPage 2003, and this chapter takes you a little further into some of the specialized tasks you might want to try as you develop your Web pages.

The tasks and techniques in this chapter all pertain to making it easier for visitors to read and understand your site. People who browse the Web really have two basic needs: They need to be able to see clearly how to get around on your site, and they need to know what you want them to click. Adding tables, frames, lines, boxes, and rollover effects all help communicate the organization and structure of your site, so that visitors will enjoy their visit enough to come back again—a concept known in Web parlance as *stickiness*.

Adding Tables to Your Pages

A new table feature in FrontPage 2003, Layout Tables And Cells, makes it easier to create and control the layout of your Web pages. Layout tables are different from standard tables that show information in a column-and-row format; a layout table is actually a framework for your Web content, and layout cells are the areas in the larger layout where Web content is placed. Consider the example shown in Figure 20-1. You can see that the layout of the page is actually comprised of a series of small frames, or cells. You can fill each of those cells with any content you'd like—text, images, navigation bars, and more.

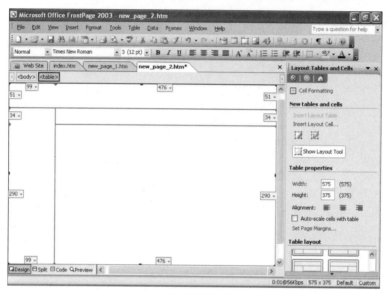

Figure 20-1   A layout table provides a framework to house the content of your Web page.

For traditional tables, you'll be pleased to see that the Insert Table feature in FrontPage is almost identical to that feature in Microsoft Office Word 2003. When you're ready to add a table to your Web page, position the cursor at the point where you want to create the table, then open the Table menu, and choose one of the following options:

- **Layout Tables and Cells**   Displays a task pane you can use to create a customized layout table.

- **Draw Table**   Enables you to draw a table freehand in the space you have available on the Web page. Using the pencil tool, draw the table in the size you want; then click and drag to draw the separator lines for rows and columns. Use the Tables toolbar, shown below, to customize your table to appear the way you want it.

- **Insert Table**   Displays the Insert Table dialog box, shown on the following page. Enter the number of rows and columns you want, then choose the layout settings that fit the space you want to use on the page. Add borders, colors, and a background if applicable. Click OK to add the table. You can then use the Table toolbar to customize the table further, by adding rows and columns, changing the alignment of text, changing the table color, or applying an AutoFormat.

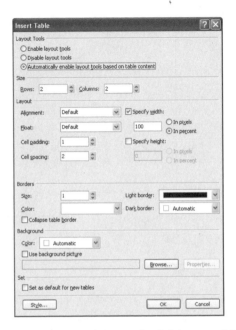

To add text to your table, simply click in one of the cells and type the information you want to place there. You also can add graphics, clip art, WordArt, and other objects to the cells in a table.

> **Aha!**   Add an Invisible Table
>
> Depending on the type of content you're adding to your site, you might want to create an invisible table that helps add behind-the-scenes structure to your site. You can use layout cells to create the framework, or just add a simple table on the page, and make the borders invisible. Simply right-click the table and choose Table Properties; then, in the Borders area, change the Size setting to 0. Click OK.

Working with Frames

If you've been tuned in to Web talk for any length of time, you know that there are some people who love *frames,* and some people who can't stand them. Some people think that frames are helpful navigation devices; others think that frames are clunky, interruptive, and annoying.

> **Lingo** A *frame* is a panel on your Web page that visitors can control independently of the other panels on the screen.

If you want to give frames a try, you'll be pleased to know that you can add frames to your pages easily in FrontPage. Some people choose to create vertical frames, positioning the navigation frame on the left, and the content area on the right. (If you save your Microsoft

Office PowerPoint 2003 presentations as a Web page, that is the way it's done.) Here's the process for adding frames to a Web page in your site:

1 Open the Web site you want to work with.

2 Click the down arrow to the right of the New tool in the Standard toolbar. Click Page.

3 Click the Frame Pages tab in the Page Templates dialog box.

4 Select the frame template you want, and click OK.

The new page appears, showing the frame style you have selected. As Figure 20-2 shows, the design isn't very exciting. But design isn't the next thing you need to worry about; you'll first need to tell FrontPage what to display in the different frame areas.

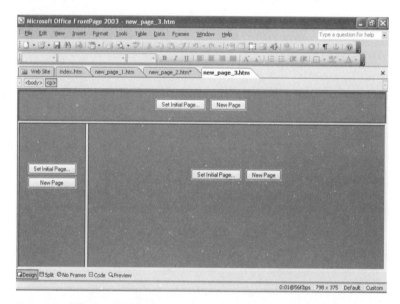

Figure 20-2 When you add a frame page to your site, you must tell FrontPage which content to display where.

If you want to add existing page content to a frame, click Set Initial Page to display the Insert Hyperlink dialog box (as shown in Figure 20-3). Select the page you want to display in the selected frame, then click OK.

Figure 20-3 When you click Set Initial Page, FrontPage displays the Insert Hyperlink dialog box, so that you can choose the page you want to use in that frame.

If you want to add new content to a frame, click New Page. That part of the frame opens, so that you can add text, pictures, and links.

5 Add the information and links as you would normally do. Then resize the frames, if necessary, by dragging the frame border in the direction you want to resize the frame.

6 Finally, preview the page by clicking the Preview tab at the bottom of the work area, then save and close your file as usual.

> **Aha!**   Preview in Multiple Browsers
>
> Because frames can behave differently in different browsers, for best results, test the display of your frames in at least two or three popular browsers before you publish your site to the Web. This helps you reduce the "Oops!" factor when you find out that people using Netscape Navigator can't see a heading underline, or that your boxes are cut off in Microsoft Internet Explorer. To preview the page, choose Preview In Browser from the File menu, then choose the browser and resolution you want to use.

Adding Lines and Borders

In the last chapter, you learned how easy it is to add pictures, WordArt, AutoShapes, and more to your Web pages. Other special items you might want to add are the graphical lines and boxes. Lines can help you show readers where one section begins and another ends on your Web page; borders can draw visitors' attention to an important point that you don't want them to miss.

The fastest and easiest way to add a dividing line to your Web page is to choose Horizontal Line from the Insert menu. FrontPage adds a line at the cursor position. You can change the look, width, color, and alignment of the line by right-clicking the line, and choosing Horizontal Line Properties. Set your choices in the Horizontal Line Properties dialog box (see Figure 20-4) and click OK to save the changes.

Figure 20-4   Modify your horizontal lines by right-clicking them and choosing Horizontal Line Properties.

Aha!   Add Custom Lines Quickly

If you want to add your own line quickly, click the Line tool in the Drawing toolbar. To keep the line straight, press and hold Shift while you draw the line. To change the color and style of the line, use the Line Color and Line Style tools on the Drawing toolbar.

Note   Remember that when it comes to adding design elements such as lines and borders, a little goes a long way. Because your ultimate objective is to create a site that is easy to navigate and fun to read (or at least informative), you don't want to make things more difficult for your readers by littering the page with unnecessary lines and boxes. Use these items sparingly and they'll be more effective. When in doubt, do without.

With that in mind, here's how to add a border to items on your current page:

1   Select the text or object around which you want to draw the border.

2   Click the Border down arrow on the Formatting toolbar. A palette of border options appears.

3   Click the border style you want, and it's applied to the selected area.

> **Aha!**   Choose a Border Alternative
>
> If you don't like a border once you've added it, press Ctrl+Z to undo your changes. Instead of doing away with the border altogether, however, you might want to experiment with other border styles to see whether there's something you like better. In addition, you can add shading to a selected area of your page by choosing Borders And Shading from the Format menu, and clicking the Shading tab. Click the Background color down arrow, and choose the color you want. Click OK to close the dialog box and return to your Web page.

Creating Rollovers

A *rollover* effect is a simple but effective way to help visitors to your Web site know what to do there. You can add rollovers to hyperlinks, so that the text changes font or color when pointed to; you can add rollovers to pictures, so that captions pop up over the image when the user positions the mouse pointer above it; and you can add rollovers that display additional buttons, rotate, or cause some other action to occur.

> **Lingo**   A *rollover* is the name of a special effect that causes a button, link, or image to change when the visitor positions the mouse on the object.

To create a rollover in FrontPage, follow these steps:

1   Begin with the page open in the FrontPage window. Make sure that Design view is selected.

2   Right-click the page area; then choose Page Properties from the shortcut menu.

3   In the Page Properties dialog box, click the Advanced tab.

> **Note**   You cannot apply rollover effects to a site that uses themes, so if you selected a theme when you created your site (as we did in Chapter 19, "First, the Basics"), rollovers won't be available to you. You can either create a new page with no theme or remove the theme from your existing site by choosing Theme from the Format menu, selecting (No Theme) in the Theme list, and then clicking OK.

4   Click the Enable Hyperlinks Rollover Effects check box; and then click Rollover Style to display a Font dialog box, where you can make the changes the rollover will display (as shown in Figure 20-5 on the following page).

Figure 20-5 Use the Font dialog box to add a rollover effect to a hyperlink, to make the link stand out when the visitor points to it.

5   After you make your changes, click OK; then click OK again in the Page Properties dialog box to return to your Web page.

6   Now click Preview to see how the rollover effect works when you point to links on the page.

> **Note**   You don't have to change these settings to create an eye-catching rollover; using a simple color change, and perhaps adding an effect also works.

Working with HTML Code

All this time we've been talking about ways to use the menus and tools in FrontPage, so that you don't have to use Hypertext Markup Language (HTML) to hand-code your pages. But I don't mean to suggest that coding is a bad thing—in fact, coding your Web page is fun and interesting, and knowing how to work with HTML gives you more control over your pages, and enables you to customize your site beyond what menus and wizards offer. If you're curious and want to see what all the behind-the-scenes code looks like, click the Code tab in the lower left portion of the FrontPage work area. The HTML tags appear within brackets in blue text, while the content you have entered (or that the wizard created for you) is shown in black text, as shown in Figure 20-6.

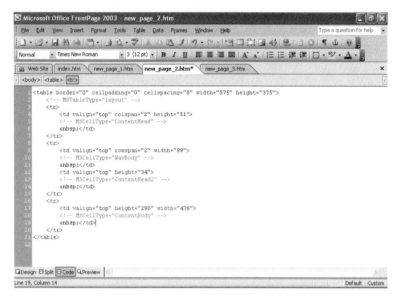

Figure 20-6   You can click the Code tab to take a look at the HTML source code for your Web page whenever you like.

Working in Split View

FrontPage 2003 also introduced the new Split view, which enables you to see both Design and Code view on-screen at the same time. This is a great convenience feature, because you no longer have to switch back and forth between Code and Design or Preview mode any time you make a coding change. Now you can immediately see the effect of your action— and revise accordingly. Figure 20-7 on the following page shows a simple code segment, and the corresponding header in Split view.

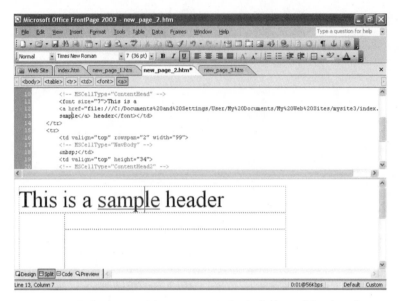

Figure 20-7   Split view enables you to see both Code and Design view on-screen at the same time.

Editing Code

If you want to try adding or deleting information on your page, you can do it in the Code window, but be sure to make a backup copy of the page before you try your hand at coding—just in case something goes wrong. To make changes in the Code window, click at the point in the code where you want to make the change, and use the Backspace key to delete any unnecessary text. You can select, copy, paste, and cut text in the Code window, just as you would in any word processing program.

Aha!   Bone Up on HTML

Before taking too much of the coding on yourself, be sure to do some homework to become familiar and comfortable with HTML prior to working on something important. Practice makes perfect, but it also involves plenty of mistakes along the way. One good way to learn about HTML (besides finding a good book to use as a guide, such as *Faster Smarter Web Page Creation*, by Mary Millhollon and Jeff Castrina), is to view other peoples' code. When you're using Internet Explorer to visit a Web site you really like, choose Source from the View menu to see the code that makes up the site. The code will appear in Notepad; you can choose Print from the File menu to save a printed copy of the source code for later review.

Using the Quick Tag Selector

FrontPage 2003 also makes a number of substantial changes in the Code Editor (a welcome improvement for die-hard HTML enthusiasts), but covering high-end coding techniques is really beyond our purposes here. One addition that will be helpful to you as you learn about HTML code is the Quick Tag Selector, a bar that stretches across the top of Code view (just beneath the page title tabs), showing the HTML tags that are used in the current document. To change, add, or remove a tag, you can simply click the down arrow that appears beside the tag when you point to it, to display a menu, as shown in Figure 20-8.

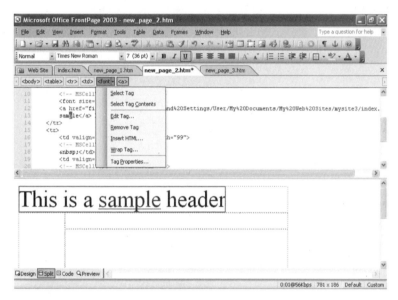

Figure 20-8 The Quick Tag Selector gives you an easy way to work with HTML tags in Code view.

Fast Wrap-Up

- Layout Tables And Cells, a new addition to FrontPage 2003, enables you to easily create a framework for the content in your Web page.

- To add a traditional table to your Web page, select the place in the page where you want the table to go, and choose Insert Table, or Draw Table from the Insert menu.

- You can add a page with frames by clicking the New tool, and choosing Pages; then select the frames template you want to use, and click the appropriate buttons to either link to existing content or add new.

- Add horizontal lines easily, by choosing Horizontal Line from the Insert menu; you can change the color, line thickness, and other settings by using the Horizontal Line Properties dialog box.

- A rollover is a special effect in which a hyperlink changes font, style, or color when the user positions the mouse over it. You can add rollover effects easily to your hyperlinks in FrontPage by displaying Page Properties, and choosing the rollover effect you want to apply.

- Although FrontPage makes it possible for you to bypass coding completely, you can easily work with HTML in Code view. To see the effects of your coding, you can click Split view to see both the code you enter, and the effects in Design view.

- The new Quick Tag Selector in Code view shows you all the HTML tags used in the current page, and makes it easy for you to change, add, or remove tags as you're coding.

Publishing Your Pages

10-Second Summary

- ■ Prepare your Web files
- ■ Use server extensions
- ■ Optimize your HTML
- ■ Publish your site
- ■ Troubleshoot your site
- ■ Rate your site's effectiveness

Okay, now we've come to the part you've been waiting for: putting that slick new site on the Web. Although there aren't many steps left, these last few are very important. In this chapter, you'll learn to prepare your files for the Web, publish the site (using a few different approaches), and then sit back and evaluate (in other words, bask in the glow of) your success.

Preparing Your Web Files

You have one more stop to make in Microsoft Office FrontPage 2003 before you publish your site on the Web. Take a moment to go back through your entire site, and make sure it's in the best possible shape. Here are some ideas of things to check for:

- ■ Preview your site in different Web browsers.

- ■ Check all links to make sure they're working correctly.

- ■ Check all contact information—including your address, e-mail, and telephone information—to make sure your visitors will be able to reach you.

- ■ Take a last look at Tasks view, to make sure you haven't left anything undone.

- ■ Click Reports on the Views bar to check the status of all the different elements in your site (as shown in Figure 21-1).

- ■ Optimize the Hypertext Markup Language (HTML) to ensure your page appears as quickly as possible.

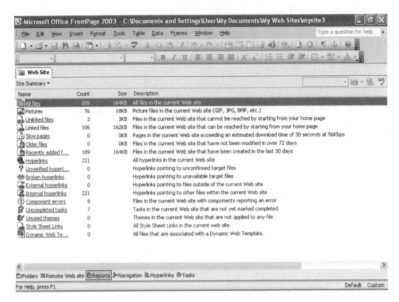

Figure 21-1 You can display Reports to see information about your site and list the elements that still need work.

Aha!   Check Your Links

You can have FrontPage check the hyperlinks in your site for you. To start the process, click Reports. The Reporting toolbar appears at the top right side of the work area, and you can click the Verify Links tool (position the pointer over the tools to see their names if necessary). In the Verify Hyperlinks dialog box, choose whether you want to verify all or only selected links; then click Start. Any broken hyperlinks will be displayed in the Report window; you can right-click and choose Edit Hyperlink to repair them.

About Server Extensions

Microsoft FrontPage Server Extensions are add-in programs that extend the capability of the *Web server* in charge of hosting your site. Extensions enable you to add such items as Web search capability, hit counters, the photo gallery we discussed in Chapter 19, "FrontPage 2003 Basics," top-10 lists, and document libraries.

Not all Web servers support FrontPage Server Extensions, so you'll need to check with your Internet service provider (ISP) before publishing your site to see whether the ISP has that capability. If not, the features you've included on your site that rely on the extensions won't function—which means that your hit counter or Web search utilities won't work.

> **Lingo** A *Web server* is the computer that stores your Web site and interacts with users who visit your site.

When you first begin working with FrontPage, Server Extensions are started by default, which means all these features are available to you as you create your site. If you find out that your ISP does not support Server Extensions, you can disable the extension features by choosing Page Options from the Tools menu, and clicking the Compatibility tab in the Page Options dialog box. Click the Enabled With Microsoft FrontPage Server Extensions check box to clear it. This turns off Server Extensions, and the features that use them in your Web design will be disabled so that you cannot add them.

If your server does not support extensions, you will publish your site to a File Transfer Protocol (FTP) server. To do this, you must know the server name, as well as your user name and password.

Optimizing HTML

In FrontPage 2003 you have to make sure your code is as tight as possible because it saves download and viewing time for your site visitors and ensures that your page appears as quickly as possible. To optimize your Web page before publishing, follow these steps:

1 Display your Web page in Code view by clicking Code or Split view in the lower left corner of the FrontPage window.

2 Choose Optimize HTML from the Tools menu.

3 In the Optimize HTML dialog box, click the items you want to remove in the optimized code (see Figure 21-2). By default, adjacent tags, empty tags, and Word-generated HTML are all removed. You can also elect to remove comments, white space, and unused styles and auto-generated content.

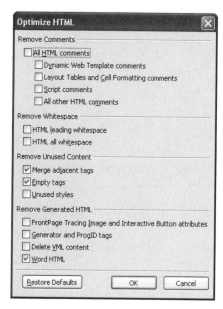

Figure 21-2 You can optimize your HTML code in FrontPage 2003 to ensure that it appears as quickly as possible.

4 Click OK to save the changes, and FrontPage optimizes your code.

Publishing Your Site

Putting your Web site on the Web is called *publishing your site* in FrontPage. The process actually involves copying the Web site—including all pages, images, and supporting files— to a remote location, or server, where your site's visitors will be able to view it. FrontPage 2003 provides the Remote Web Site view so that you can easily see and manage the files you're working with on your local system and on the remote destination.

You begin the process of publishing your Web site by choosing Publish Site from the Files menu. If you've changed anything on the site since the last time you saved the file, FrontPage will prompt you to save the file before publishing. If you see this prompt, click OK. FrontPage will automatically display the Remote Web Site view, and if you have not yet set up a remote Web site, a prompt will ask you to click Remote Web Site Properties (in the upper right side of the Remote Web Site view) to do so. In the Remote Web Site Properties dialog box (see Figure 21-3), choose the type of server to which you'll be publishing (the default selection is likely to be the one you want, unless you intend to use FTP to transfer the file).

Figure 21-3   Choose the server type you're publishing to in the Remote Web Site Properties dialog box.

Next, enter the destination for the Web site files, and click OK. A connection dialog box will appear, asking for the user name and password for the server access (see Figure 21-4). Enter your information and click OK.

Figure 21-4   FrontPage will request your user name and password, so that a connection with the server can be established.

Once the connection is established, the Remote Web Site view displays the Web files on your local system, as well as the folders on the server (see Figure 21-5). To publish the site, simply click the Publish Web Site button in the lower right corner of the Remote Web Site window.

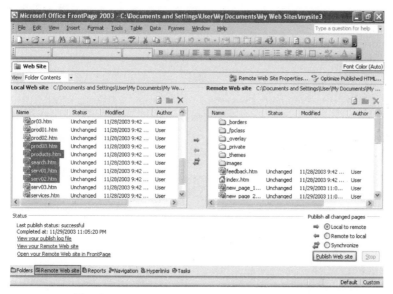

Figure 21-5   Click Publish Web Site to copy the Web site files from your local system to the Web.

Aha!   Update Your Site

Later, you can use the Synchronize option in the Publish All Changed Pages area of the Remote Web Site view to publish only pages you've modified. FrontPage will compare the files on the local and remote sites and update any that have been changed since you last published to the Web.

Troubleshooting Your Site

Anything worthwhile takes a little effort. Most of the sites I've published have at least a couple of glitches to work out after I publish them. A link doesn't work on this one, or the form looks funny on that one, or an animated image doesn't rotate the way it's supposed to. It's almost inevitable that I'll have some tweaking and moving and resizing and resaving to do. This is all a learning process, and because of the changing nature of the Web, and because of the continual upgrading that goes on at the server level at Web hosting companies, we have to be persistent in figuring our way around the variables that we encounter. When your page isn't loading or working as it should, approach it as a puzzle, not a dead end. There's an answer there somewhere—and if you keep looking for the fly in the ointment, sooner or later you're sure to find it (just remember to wash your hands before you come back to the keyboard, okay?).

Here are some of the more common problems that occur when you are publishing Web sites with FrontPage:

- **The computer is disconnected from the system.**   This may be a server error; the system might be down, or you might have been temporarily disconnected. Check your Internet connection. If the connection is fine, try publishing again shortly to see whether the error has resolved itself.

- **The server isn't recognizing my password.**   Passwords are case-sensitive, so make sure that you're entering the password correctly. If you still get the error, your server might be having difficulties. Wait a few minutes and try again. If all else fails, call your ISP to see whether there is a server problem.

- **My hit counter (or some other site element) isn't working.**   If one of your Web components doesn't work as you thought it would, check with your ISP to make sure FrontPage Server Extensions are installed.

- **I uploaded the site successfully but when I try to access the site on the Web, I get a "Page not found" error.**   Double-check the location of the files on the remote server. More than once, when publishing a new site, I've published files to a subfolder instead of the primary Web container. When in doubt, ask your ISP or administrator to verify the server location for your site.

Rating the Effectiveness of Your Site

So how does it look? Does everything work? Do the pages scroll as you intended? Remember that, whether your site looks great or needs a total makeover, designing for the Web is 10 percent splash and sparkle and 90 percent functionality.

Here are some questions to consider (and maybe to ask others, if you're a brave soul) when you want to know whether your Web site hits the mark:

- Is it easy to know where to click to move from page to page?

- Are the colors inviting?

- Is the text easy to read? Is it the right font, size, and style?

- Is the page too crowded?

- Do the special elements work well, or are there too many of them?

- Will users with different kinds of browsers be able to use the frames, and see the graphics you've added?

See Also To get more information, tips, and ideas you can use with FrontPage, subscribe to the Microsoft FrontPage Fan-Zine by going to *www.microsoft. com/office/ using/newsletter.asp.*

Remember that your site is a work in progress and that the more you experiment, the more you'll learn. Keep your eyes open for the designs you like, and try your hand at new, cool Web techniques as they catch your attention. Most of all, have fun with this fascinating medium, and get comfortable—because it's the fast wave of the future. In fact, it's a fast and *smart* wave of the future, rolling right alongside Microsoft Office Word 2003, Excel, Outlook, PowerPoint, and Access. I hope this quick trip through the Microsoft Office System has provided you with the know-how and the inspiration to put these fine tools to work. Enjoy your increased productivity and efficiency and, most importantly, do something *fun* with all that time you're saving!

Fast Wrap-Up

- Before you publish your Web site with FrontPage, do a quick check to make sure everything is working as you intended.

- Use Reports on the Views bar to show the status of different elements in your site.

- Optimize your HTML code to ensure your site is as fast and efficient as possible, by choosing Optimize HTML from the Tools menu.

- Click Verify Hyperlinks to have FrontPage check all the links in your site and display any problems. Fix broken links by right-clicking a broken link, and choosing Edit Hyperlink.

- Publish your site to the Web by selecting Publish Site from the File menu.

- Set up a Remote Web Site to accept your published site. Once you've published the site, you can sychronize files between your local server and remote server, and do quick updates on only those pages that have been changed since the last transfer.

Installing the Microsoft Office System

A

10-Second Summary
- ■ Prepare to install
- ■ Install the Office System
- ■ Change your installation
- ■ Detect and repair problems

Once upon a time, installing programs was a hit-or-miss effort that required plenty of coffee, and more than a little luck. Today, using Microsoft Windows XP and the Microsoft Office System, installing involves little more than putting the CD in the CD-ROM drive, and having the numbers you need handy.

Knowing how to install and uninstall programs is helpful for those times when you want to make changes to the components you have installed in the Office System, add new programs, or remove programs you're not using.

> **Note** If you are using Office on a network, be sure to talk with your system administrator for more information before you make any changes to the programs installed with your version of the Office System.

What You Need to Install the Office System

The most important things for installing the Office System are, of course, a computer and the Office System. Here's the "essential ingredients" list the Office System needs in order to run on your computer:

- ■ A personal computer with a Pentium 133 MHz or higher processor (Pentium III is recommended)

- ■ Microsoft Windows 2000 with Service Pack 3 (SP3) or Microsoft Windows XP

- ■ 64 MB of RAM (but 128 MB is recommended), with an additional 8 MB for each application you intend to run simultaneously

- ■ At least 245 MB disk storage space

- CD-ROM drive

- SuperVGA or higher resolution monitor

- Mouse, trackball, touchpad, or other pointing device

- Printer (optional)

- Modem (optional, for Internet-related features)

- Microphone (optional, for speech features)

- Graphics tablet (optional, for handwriting recognition)

Before you install, be sure to make a backup of all your important files, just in case there's a glitch and something goes wrong. That's not likely, but it's always better to be safe than dataless.

> **Note**   If you will be using the Shared Workspace features (in Microsoft Office Word 2003, Excel, and PowerPoint), creating Meeting Workspaces (in Outlook), or creating data-driven Web sites (in FrontPage), you need to install and run Microsoft Windows SharePoint Services. For more information on SharePoint Team Services V2, visit *www.microsoft.com/sharepoint/*.

Installing the Office System

To install the Office System on a single-user system, close any programs you have open, then insert the first Office System CD in your CD-ROM drive. The auto-install utility begins and walks you through the process, helping you choose the folder where you want to install the program, allowing you to choose the components you want to install, and more. When the installation is complete, Windows displays a message box. Click OK to complete the process.

Changing Your Office Installation

At some point down the road, you may want to make changes to the way you've got Office installed. You might want to install Access, even though you skipped it before; or perhaps you aren't using FrontPage, and you want to remove it to free up more disk space. When you want to change the installation, choose Add Or Remove Programs from the Control Panel, then click Change Or Remove Programs. A list of currently installed programs appears (see Figure A-1). Click the Microsoft Office System entry (the name will vary, depending on which version you've installed) and two buttons—Change and Remove—become visible.

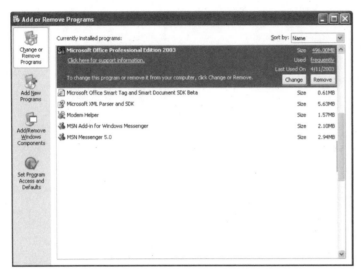

Figure A-1   Use the Change or Remove Programs feature to change your Office installation.

Click the Change button. The Windows Installer begins, and starts the Microsoft Office System Setup utility. You can then follow the Wizard's prompts, and make the changes you want to your Office installation.

Repairing after Installation

If you find that an update file or accessory doesn't work right after you install it, you can repair the file from the Add Or Remove Programs dialog box by following these steps:

1 Click Start, and choose Control Panel.

2 Click Add Or Remove Programs, and select the program or utility that isn't working properly.

3 Just beneath the program name, select Click Here For Support Information.

4 In the Support Info box (see Figure A-2), click Repair. Windows Installer starts and reinstalls the program, hopefully correcting the problem.

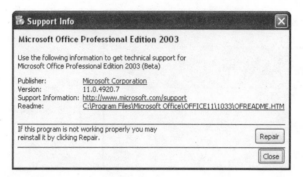

Figure A-2 You can repair installation problems while you're still working with Change or Remove Programs.

Note   I mentioned this earlier in the book, so I'll just add a reminder here: If your version of Office begins acting strangely—that is, taking a long time to update the screen, operating slowly, inserting unwanted characters at odd places—it could be that a file the program needs has become damaged. The Office System includes a utility that will fix that for you automatically. To repair the problem from within the application you are using (Word, Excel, Outlook, PowerPoint, FrontPage, or Access), open the Help menu and choose Detect And Repair. In the Detect And Repair box, choose whether you want to restore your shortcuts, or return the computer to its default settings. Click Start to have the Office System search for problems and repair the files.

The Office System Shortcut Keys

As you've learned throughout the book, one of the benefits of the Microsoft Office System is transferable knowledge: You can learn certain tasks—such as printing, saving, opening, and closing documents—in one Office application, and then apply that knowledge (and the same keystrokes) in other applications. This list brings together all the Office shortcut keys you'll be using with the various programs. Commands followed by a program name in parentheses (for example, Delete *(Outlook)*) indicate that the shortcut key is available only in that program for that purpose.

To do this	Press this:	Found in this menu:
New	Ctrl+N	File
Open	Ctrl+O	File
Save	Ctrl+S	File
Print	Ctrl+P	File
Undo	Ctrl+Z	Edit
Repeat	Ctrl+Y	Edit
Cut	Ctrl+X	Edit
Copy	Ctrl+C	Edit
Delete (Outlook)	Ctrl+D	Edit
Mark as Read (Outlook)	Ctrl+Q	Edit
Mark as Unread (Outlook)	Ctrl+U	Edit
Move to Folder (Outlook)	Ctrl+Shift+V	Edit
Paste	Ctrl+V	Edit
Select All	Ctrl+A	Edit
Find	Ctrl+F	Edit
Replace	Ctrl+H	Edit
Go To	Ctrl+G	Edit
Rename (Access)	F2	Edit
Refresh (Access)	F5	Edit
Reveal Tags (FrontPage)	Ctrl+/	View
Task Pane	Ctrl+F1	View
Slide Show (PowerPoint)	F5	View
Navigation Pane (Outlook)	Alt+F1	View

To do this	Press this:	Found in this menu:
Refresh (Outlook)	F5	View
Hyperlink	Ctrl+K	Insert
New Slide (PowerPoint)	Ctrl+M	Insert
Bookmark (FrontPage)	Ctrl+G	Insert
Cells (Excel)	Ctrl+1	Format
Reveal Formatting (Word)	Shift+F1	Format
Remove Formatting (FrontPage)	Ctrl+Shift+Z	Format
Properties (FrontPage)	Alt+Enter	Format
Mail (Outlook)	Ctrl+1	Go
Calendar (Outlook)	Ctrl+2	Go
Contacts (Outlook)	Ctrl+3	Go
Tasks (Outlook)	Ctrl+4	Go
Notes (Outlook)	Ctrl+5	Go
Folder List (Outlook)	Ctrl+6	Go
Shortcuts (Outlook)	Ctrl+7	Go
Folder	Ctrl+Y	Go
View Show (PowerPoint)	F5	Slide Show
Next Pane	F6	Window
Spelling and Grammar	F7	Tools
Research	Alt+Click	Tools
Thesaurus (FrontPage)	Shift+F7	Tools
Track Changes	Ctrl+Shift+E	Tools
Address Book (Outlook)	Ctrl+Shift+B	Tools
Find (Outlook)	Ctrl+E	Tools
Advanced Find (Outlook)	Ctrl+Shift+F	Tools
New Mail Message (Outlook)	Ctrl+N	Actions
Follow Up (Outlook)	Ctrl+Shift+G	Actions
Reply (Outlook)	Ctrl+R	Actions
Reply to All (Outlook)	Ctrl+Shift+R	Actions
Forward (Outlook)	Ctrl+F	Actions
Help	F1	Help

The Microsoft Office System: Additional Resources

Throughout this book, we've touched on ways to get you up to speed and working quickly in the Microsoft Office System. But, as you've no doubt noticed, there is *much* more to discover in the Office System. We've only touched the tip of the iceberg here when it comes to some of the great new features like Extensible Markup Language (XML) support, Information Rights Management (IRM), online collaboration, and dynamic Web publishing. There's much more to learn!

This appendix lists some of the higher-level books Microsoft Press publishes on each of the various Office System applications. In addition, you'll find a listing of Web sites that can give you more information about the new complementary Microsoft programs—such as OneNote and InfoPath—that work alongside the Office System. Finally, you'll find the link to Microsoft newsgroups, a consistently helpful place to go when a particular Office issue has you stumped.

Book Resources

These books are available from Microsoft Press to help you learn more about the various offerings in Office System. To find out about the books listed here, visit Microsoft Press online at *www.microsoft.com/mpress/*.

- *Introducing Microsoft Office 2003 InfoPath*, by Acey Bunch (Microsoft Press, 2003). Learn about this new native-XML tool, and discover how to develop InfoPath solutions for your organization from a member of the InfoPath development team.

- *Microsoft Office System Inside Out 2003 Edition*, by Michael J. Young (Microsoft Press, 2003). Use this comprehensive reference to explore each of the core Office System applications in depth, and find out how you can make the most of the enhanced collaboration and communication features in this release.

- *Microsoft Office Word 2003 Inside Out*, by Mary Millhollon and Katherine Murray (Microsoft Press, 2003). Learn the ins and outs of high-end Microsoft Word 2003, and create your own expert business documents.

- *Microsoft Office Excel 2003 Inside Out*, by Mark Dodge and Craig Stinson (Microsoft Press, 2003). Find expert information on using Microsoft Office Excel 2003, and develop sophisticated Excel worksheets using the newest features.

- *Microsoft Office FrontPage 2003 Inside Out*, by Jim Buyens (Microsoft Press, 2003). Get the latest-and-greatest ideas on using Microsoft Office FrontPage 2003 for high-level site design and publishing.

- *Microsoft Office Outlook 2003 Inside Out*, by Jim Boyce (Microsoft Press, 2003). Learn more about the many changes in Outlook 2003, and find out how you can use the new features to better organize the way you work with groups and individuals.

- *Tablet PC Quick Reference*, by Jeff Van West (Microsoft Press, 2003). A full look at the range of features available on your Tablet PC that shows you how to use your Tablet with Office applications.

- *XML Step by Step, Second Edition*, by Michael J. Young (Microsoft Press, 2002). This book teaches you how to understand and apply the latest XML technology and standards. A great companion book for those who want to take full advantage of the widespread XML support in the Office System.

Web Resources

These resources provide links to specific sites for more information. Be sure to sign up for the Microsoft newsletters related to the applications you use most often.

- Microsoft InfoPath: *www.microsoft.com/office/preview/infopath*

- Microsoft OneNote: *www.microsoft.com/office/preview/onenote*

- Microsoft SharePoint Portal Server: *www.microsoft.com/sharepoint/*

- Information Rights Management: *www.microsoft.com/office/preview/editions/ technologies/irm.asp*

- Microsoft Office Newsletters: *www.microsoft.com/office/using/newsletter.asp*

- Microsoft Newsgroups: *http://communities.microsoft.com/newsgroups/ default.asp?icp=Prod_officebeta&slcid=us*

The Microsoft Office System: The Big Picture

D

Throughout this book, we've been focusing on the fastest and smartest ways to get tasks done, using the various Microsoft Office applications. But sometimes it's nice to slow things down a bit, and understand some of the theory and insight behind the fast and functional changes with which we work every day. For that reason, this appendix gives you a fuller picture of the new changes in the Microsoft Office System. You'll learn what challenges developers were attempting to address, and see how the new and improved elements in Office meet those identified needs. You'll also learn more about the overall changes in the different applications, and see how the new features can fit into your own day-to-day work.

Computing Today

It's the dream of every information worker: programs as flexible as you are, powerful enough to capture, process, and produce information in a variety of forms—but simple enough to master in a short time. And seamlessly integrated with intranet and Internet resources, so that you can find what you need when you need it, and apply it almost instantly.

The last few years have taught us many things. We've learned that our simple, interpersonal communication is as powerful, and packed with information, as the reports and analyses over which we labor. We've discovered that working in groups brings far greater benefit, in terms of creativity, vision, specialization, and error-trapping, than working solo, one-project/one-person, alone behind our office walls. We now know that physical distance doesn't limit us in a time of virtual meeting rooms, online conferences, instant messaging, and collaborative scheduling. We don't have to run down the hall to check a fact when we can ping someone, using instant messaging, right now.

"What's possible" has been stretched to include faster, more efficient, farther-reaching, and more flexible rules about how we complete our work. And our quickly evolving understanding of what's possible at work drives the call for faster, more flexible, and more efficient tools to get the job done. That's where the Office System comes in.

The Challenges Information Workers Face

The worldwide community of Office users totals more than 300 million people (now that's a big family!), and the needs and wishes of this vast audience are as diverse as the industries and countries they represent. The experience level of those users ranges from brand-new novice user, to advanced user, to developer/expert. Some users would choose speed over power; others want greater flexibility with third-party products; still others want the new Office to be more secure, more stable, or more streamlined in one area or another. All want easier access to information, the ability to smoothly apply data across the range of applications, and processes and procedures that can be personalized to provide solutions for their own unique business challenges.

The Office System is designed specifically to meet the biggest challenges that people who work with information typically face:

- **Information fatigue**   We deal with lots of data—from reports and Web sites to meetings and phone calls. We listen to presentations, watch television, hear Web broadcasts, and go to seminars. We receive thousands of e-mails a week, subscribe to online newsletters, and visit discussion and newsgroups. Information flies at us from all directions at all times, in a huge array of forms. How do we sift through the glut of data we absorb, and keep only what is useful for our particular job, team, or company? The tools in the Office System for grabbing notes, recording ideas, and sharing thoughts instantly enable you to save and act on ideas as they occur, reducing their chances of being buried beneath a pile of not-so-important reading.

- **Inefficient collaboration**   The concept of workgroups is a terrific one, but it's often an idea that needs a long evolution. How many people worked on your last annual report? Who managed the process? How many hours did your manager spend trying to find suitable meeting times and places? Did using a team approach save you time, or cost you more? The new Office System includes great enhancements for working collaboratively, including a new meeting workspace service that helps you organize and facilitate meetings online.

- **Disconnected islands of data**   Does this sound like your office? Accounting prepared a document last spring that described each of the products in your 2002 line, breaking down the costs according to your various departments. As you're preparing your proposal for the three new products you want to introduce in 2004, you find out that the document was created in Word, but was not part of an Excel spreadsheet. Which means that, when a manager went in and

corrected the amounts later in the year, the new totals were never updated. So
you have a choice: You can use the previously corrected document, and go in to
make the cost corrections by hand, or you can use the Excel spreadsheet with the
correct values (but not the cost-center calculations you want), and re-create the
information you need. What a lot of work! The Office System helps you use your
data more efficiently, by providing Smart Documents, InfoPath, and improved
smart tags—as well as enhanced support for Extensible Markup Language
(XML), which enables you to store your data independent of its form, and use it
to produce a variety of end results.

- **Lack of business process integration**   Even in the smoothest businesses, there is
  often a lot of overlap in terms of business process. One department replicates what
  another department is doing at the other end of the building. With enhanced collaboration features, and improved support for XML, the Office System can help
  you cut down on duplication of effort, and allow all departments to share access to
  information that would support each of their efforts in unique ways.

- **Under-utilization of productivity tools**   Each of the core applications in Office
  are so feature-laden that many businesses don't use them fully; we tend to perform
  a specific number of tasks with each program, without a sense of how they could all
  work together to improve and expedite our business processes. The Office System
  makes productivity improvements in each of the core applications—Word, Excel,
  Outlook, Access, and FrontPage—and enhances the easy way the applications
  work together to make your work time more productive and more efficient.

Any new release of a software product will fix things that fell short in the last version, but this
new version of the Office System brings much more to the table than corrective measures.
Although the Office System does lessen Outlook's clunkiness, enhance stability, and beef up
security, it's the exciting innovations in the Office System that are likely to inspire you to take
a closer look. Whatever your particular obstacles may be right now—communication dead-
ends, repetition of effort, security holes, under-use of existing data and processes, workgroup
struggles, or something else—the Office System may have a shot at dissolving them. In the
next section, you'll see how this version of Office is more than a collection of bug fixes and
error controls. Instead, it's a new, highly flexible, and fast platform that enables you to capture
information instantly, share ideas easily, work with data efficiently, and produce results in a
variety of forms that fit the task you want to accomplish today.

The Office System Answer

The Office System is designed to support the entire life cycle of an idea—from that first spark in the back of your head, to the brainstorming meeting with Product Development, to the project management and final production of the end result. Each aspect of Office—the core applications, the online services, the customizability of key features, the instant communication, the underlying XML support—supports a way you can capture, explore, contribute, and build on your ideas. With an emphasis on communication and collaboration, the vision for the Office System includes these important aspects of working with information effectively:

- **Capturing ideas wherever and whenever they spring up**　With support for the Tablet PC in all core applications, you can jot notes on your tablet in a meeting (or on your Pocket PC) and then e-mail them directly to others on the team. You can save, store, and file information in a variety of ways, including XML, which gives you the ability to pull it into an almost unlimited number of forms.

- **Communicating instantly with integrated messaging**　Now Windows Messenger is built right into Outlook (and appears as smart tags when you type recognized names in application documents), which means you can see whether others in your contact list are currently online. And if they are, you can ask a quick question, or send a fast update, while you're thinking about it.

- **Collaborating more effectively with enhanced team features**　Improved collaboration features in the major applications, as well as improvements in Microsoft SharePoint Team Services makes collaborating—working with others both inside and outside your organization—easier to manage than ever before. With new meeting and document workspaces, you have a place for gathering and discussing (and revising), anywhere you have access to the Web. You can also customize templates for your SharePoint site, compare calendars, set alerts, and create customized lists for the way you organize and view your site.

- **Creating a personalized collection of services you need and want**　The new Microsoft Office Online site is an online collection of templates, supports, and services that not only help you answer questions about Office, but also extend its core functionality, by offering complementary products and services to help you get your work done—the way you want to do it.

- **Making your data go farther with XML**　XML is changing the way we work with information, by enabling us to separate our data—the document's structure and meaning—from its format (Word document, Excel spreadsheet, Access report, and so on). Because the data is stored separately, using a structured, self-describing language, the data itself can be used in many different forms, producing a variety of end results. This allows you to use the same data to create a brochure, a Web site, a report, articles, and more. This means that you will save time creating what you want to create, instead of copying existing documents, removing formats, and starting again. Not only can you tag and work with XML in Word, Excel, and Access (in the Office System Professional versions), but Smart Documents use XML to also bring this enhanced functionality to Word and Excel—and InfoPath enables you to prepare sophisticated forms to gather and re-use information.

- **Simplifying the upgrade and deployment process**   Adding new software always involves a learning curve and, depending on the size and structure of your organization, it may be a major undertaking. The Office System takes a shot at resolving upgrade challenges by adding a new Custom Installation Wizard, and Custom Maintenance Wizard, for corporate deployment. For individual users, the Setup interface and process has been improved, stabilized, and expanded to be more accessible for everyone.

The next section looks more specifically at ways the Office System meets the needs of individual information workers, small businesses, and large corporations, by offering new and improved products and services that make communication, collaboration, and data application easier and more flexible than ever before.

What's New in the Office System?

With a focus on connecting people, processes, and information, the Office System has positioned itself to be flexible enough to enable you to capture ideas in whatever form they occur. Then use them to create documents (including spreadsheets, reports, e-mail messages, Web pages, and more) individually, or as part of a group, and save them in such a way that they can be ported to all kinds of different products. Put simply, the new features enable you to gather data easier, work with it more efficiently, and save it in such a way that it will save you time, hassle, and more work later.

Improvements in Setup

One of the first changes you're likely to notice as you install the Office System is the simplified installation process. Gone are the glitches and hitches of earlier versions, and because Office doesn't modify the system files, you don't have to go through the traditional reboot stage after installation is complete. Office gives you the choice of creating a local cache for installation files, which enables you to repair, install on first use, and update Office later, without using the CD. In a corporate environment, the new Custom Installation Wizard will walk you easily through the setup process.

The Office System: Top 12 Things You Need to Know

1   This version of Office has a greater number of features, and more support for collaboration than past Office releases.

2   The Office interface now uses Microsoft Windows XP themes, so that users can rely even more on consistency between programs.

3   The Office System includes Outlook additions, and enhancements that make communication easier, faster, and smarter.

4   SharePoint Team Services uses Microsoft Windows Server 2003, and giving you a cutting-edge, secure, collaborative team option that you can use from any point of Web access.

5   The Office System takes a huge step toward extending the usefulness of data, with full support for XML in Word, Excel, and Access (in the Office System Professional versions only).

6   Smart Documents, smart tags, and InfoPath enable you to create intelligent documents that are easier for end users to work with, and save data in a secure, structured form that can be applied in unlimited ways.

7   Seamless integration of Microsoft Office Online broadens your resources with a click of the mouse, and gives you access to training, upgrades, solutions, and marketplace services.

8   The new Microsoft Office OneNote tool allows you to capture thoughts on the fly, in your own handwriting (or in doodles, recorded audio, and more), and port them to applications as usable data.

9   Improved customer service channels help keep the Office System customers in touch with Microsoft, and with each other.

10 Enhanced security features and improved setup make upgrading, deploying, and maintaining Office easier.

11 Information Rights Management (IRM) enables you to control who has access to your proprietary documents, and limit the tasks (copying, forwarding, printing, and more) that anyone can perform.

12 Many new design and functionality features in the core applications make using Office a more pleasant, efficient, and productive experience.

Changes in the Office System User Interface

The next obvious change you'll notice in the Office System is the new look and feel. Office now sports a more "sophisticated" look, following the color schemes and element designs used in Windows XP. You'll notice a similar theme right from first use—a "pipe" effect, and gradient colors in the task panes and menus; changes in the menu options and task panes (see Figure D-1).

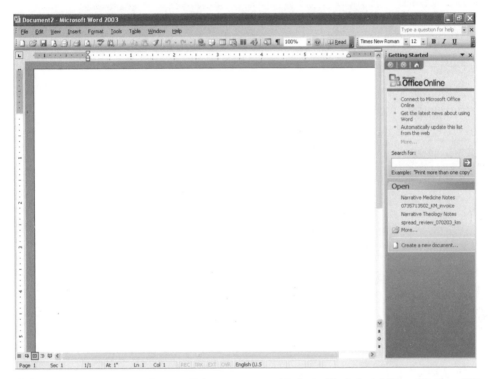

Figure D-1   The new Office System UI has a more sophisticated look that follows Windows XP themes.

After considerable research on what users want, the Office team went with this new look. Because so many users "spend all day in Office," they wanted to provide a more polished look for experienced users. The task panes have been enhanced to show the subheadings on a second color bar, making it easy to see, at a glance, where one grouping of commands ends and the next begins.

Some of the individual applications include significant interface changes as well. In Outlook, for example, you'll find a three-column view that enables you to preview a received e-mail message without scrolling (see Figure D-2). You'll also find an instant-message-like preview that pops up, showing the first few words of each incoming e-mail message so that you can see what's coming in, without leaving your current task, or even taking your hands off the keyboard.

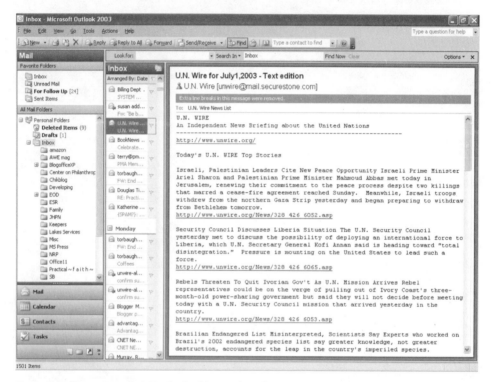

Figure D-2   You can customize Outlook's new interface to rearrange the column format, if you choose.

Seamless Integration with Microsoft Office Online

Another big change, which involves both the look and feel, and functionality of Office, is the increased integration with Microsoft Office Online. Links to more Office resources are no longer buried in the Help menu, as Office on the Web. Now, links to information online (including Thesaurus, Encarta, and more) are built right into the task pane in each of the core Office applications (see Figure D-3).

Figure D-3   You can get Help from both your local system and from the wider resources available on Microsoft Office Online.

Office Online will be more than just how-to articles and help resources, however. The new site will have the same look and feel as the rest of the Office System UI, and will offer a number of new features, including these:

■   The Assistance Web page on Office Online provides articles to help you find the answers to common questions, explore key features in each of the programs, and look for specific help in newsgroups, or report a problem.

■   Training offers online classes, Web-based interactive training, and self-paced practices. In the Training section of Office Online, you'll find specific task-oriented projects to help you accomplish a particular goal (for example, create a baby growth chart, a party guest list, or a car for sale sign). You'll also find more general application-oriented introductions (create an outline in Word or use Excel as a calculator), and explore online courses in each of the primary office applications (Word, Outlook, Excel, FrontPage, Access, and PowerPoint).

■   Templates provides you with all the templates you could ever want for use with the Office System: calendars and planners, financial templates, project templates, and much more—for all kinds of industry (see Figure D-4 on the following page).

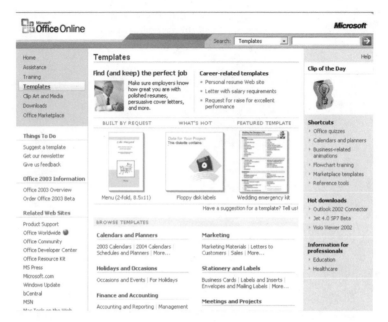

Figure D-4   The Templates area of Microsoft Office Online is a jackpot of templates for any kind of document you need to create.

■   The Clip Art and Media link on Office Online allows you to download thousands of pieces of clip art and animations for use in your documents and business (or fun) presentations.

■   Downloads enables you to check for Office updates, gives you the latest information on the Office System, and lets you know when new information is available.

■   In the "Things To Do" area of Office Online, you'll notice enhancements in the feedback loop. Now you can report a problem online, or even suggest new content for the site.

■   Office Marketplace offers Web services that complement the services included in the Office System. For example, you might use the Marketplace to find someone to convert your PDF files to Word documents, translate your German reports into English, or find an online fax service. The Marketplace is open to third-party vendors offering Office-related products and services.

A Farther Reach for Research

The Research task pane (available in the Tools menu, or by Alt + clicking) enables you to search through online references of your choosing to do research on a given topic. If you frequently search scientific journals, grant-making announcements, academic writings, or any number of other online sources, you can add them to your research options, and perform the search easily in the Research task pane (see Figure D-5).

Figure D-5 The Research task pane extends your research options, by scouring the online resources you select.

Capturing Ideas as They Occur

If your work relies on good note taking, the new OneNote application may make your professional life a lot easier. OneNote is a new utility that enables you to capture, store, organize, and use the notes you create. No more retyping text from wrinkled napkins or the backs of envelopes. If you've got OneNote on a Tablet PC, a Pocket PC, or installed on your regular work computer (with a writing pad peripheral), you can write, draw, or speak your notes as they're happening. OneNote even time stamps and saves the information for you automatically. Once you capture them, you can organize, use, and share notes of any kind as needed, whether it's an audio clip of catch-phrases for your newest product, a diagram showing the potential restructuring of your business, a quick bit of conversation with a developer you just met, or a follow-up task list for the team.

OneNote is exciting, because it works the way you do, enabling you to capture those good ideas that often lose their sparkle (or disappear altogether) when you're trying to recall your inspiration later. The interface is easy to use, whether you're typing at your desktop or sketching on your Tablet (see Figure D-6 on the following page).

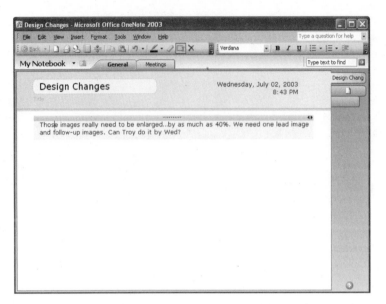

Figure D-6 Office OneNote helps you capture good ideas wherever they occur, and use them seamlessly in your Office applications.

Outlook for Small Businesses

Another addition that fits in the "capturing information" category is the introduction of Microsoft Outlook with Business Contact Manager. This application allows owners of small businesses to capture and organize crucial information on leads, contacts, and events. The Business Contact Manager enables users to manage customer information and relationships in one common utility, import information from other contact managers (such as ACT!), and use data tables and lists from programs such as Excel and QuickBooks.

Enhanced Collaboration with SharePoint Team Services

At its essence, SharePoint Team Services is a Web service that enables teams and workgroups to collaborate more easily. Users can create shared documents, and document workspaces, while working in Word, Excel, and PowerPoint. Creating a new SharePoint Team Services site for collaborative documents can be as easy as e-mailing a shared document. Additionally, access to SharePoint Team Services is built into FrontPage, where users can create simple, or customized, SharePoint pages, by selecting a wizard, and walking through the process. A SharePoint Team Services site helps teams get organized, communicate with each other, schedule events, and collaborate on documents.

SharePoint Team Services was first introduced in Office XP, and have been significantly enhanced in the Office System. Now you and your team can use document workspace templates to make document collaboration easier than ever. And the Shared Workspace functionality is built right into Word's Tools menu, so that you can move seamlessly to the shared space without ever leaving Word. The new Meeting Workspace feature enables business professionals to create a repository for meeting-related information, and keep it in a secure, team-accessible space—or to schedule, and host, a meeting online (see Figure D-7). Other enhancements in SharePoint Team Services make customization of sites easier, and add new list and field types for fuller data management.

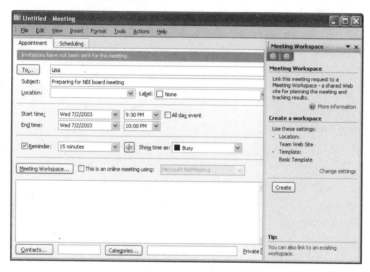

Figure D-7   Users can create a Meeting Workspace when they are setting up a meeting in Outlook.

Extending Data Functionality with XML

XML (Extensible Markup Language) is a new language standard that enables businesses, individuals, and developers to create documents in which the data is stored independently of the form in which it is presented. This means, for example, that the data in an XML document is stored as one set of information, and the format of the data (the way in which it appears) is stored separately. Because the data is self-describing, it can be used seamlessly in other types of documents (reports, letters, databases, spreadsheets, and Web pages, for example), without the need for retyping the data, or for the laborious task of copying sections of documents, stripping out formats, and applying the information as needed in another form.

The Professional Editions of the Office System include full support of XML in Word, Excel, and Access, with features and helps that enable users to take advantage of XML, using existing schemas, or schemas customized for their own business needs. The Standard Editions of the Office System include only the ability to save documents, worksheets, and data in XML format.

Making Your Documents Smarter with Smart Documents, InfoPath, and Enhanced Smart Tags

What would you call a document that can arrive via e-mail or Web download, do its own security checks upon opening, and offer users or readers contextual helps in the task pane while they review or modify the document? The Office System smart documents are documents built on XML schemas, which allow developers to create customized documents with contextual help, context-sensitive prompts, content suggestions, data lists, or links to additional resources. Smart documents are supported in Word, Excel, and PowerPoint, and take interactive, specialized document creation and application to a new level.

Smart tags, which were introduced in Office XP, have been enhanced in the Office System. Now developers can create more powerful smart tags, with a larger range of actions and applicability. Smart tags are now available in PowerPoint and Access for the first time, and developers can create smart tags with cascading menus, giving users a greater range of choice, and developers more room for customization.

InfoPath is a new offering in the Office System that enables businesses and individuals to really apply the power of XML. On the front end, InfoPath looks like highly interactive, customized forms, with contextual prompts; on the back end, InfoPath consists of highly structured XML documents that gather the entered data for re-use and re-application in an unlimited number of ways. InfoPath comes with sample forms that can be used as-is, or modified to specific business uses. InfoPath also includes forms for developers that illustrate the various ways it can be designed to fit into existing business procedures.

Improvements in the Office System Security

Enhancing collaboration and sharing ideas and projects are great ways to improve productivity and creativity, but there are inherent risks. For that reason, security has been an important development component in the Office System. Many of the security-related changes are actually transparent to the user, and are built into the infrastructure of Office and its core applications. Now, however, Microsoft Internet Explorer and the Office System share the same trusted certificate list, making it easier for you to manage accepted sites. The Office System also improves compatibility with third-party anti-virus software.

Additionally, Windows Rights Management now enables users to control who has access to sensitive documents, and permits document owners to control the editing, formatting, and distribution of the document. Additional protection features have been built into each of the core Office applications as well, to provide greater security against unwanted changes and circulation of sensitive documents.

The Office System Productivity Enhancements

On top of all the new features, tools, and technologies in the Microsoft Office System, you'll find many productivity enhancements in each of the core applications, as well as additions to the Office System as a whole. This section gives you a quick look at the wide range of enhancements that can make your work easier, more productive, more secure, and more flexible.

Using Ink

Most people grumble about their handwriting, yet they still feel more comfortable jotting notes on a legal pad than they do typing those same notes into Word. What if you could do both? Sitting in a meeting or a coffee shop, you can scribble notes on a Tablet PC (or the graphics tablet attached to your desktop computer), and watch your own doodles become data.

Ink enhancements in the Office System make handwriting a viable option for entering, and working with, text, numbers, and slides in Word, Excel, and PowerPoint. Now Tablet PC users can write information, and allow the application to transform the data to typed text, or keep it as handwriting. The Write Anywhere feature allows you to turn most of your Tablet PC into a writing surface. This means you're not limited to the Input Panel that appears at the bottom of your tablet in portrait mode. You can customize the Ink feature by making these changes to Write Anywhere:

- Add the Write Anywhere button to the title bar

- Change the color and thickness of your writing

- Modify the "wait time" between the time you write or draw, and the time the input is displayed

Word automatically converts handwriting to typed text, but you can elect to leave your notes hand-written if you like. To do this, you simply enter your text in the Writing Pad of the Input Panel, and click the down-arrow to the right of the Send button. From the displayed list, click Send As Ink. The data is placed in the document at the cursor position—but it's your handwriting, not typed text, that appears.

> **Note** The Send As Ink feature works as a toggle, so Word will continue inputting your handwriting as ink, until you choose Send As Text.

Inking Modes

When you're using Ink on the Tablet PC, three new toolbars are available to you:

- Ink Annotations turns on the annotations feature, so that you can add notes on documents, slides, or spreadsheets. A toolbar provides tools for choosing line color and thickness, using an eraser, selecting objects, or stopping annotations.

- Ink Comments enables the Input Panel or the Write Anywhere feature, so that you can add comments directly into the document at the cursor position. A toolbar with only two options—Draw Ink and Erase Ink—appears when you choose Ink Comments.

- Ink Drawing and Writing displays the Drawing Canvas (and accompanying toolbar), so that you can write or draw a diagram directly into your document. You also can change ink colors and thickness, and erase ink as needed.

Bubble Comments in Word

Comment bubbles were a new addition to Word 2002, enabling users to view and respond to comments (in Print Layout and Web Layout views) in bubbles in the right margin of the document. The Ink feature in the Office System allows you to use Word's bubble comments feature, and also provides for handwritten and drawn comments inside the bubbles. This enables you to enter the traditional comments, but use a variety of handwritten, typed, or mixed comments.

> **Note**   Using comments in this way is preferable to using annotations in situations where you have several reviewers commenting on a document. Comments can be tracked, hidden, or organized by reviewer, whereas annotations can only be hidden or displayed.

Cell-Centric Comments in Excel

In the Office System, ink annotations you add to your Excel spreadsheets are anchored to the cell that was selected when you created the ink note. This means that, no matter how the worksheet may change (cutting and pasting an annotated range from one worksheet to another, inserting or removing columns, etc.), the annotation stays with the cell to which it is linked.

PowerPoint Annotations

Ink may seem like an intuitive feature in PowerPoint; in fact, the Pen option has been around in PowerPoint for several generations. Ink is helpful for drawing those circles and arrows on current slides when you are giving presentations. Ink can be a dramatic addition to a slide showing a table, diagram, or a chart. In fact, in PowerPoint 2003, you can create entirely hand-drawn slides, if that fits your presentation needs.

Ink in Outlook

Finally, ink in Outlook enables you to write your e-mail messages longhand, draw maps to the downtown bookstore, sign your name with a real signature, or make notes on an e-mail message you're forwarding. Additionally, you can write out your to-do list, add the items to your task view, and create Calendar entries, using ink.

Internet Faxing

The Office System builds in the option of using an Internet service to send a fax from within Word, Excel, or PowerPoint. Relying on partnerships in the Microsoft Office Marketplace, Office enables you to choose Send To in the File menu, and select the new Fax Service option.

The first time you choose the Fax Service option, a prompt lets you know that you need to sign up for an Internet fax service. When you click OK, you are taken to the Office Marketplace Web site, where you can choose a fax service provider. After that, you'll be able to send and receive faxes automatically, while you work in your favorite applications.

IRM (Information Rights Management)

IRM (Information Rights Management) technology is a new addition to the Office System that enables you to limit others' accessibility to your critical business documents. IRM actually protects the document at the file level (as opposed to network level), giving users controls, which can allow or disable features that could be used to forward materials to people outside the organization, or to change valuable data that shouldn't be modified.

IRM: Quick Facts

Here's a quick look at some of the key features of IRM:

- Information Rights Management is available only in Office Professional Edition.

- IRM is a document-protection model that works at the file level. You control the level of permission by choosing Permission from the File menu, and selecting Unrestricted Access (the default), Do Not Distribute, or Restrict Permission As, and setting the restrictions you want to apply.

- Features for protected documents can be disabled to block forwarding, e-mailing, faxing, printing, or editing.

- Users can set expiration dates for documents, so that they will not be viewable past a certain date.

- For more information on IRM, go to Microsoft Office Online, click Assistance, and search for *Rights Management*.

All businesses have sensitive data that they want to ensure stays within the limits of the organization. Payroll information, private personnel data, critical strategic information, specifications for new products, and valuable market research are just a few of the documents organizations want to keep private. By using the IRM features in the Office System, organizations can limit how far a document can travel, and control what can be done with it. For example, the forwarding, copying, and printing features might be disabled for a sensitive e-mail message; attached documents are similarly protected.

Picture Manager

The new Microsoft Office Picture Manager gives you a set of image-editing tools, when you are working with pictures on your local system, or on your SharePoint Team Services sites. When you, or your team members, create picture libraries, you can upload images from your local hard drives, or network drives; import images from digital cameras or scanners; and post images to the team site, using Picture Manager.

When you click an image in a picture library, and then click the Edit Picture tool, the Microsoft Picture Manager opens (see Figure D-8). This utility enables you to perform basic image-editing functions on the selected picture. These editing possibilities include the following:

- Change brightness and contrast
- Alter the color of the picture
- Crop the image
- Rotate and flip the image
- Remove red eye in the photo
- Resize the picture

Figure D-8   The Office Picture Manager is a new tool with the Office System that enables you to edit your pictures.

Aha!   Correcting Images Fast with Auto Correct

The easiest modification is the one to try first: click Auto Correct to cause the Picture Manager to correct the color and brightness of the selected image for the best possible display.

You can also use the Picture Manager to print pictures, export images to other file formats, e-mail pictures to friends and coworkers, compress images, and work with images in batches for export, conversion, or print processes.

Microsoft Office Document Imaging

Microsoft Office Document Imaging, which is made available with Microsoft Office Tools in the All Programs submenu, has gone through a significant growth spurt. Now the utility includes three toolbars instead of one (Views, Annotate, and Standard), offers improvements in OCR (optical character recognition) technology, provides a search feature, and allows annotations on the documents you scan, convert, and use (see Figure D-9).

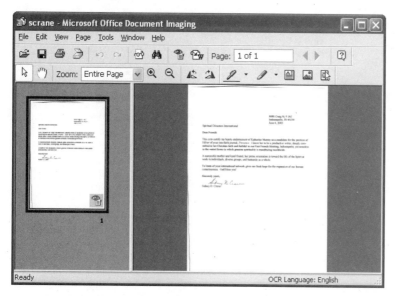

Figure D-9   Office Document Imaging includes a number of enhancements, such as the annotations feature to support ink capability throughout the Office System.

Summary

This appendix has given you a glimpse of the big picture of the Office System changes, as well as a closer look at the many enhancements in the various applications. From the Office-wide addition of Ink and Tablet PC support, to IRM (Information Rights Management), to the individual enhancements in each of the core Office System programs, the changes throughout Office are designed to help you work the way you work best. The streamlined procedures, flexible data formats, improved tools, and seamless integration with Web services, and XML-based technologies throughout Office will enable you to expand the effective use of your data, throughout your department or across your entire enterprise.

Index

Symbols and Numbers

A

X

Y

Z

Katherine Murray

Author Katherine Murray has written dozens of computer books since the early 80s. Blessed with a genetic geekiness (her father *still* programs in RPG) and a fascination for doing things quickly and efficiently, Katherine is enthusiastic about mapping out ways people can use technology to their advantage so they can get on with the important things in life—walking the dogs, swimming with the kids, rollerblading at sunset, or cooking a gourmet meal. In addition to her many technical books, Katherine has written extensively for families and  publishes a number of weblogs: *BlogOfficeXP,* providing tips and thoughts for Office XP users; *Practical Faith,* sharing simple stories of everyday faith; *Chikblog,* a blog for women over 40; and *The Horton Chronicles,* a group blog focusing on quirky bits of media coverage we may be missing. To find out more about Katherine or locate one of her weblogs, visit *www.revisionsplus.com/kmurray.html.*

Get a **Free**
e-mail newsletter, updates,
special offers, links to related books,
and more when you
register online!

Register your Microsoft Press® title on our Web site and you'll get a FREE subscription to our e-mail newsletter, *Microsoft Press Book Connections.* You'll find out about newly released and upcoming books and learning tools, online events, software downloads, special offers and coupons for Microsoft Press customers, and information about major Microsoft® product releases. You can also read useful additional information about all the titles we publish, such as detailed book descriptions, tables of contents and indexes, sample chapters, links to related books and book series, author biographies, and reviews by other customers.

Registration is easy. Just visit this Web page and fill in your information:

http://www.microsoft.com/mspress/register

Microsoft®

Proof of Purchase

Use this page as proof of purchase if participating in a promotion or rebate offer on this title. Proof of purchase must be used in conjunction with other proof(s) of payment such as your dated sales receipt—see offer details.

Faster Smarter Microsoft® Office System—2003 Edition
0-7356-1921-2

CUSTOMER NAME

Microsoft Press, PO Box 97017, Redmond, WA 98073-9830